Practical Social Research

Project Work in the Community

David Hall
and
Irene Hall

Consultant Editor: Jo Campling

MACMILLAN

First published 1996 by
MACMILLAN PRESS LTD
Houndmills, Basingstoke, Hampshire RG21 6XS
and London
Companies and representatives
throughout the world

ISBN 0–333–60673–6 hardcover
ISBN 0–333–60674–4 paperback

A catalogue record for this book is available
from the British Library.

10   9   8   7   6   5   4   3   2   1
05   04   03   02   01   00   99   98   97   96

Printed in Malaysia

Contents

Contents

Contents

Contents

Contents

Contents

List of Tables

List of Figures

Glossary

Client organisation: Used to denote the group with whom the research has been negotiated. A representative from this group is the recipient for the **Client report** produced by the student(s) as a result of their agreed practical research project.

Client report: The outcome of practical research, addressing the issues negotiated with the client organisation and written in everyday language. May include recommendations for action.

Community practitioner: Term currently used in Britain to denote those active at the locality level in providing welfare services.

Gatekeeper: Individual in an organisation with the power to grant access to a researcher.

Housing co-operative: A form of housing provision in Britain where residents are tenants of housing which they own in common (with government grant assistance), and which they are usually involved in planning, designing and administering.

Informant: Term used to denote the individual who is being asked for information, whether by interview or survey. Used instead of 'interviewee' or 'respondent' (also in common usage) as such an individual possesses the information which is the basis of the study – s/he is the 'expert'. However, a study for women partners of prisoners could not use this term because of the negative connotation of 'informing'.

Learning difficulty: Term currently used in Britain in preference to 'mental handicap' or 'mental retardation'.

Local authority: British term for local government at town, city or metropolitan area level which provides a number of services for residents and levies taxes.

Methodology report: Used to refer to a report which students may provide for their academic department as a reflection on their research experience and demonstrates the lessons they have learned about methodology in the everyday world.

Service user: Term in current usage which denotes the beneficiary of services, often of social care, from voluntary or statutory organisations. Used in the book in preference to 'client' – to distinguish from the official providers of the service (the client organisation).

Special needs: Term increasingly used in Britain in preference to 'disabled'.

Sponsor: Individual with influence who promotes research by providing researchers with the means and/or contacts for undertaking it.

Stakeholder: Refers to everyone in an organisation as provider or recipient of service, paid or voluntary staff who has some interest (stake) in the quality of service provided.

Survivor: Used as a non-stigmatising term instead of victim, as in survivor of rape

Voluntary organisations: Non-profit organisations, often either registered charities or voluntary associations, which usually include volunteers among their workers. In Britain increasingly dependent on paid staff, and major providers of specialised services to local authorities who contract to 'buy' such services (provided by, for example, residential homes or day centres). Called the Third Sector in the USA.

Introduction and Acknowledgements

This book is written as a guide to students wanting to become involved in practical social research in the local community. In particular it is addressed to undergraduate students participating in small-scale research projects as part of their assessed work, though we hope that the book will also be useful for anyone who wants a general understanding of social research.

The type of research being presented here is 'applied' research, or what Hakim (1992, p. 3) calls 'policy research' as opposed to 'theoretical research'. It is about working with those active in the community to produce information which meets their requirements. It is focused on research which leads to action and has a specific intended audience. It requires communication in 'plain English'.

When a research project is undertaken with the particular needs of a local group or organisation in mind, then the actual carrying out of the research is only one stage of involvement. It is preceded by negotiations to define the scope and provide access for the research. It is concluded by the writing and presenting of a report, which may include recommendations for action, to the organisation. Such a group or organisation is the 'client' for applied research.

As illustrations of how this can work, throughout the book examples of student projects are presented where the client organisation has been in the voluntary or non-profit sector of social welfare. Suggestions are made for how students can develop this practice for themselves and how potential difficulties may be anticipated and worked around, again using examples from actual projects.

1

The emphasis is on doing research projects in the 'real world'. Like Robson (1993, p. xii) we are dubious about a term which suggests that university institutions exist in an unreal world, but feel that research outside the academic confines offers a quality of involvement and learning opportunity which tends to be missing from more conventional forms of teaching and learning about research and research methods. That is why we also consider what students have to gain from this practice in terms of personal transferable skills, how teamwork can be employed within projects and what students working in teams need to look out for, and finally how such learning can be incorporated into the practice of academic assessment.

Research as a process begins with the development of an idea – in this case an idea that can be shared with community practitioners. From there the book moves through a number of stages: negotiating with a client organisation, designing the research strategy, selecting the research methods to be used, analysing the data and writing reports. In applied research, reports are required for two audiences, the client organisation and the academic department. Each will be different in style and content: one is practical, down to earth and brief; the other is scholarly, reflexive and self-evaluatory – and also brief!

Although the focus is on practical research, we do not want students to fall for the 'cookbook' type of research, choosing research methods off the shelf to suit predefined problems. Instead, because research, and especially applied research, does not exist in a vacuum we think it important that our discussion considers at an early stage the philosophical issues underlying methodology and choice of methods. Throughout we emphasise the importance of ethical considerations in working with client organisations or service providers and their service users.

The book is divided into three parts covering the stages before, during and after fieldwork. Part I includes an overview of how research can be effective in partnership with community organisations, along with detailed suggestions on how to go about setting up a specific research project. In Part II the context of applied community research is used to explore the methods of data collection and analysis from the two major traditions in social science, the scientific or survey method and the ethnographic. Part III covers the steps in producing project reports which will identify key findings and meet the requirements of client organisations and academic disciplines.

The model that we adopt and here propose is that of producing research in *partnership* with local community organisations. Community needs are met at the same time as worthwhile academic and transferable skills are developed. A research project on this basis avoids being exploitative either of the student or of the client organisation. Both parties receive benefit from the project and students have the satisfaction of knowing that their work should contribute to improving service provision in the light of the information which the research has produced.

As tutors we are enthusiastic about the benefits of such research projects not just for the client organisations but also for the students. We have seen students grow in confidence and self-assurance as they develop academic and practical skills through this experience. Although such projects are never an 'easy option' nor always problem free – in fact they can be uncertain and nerve-wracking at times – students overwhelmingly have found this type of research enjoyable and satisfying to do.

In this extract from a methodology report one of our students reflected as follows:

> I have personally learned a lot by carrying out this research. For me the learning was based on research techniques and personal enhancement. One of the major skills I have learned is the ability to feel easy with people unknown to me and in some respects to make them also feel at ease. . . . If anything at all has come out of this project I think it has been the confidence that I have gained in myself to make decisions and to work alone to a large degree . . . and to accept criticism. (Navarro, 1992)

In writing this book we have been influenced by a wide range of sources as debate and publishing in the area of methodology and methods burgeons, as well as by our own experiences of different styles of research. We wish to express our gratitude to all those who have helped in the formulation of our ideas and in the practice of social research. Particular mention must be made of colleagues such as Tony Lane, Brian Corby and Graham White for their advice and support. We are grateful too for the comments and guidance of Jo Campling and Catherine Gray at Macmillan, and to the anonymous reviewers for their helpful and pertinent observations on earlier drafts. Needless to say, they are in no way responsible for any faults that remain.

We are also grateful to Aldine de Gruyter, Dr. Walter L. Wallace and Polity Press for permission to reprint Wallace's diagram of the scientific method, to the Open University Press for permission to use Parker et al. diagram of the snowball sample, and to the British Sociological Association for permission to include in the Appendix its Statement of Ethical Practice.

We wish to mention with special thanks the voluntary groups and organisations on Merseyside and elsewhere which have hosted the research projects mentioned in the book, and those which have also given permission for examples from their reports to be included. For reasons of confidentiality they all remain anonymous.

We thank also all the students whose work has been our inspiration and some of whose projects have been used as examples: Frank Ainsbury, Susan Ainscough, Dorothy Ashton, Angela Bergquist, Beverley Bethel, Janet Bevan, Georgina Black, Carmel Brady, Clair Bryan, Pamela Caldwell, Anita Callaghan, Clare Calvert, Richard Cant, Paula Carroll, Michelle Casey, Viv Chaloner, Karen Christian, Caroline Coles, Helen Connolly, Ann Crotty, Ceri Daniels, Julia Davitt, Deirdre Doherty, Sue Dorricott, Stuart Eckford, Karen Gillet, Toni Gleave, Jade Gooch, Susannah Greenwood, Christopher Haigh, Paula Hall, Marilyn Hamilton, Sarah Harland, Paul Higgins, Leslie Highton, Simon Jenkins, Charlotte Johnson, Diana Jones, Ruth Khan, Rebecca Riley, Christina Lawrence, Kathryn Lee, Gwen Lightfoot, Joanne Mayson, Jane McKelvey, Paul McKeown,

Introduction and Acknowledgements

Jane Meehan, Helen Milor, Aisha Mohamed, Eileen Morgan, Emily Morrell, Emmanuel Mufti, Shona Murray, Kate Mutton, Alison Navarro, Carole Nixon, Susan O'Dea, Lisa Omar, Charlie Phillips, Hannah Pool, Sally Pugh, Helen Quinn, Sara Ray, Debbie Raymond, Layla Roberts, Les Roberts, Sally Small, Celia Sullivan, Alice Tilley, Alex Tucker, Colin Scaiff, Edward Surrey, Elizabeth Wakefield, Sally Walters, Elaine Warren, Rachel White, Pauline Williams, Brendan Woodhouse, Clare Woodward, Angela Wray, and Karen Wright.

Undoubtedly, fewer of these projects could have been initiated and negotiated without the services of Interchange, a charity aiming to link the resources of higher education with community groups to meet their information needs. We have been involved from its inception over a number of years in creating a structure for Merseyside which supports student projects in the community, responds to organisations' requests and offers a model of sound practice in forging links between higher education and the community. So we are truly grateful for the support of Alison Thornber as Interchange Co-ordinator and Anne Merry as Director of the Centre for Academic Practice at the University of Liverpool in facilitating applied research. We acknowledge too the financial contributions of the University of Liverpool, Liverpool Institute of Higher Education, and Liverpool John Moores University as well as much-needed donations from industry and local charitable funds to Interchange.

DAVID HALL
IRENE HALL

PART I

PART 1

1
Philosophy and Practice of Applied Social Research

The aim of this chapter is to encourage students to undertake their own research project, by outlining the steps to be taken which are detailed in later chapters. In doing so, we set out a philosophy for research based on participation with local groups and organisations and present an ethical basis for research practice which emphasises respect for informants' autonomy. Finally we discuss the personal transferable skills which can be developed through social research, including the advantages (and the drawbacks) of teamwork.

The research adventure

Research has been called a 'journey of adventure' (Miller and Crabtree, 1992, p. 3) and statistics a 'spectator sport' (Jaeger, 1990). Phrases like these attempt to inject some interest into the topic of 'research methods', notorious for its ability to put students off because it is often perceived to be difficult, boring or just plain irrelevant.

But does it have to be like that? Experience has proved that students are able to undertake worthwhile research projects which are not just paper exercises but can make a real contribution to resolving a problem facing a client organisation. So what we are trying to do is to take the

9

general principles of social research and show how these can be applied in small-scale research projects in the real world – which at the same time are of practical use to those involved. Here are some comments offered by students on the effect that doing such research has had on them.

> It's a different discipline from an essay. If you read about it, there's no way you'd get the feel of it without doing it.

> It's so completely different from what you've ever done before. It's what you've put into it, all your own work.

> You have responsibility because of the contract. You're doing something for someone.

> Teamwork is the most important thing for me. We're very supportive. It's amazing how different we all are through doing it.

Projects based on 'real world' research are far from easy: another comment was,

> I didn't realise how hard it was.

and yet at the same time it could be 'a good laugh'.

Why practical research?

Social research involves engaging with the world. Blaikie defines it in terms of:

> exploring, describing, understanding, explaining, predicting, changing or evaluating some aspect of the social world. (Blaikie, 1993, p. 4)

This is a broad invitation, and the examples in the book demonstrate the variety of ways this may be interpreted in an actual project. Research answers such questions as:

- what is happening?
- why is that happening?
- how does that affect people?

In applied research these questions are supplied by the researcher and the client, and the answers have to make sense to both. The results of research are published, for publication is an essential conclusion to the research process (Gilbert, 1993, p. 328) which both communicates and persuades. As Stacey (1969, p. 134) has argued, applied research may require more than one report – to the client and to the academic audience – with different styles and different emphasis.

However, research in practice rarely runs with textbook smoothness and first-hand involvement in project work reveals the reality behind so-called 'hygienic' accounts of research (Stanley and Wise, 1993). Messes, mistakes and false starts do occur and researchers have to learn problem-solving techniques to deal with them. The academic and dry treatments of methodology in textbooks come to life through the experience of conducting research for oneself.

Many courses in research methods require students to conduct interviews and carry out surveys for precisely the reasons suggested above. Family, friends, acquaintances and other students are often used as willing (or coerced) participants in a project. Sometimes students may conduct research in another setting – in an organisation outside academia. Often in this case, however, the student's concern is primarily (and understandably) to use the organisation for the purposes of finding people to interview or survey and the results are set within the context of an academic theory or set of concepts being developed and tested. Such research is not primarily designed to be of practical application.

This book advocates a different approach based on developing research projects which are planned from the outset to be of value to a client organisation. The aims and objectives of such projects are therefore negotiated to be acceptable and make sense to the group being studied as

11

---

1 **Partnership**
The research relationship is between equals and is not exploitative: the client organisation is not being 'used' merely to develop academic theory or careers nor is the academic community being 'used' (brains being picked). There is a genuine *exchange*. The research is negotiated.

2 **Learning experience**
Both partners should learn from the experience.

3 **Empowerment**
Informants are respected as 'experts' in the social process under research. The style and methods of research are collaborative. The research should enhance the situation of informants.

4 **Communication**
All communications should use appropriate language and should be clear and well structured, showing awareness of and sensitivity to the ethos of the client organisation.

5 **Quality result**
The final report should be a quality product which meets the need of the client organisation and satisfies standards of academic integrity. To enable this, supervision needs to supportive and thorough.

6 **Assessment**
Criteria should be developed which will measure the student's work on a broader scale than that used to evaluate traditional academic work.

7 **Ownership**
The organisation has the right to own and distribute the report, subject to authorship being credited. Copies of the report will be retained by the students and their supervisors.

8 **Funding**
Students should not be out of pocket through doing the research. Wherever possible the client organisation should supply the modest expenses of the student.

9 **Ethics**
Students should adhere to the ethical guidelines of the appropriate professional association (for example, BSA, BPS); confidentiality and the rights of informants to give or withhold consent must be respected.

Figure 1.1 Philosophy for applied social research

well as to satisfy the requirements of sound methodology and provide a good learning experience for the students.

Philosophy of research

Our philosophy for applied research outlined in Figure 1.1 is based on recognising how the researcher depends on the co-operation of others. In the conduct of research, organisation members become informants – their role changes and they become the providers of information, the people who have the knowledge which the researcher is seeking. Rather than the researcher being the 'expert' using people to gain knowledge, we recognise the informants as the 'experts' and the client organisation with whom the research has been negotiated as the partner.

This is in contrast to the extreme of 'quick and dirty' research noted by writers who have criticised the exploitative nature of some traditional academic research, motivated by the need to publish quickly and often (Jayaratne, 1993, p. 115). As Bell has commented, much sociological research 'is done *on* the relatively powerless *for* the relatively powerful' (Bell, 1978, p. 25).

Furthermore, writers such as Oakley have drawn attention to the instrumental orientation of masculinist rational scientific method to its subjects and have proposed alternatives. Oakley argues that

> in most cases, the goal of finding out about people through interviewing is best achieved when the relationship of interviewer to interviewee is non-hierarchical and when the interviewer is prepared to invest his or her own personal identity in the relationship. (Oakley, 1993, p. 229)

The recommendation made in this book as a positive course of action is for that style of research participation which has become known as '*collaborative research*' (Lee, 1993, p. 156; Everitt *et al.*, 1992).

Developed from an understanding of how social research has fed off minority communities to provide academic advancement without doing anything for the members of those communities, collaborative research aims to:

> facilitate indigenous social action programs by supplying data and results which could make significant contributions to the effectiveness of [residents'] efforts. (Schensul, quoted in Lee, 1993, p. 157)

Collaborative research has implications for the way research is conducted, as in Oakley's advocacy of non-hierarchical interviewing. It is also incompatible with covert research methods, where the researcher conceals from subjects the fact that research is being undertaken or the true reasons for the research (Everitt *et al.*, 1992, p. 128). Instead collaborative research treats people as individuals with rights – to know what is going on around them and to be able to give or withhold consent.

Guidelines on research ethics such as those produced by the British Sociological Association (see Appendix A) are helpful in drawing attention to the issues of privacy, confidentiality and voluntary consent, and in making the researcher responsible for the methods that are used without imposing a restrictive code of conduct (Hornsby-Smith, 1993, p. 63). Students should be aware of such guidelines; but for collaborative research which takes partnership seriously, it is essential to be as open as possible about the research. Covert research may be justifiable in particular limited circumstances but researchers using covert methods often suffer because they are not free to ask the questions they would like to, or observe areas or activities they would wish to. The most important objection, though, to covert research is the exploitation of people who are observed without their consent and who may be further damaged when research findings are published.

There is a possible danger in collaborative research that the researcher becomes partisan, co-opted as an uncritical agent of the group or organisation being researched. When one has enjoyed the hospitality of a group it may become harder to offer criticism of their efforts. Douglas has argued that field research does not always take place in an atmosphere of openness and honesty – the classical paradigm of co-operation between the researcher and 'his' subjects. Instead, Douglas claims:

> many of the people one deals with, perhaps all people to some extent, have good reasons to hide from others what they are doing, and even to lie to them ... conflict is the reality of life; suspicion is the guiding principle. (Douglas, 1976, p. 55)

For this reason he argues for what he terms *investigative field research* based upon a conflict paradigm. To avoid being deceived, the researcher – like any competent adult – has to be aware of the ever-present possibility of mis-information (unintended falsehoods), evasions, lies and fronts (socially shared and learned lies). Nevertheless Douglas concludes that social research necessarily relies on co-operative methods, building up friendly and trusting relations with informants, while checking out information wherever possible, 'for the investigative researcher likes and trusts informants, but never more than necessary' (Douglas, 1976, p. 133).

As for the objection that researchers may be 'captured' by one of the interest groups in a community and hence lose their objectivity, this scarcely arises for the relatively small-scale projects of community-based research which are advocated here.

A more cogent possibility, of findings arising which are contrary to the organisation's expectations or in some ways critical of the organisation's performance, should however be recognised at the earliest stages. Where this does occur the main participants in local organisations are often already self-critical, so that ways and means can be found for handling negative findings within the context of a reporting relationship which develops as the research progresses.

Everitt *et al.* point to the ethical difficulty surrounding publication of *evaluation* studies where the organisation concerned is lobbying for a continuation of funding. They warn that widespread publication of findings that cast doubt on a particular social programme, when at the same time there are attempts by the funding authority to reduce budgets may not be the most effective way of continuing with the programme and pursuing the direction of work, albeit with changes and modifications arising from evaluation. (Everitt *et al.*, 1992, p. 129)

By investing ownership of the client report with the organisation, the practice advocated here ensures that the internal management of the organisation is aware of the findings. In many cases they would then wish to go further and present the report to external agencies – but that is a decision for them to take and not one that a participatory researcher can make for them. Where wider academic publication is desirable, then this, like the original research, becomes a matter for negotiation.

The client organisation

Practical social research involves matching the interests of a student in the social sciences with the interests of a local group or organisation. Non-profit voluntary or third sector organisations (Salamon and Anheier, 1992, p. 126) providing services for a specific section of the community offer many opportunities for research projects, on condition that access and terms of research can be negotiated. The reasons why we suggest partnership in projects with these organisations are as follows:

- Such organisations are often involved in activities of social welfare which are of interest to social science students. For instance, they may provide services for special needs (disabled) people, ethnic minorities, women, children and the elderly. Or they may be involved in local community-based social and economic development. Such activities have implications for social policy and often relate to wider issues in students' courses.
- Voluntary organisations frequently do not have the re-

sources, in people or finance, to carry out their own research, so student involvement is a direct and positive benefit to them. Many organisations are now contracting with local government to provide services. In order to win their contracts they have to show that they are evaluating service provision from the viewpoint of the users. A student project based on independent evaluation is therefore often a welcome addition to this process.

• Working with voluntary organisations avoids problems of the exploitation of free student labour which might arise if research were being done for commercial organisations. Students often feel motivated by working for groups aiming to improve the quality of life for disadvantaged or underprivileged people.

• Research in partnership with community organisations means that the student's work is more likely to be used for the benefit of others than a report written for academic purposes – which may end up simply gathering dust on a shelf.

Gaining access

There may, however, be difficulties in gaining access to situations and informants in the kinds of areas which interest social scientists. Researchers refer to those who have the power to ease access to groups and institutions as 'sponsors'. 'Gatekeepers' are those who can permit or withhold access (Lindlof, 1995, pp. 106–10). Where an educational institution has become known for working with community groups, then invitations or opportunities for projects may be offered and sponsorship found. Otherwise, if possible, it makes sense to make an approach through an organisation with which personal contacts have already been established. If that is not possible, then a specific request needs to be made to the relevant gatekeeper. We deal with the practical aspects of this negotiation at greater length in Chapter 3. Here we note some general concerns.

First of all, the organisation has to be satisfied that the

student is a person who can be trusted to act responsibly and not to upset its own members and contacts. Students have a degree of status as people in higher education with some knowledge and experience in social issues, although the 'student image' can also attract negative labelling. But the most important part of acceptance is personal and derives from how the student presents herself or himself to the organisation, because trust tends to be based on experience.

Second, the organisation needs to know that what is being proposed will not result in exploitation of the organisation for selfish academic ends but that the project will make a contribution to the organisation's own information gathering or evaluation of services.

Third, the organisation needs to be presented with a clear rationale for the project, based on showing what the student has to offer in terms of skills, time, expertise and academic support.

Finally, the researcher needs to be aware that access is not something granted unconditionally and without restrictions for the duration of the project. Instead it is common to find that access has to be negotiated afresh with different sets of informants; that an organisation manager's permission does not release the researcher from the requirement of obtaining consent from her staff as well; and that sensitive information requires further access permission which may only be granted after the researcher has initially proved herself or himself to be reliable and able to fit in.

Stages of research

Gaining access is part of the first stage of research, preparation for the project. The next two stages are fieldwork and analysis, followed by the writing of reports. Each stage involves the client organisation, and a detailed order can be specified.

(a) *Preparation*

1. Initial formulation of concerns by the student and the organisation

2. Negotiation on a feasible project, to include outline choice of research methods and identification of potential informants

3. Development of research brief for the organisation, including types of questions to be asked, and how they are to be answered

4. Development of research action plan and timetable for research

(b) *Fieldwork*

5. Trying out research methods

6. Data collection using the methods selected in the research brief

7. Initial feedback to the organisation and revision to action plan as necessary

(c) *Analysis*

8. Checking and verification of data

9. Analysis of the data

10. Drawing conclusions

(d) *Reporting*

11. Writing the report for the organisation, with recommendations where appropriate

12. Writing a separate methodology report for the academic department

The text follows through this order in the arrangement of the chapters to offer discussion of varieties of methods of social research and to suggest ways of tackling the practical issues of setting up and completing a project with a community organisation. However, before moving on to think about research strategies, we wish to invite students to consider what they may hope to gain at a personal level from participating in a research project and how they can plan to work collaboratively.

Personal transferable skills

As well as using specific skills related to research methods which are covered in Part II, social research provides the opportunity to exercise and develop what have been termed *personal transferable skills*. What are these skills? In contrast to the technical and academic skills of being able to plan and execute research, personal transferable skills are those general abilities which come from exercising initiative, taking responsibility and working with others. They are rarely taught explicitly but tend to be picked up through experience.

Nevertheless, these are the kinds of skills which employers increasingly are demanding from job applicants. For example, a study by the University of Sheffield Personal Skills Unit (Education for Enterprise, 1992, p. 34) showed that the kind of abilities which employers were most frequently looking for, in order of importance, were:

1. Oral communication
2. Teamwork
3. Enthusiasm
4. Motivation
5. Initiative
6. Leadership
7. Commitment
8. Interpersonal skills
9. Organising ability

A research project work is one way of developing these abilities. A successful project requires a personal input of this kind and can demonstrate through the eventual reports that such skills have in fact been exercised.

Much emphasis, as can be seen from the list above and from other similar surveys (Tate and Thompson, 1994, p. 130), is placed on communication, on drive and initiative, on problem solving and on teamwork. The Education for Enterprise Unit of Teesside Polytechnic (1992) has amplified and clarified what employers are looking for, as follows.

- **Ability to communicate** – this covers the clear presentation of complex information in written and oral reports; tailoring the information and methods of presentation to the audience; and active listening, responding to and interpreting the views of others.
- **Planning skills** – the ability to set and achieve meaningful goals, and to develop contingency plans to deal with problems; time management skills; the establishment of priorities, and the balancing of short-term with long-term objectives
- **Teamwork and leadership** – to be able to work with and through others, having a positive impact on co-ordination as leader or facilitator; understanding the dynamics of groups, and the various roles of members.
- **Specific abilities** – in particular, computer literacy, numeracy and the application of technology, to include familiarity with word processing, spreadsheets and statistical packages
- **Drive or achievement** – 'self-starting', motivation and the ability to work to deadlines, coupled with willingness to take a degree of risk
- **Problem-solving and decision-making** – a willingness to tackle difficult as well as easy problems; the ability to review issues systematically and to make informed judgements; and to know when further information or support is necessary
- **Orientation to change** – showing flexibility in a dynamic environment by evaluating the impact of one's own actions and learning from the experience

21

- **Willingness to continue learning** – knowing how to learn rather than having specific skills, coupled with a commitment to continued self-development

Teamwork and group projects

Each formulation of personal transferable skills makes mention of 'working co-operatively in groups' or some other similar reference to teamwork. It has already been suggested that participatory or collaborative research involves an element of working co-operatively with practitioners and informants. Many practical research projects can be successfully completed by individual students and do not require teamwork among students. However, the option of students forming teams to do projects is well worth considering as it offers the potential of extending the scope of the work undertaken and the learning opportunities. Teamwork is such an important aspect that it is considered in some detail below.

Writing from an industrial perspective, Bailey argues that teamwork skills are essential to the future of industry in this and the next decade. She contends that *teamwork* is:

> one area where there is a major difference between the ways in which education and industry operate . . . In general, our education system is based on individual work and collaboration is frowned on . . . Understanding and being able to apply what is learned to a real-life problem is often neither examined nor rewarded. The ability of students to work with colleagues to 'deliver the goods' by a set date is given little prominence, despite being a key element of the world of work. (Bailey, 1990, p. 69)

Teamwork provides a setting in which transferable skills can be developed. For teamwork demands a great deal of the individual, not just in terms of being able to 'get on' with others. It is also about the ability to communicate well, both verbally and in writing, and to be sensitive to the feelings and needs of others: 'It concerns trust and the ability to share ideas – to gain kudos for the group rather than the individual' (Bailey, 1990, p. 69).

Team dynamics

Applied social research where there is a defined objective within a finite timescale is often appropriate for teams of students working in small groups. Teams of between 2 and 5 members can do much useful work. Much larger than that and the group becomes more difficult to co-ordinate and communication problems can arise. A team of researchers has obvious advantages in sharing the workload or expanding the range of the research – for example, by interviewing larger samples of people, or by using different styles of research within the same project, or both. Less obvious is that students can try different and more unusual techniques, such as joint interviewing, where two researchers conduct an interview together.

A team is also an important source of support for individuals and a sense of obligation to other team members can help keep everyone to an agreed time schedule for the work. On the other hand, teamwork can create stresses through dependency on others and disagreements over what should be done.

If teams are to work and not fall apart in dissent and mutual recrimination, then certain principles need to be recognised and discussed. These are:

1. Group development
2. Unwritten contracts
3. Team roles and leadership.

Group development

Tuckman's (1965) stages of group development:

- Forming
- Storming

- Norming
- Performing

demonstrate that groups do not just happen to work effectively, but relationships have to be built up and understanding and trust between members has to be fostered. Partly this involves bringing to the surface rather than hiding any conflict over objectives, methods of operation or the roles of the different members. Tuckman's suggestion is that it is only when common norms and objectives have been agreed that a group can become effective. This final stage of 'performing' is preceded by more conflictual stages as people hammer out agreement on the common objective and their contribution as well as that of the others towards it.

Where students are allowed to form a self-selected team, prior acquaintance with each other may help to reduce conflict and problems. The self-selected team has a background of past activity and knowledge of each other to draw on and initial levels of trust and mutual obligation are already in place. However, the experience of project work together, which is far different from ordinary acquaintance, may severely strain even such a relationship.

The alternative, the purpose-formed team, begins with that initial process of forming to undertake a specific project. For research projects of the scale and complexity that are being considered here, extending over most of an academic year, the risks of incompatibility among team members are severe and such teams would require a careful watching brief from supervisors. Our practice has been to opt for self-selected teams where possible, though obviously this restricts the possible combinations. The individual project is then valuable for students who feel that they do not wish to work with other students.

Unwritten contracts

In contrast to formal contracts which are written agreements (like the agreements produced with and for the

24

client organisations), unwritten contracts are based on understandings about expected behaviour which are not formally specified. These are mostly unconscious as long as the expectations are observed, but can create stress and disturbance if they are broken. Yet because the expectations have not been voiced and team members do not wish to damage the team, they may feel unable to express their dissatisfaction or negotiate to reach agreement.

To deal with this it is a good idea to discuss explicitly the following questions:

- What do I expect of the other members of this group?
- What do the other members of this group expect of me?

These can form the basis for a short brainstorming session.

Some of the issues which might be raised and which can be divisive if expectations are breached, are:

- listening to suggestions from others
- accepting advice from members who have most expertise in the topic
- meeting regularly and punctually
- sending in apologies beforehand if absence is unavoidable
- sharing the workload equally by doing work of equal value
- being able to express differences of opinion without argument
- resolving differences calmly and logically
- carrying out individual tasks delegated by the group
- sharing the most difficult or boring tasks.

Other issues may have to do with dealing with external circumstances, such as:

- not giving lower priority to the team project in order to boost one's individual performance on other courses
- making allowances and covering for team members with justifiable reasons for absence, such as illness or family problems.

Flagging up these issues through discussion at an early stage can be helpful in establishing a baseline of mutual responsibility, and avoiding situations where one or more members of the team become critical of the behaviour of others, but do not feel able to mention it to them for fear of damaging or destroying the team, with consequences to their own performance. Such discussion may also deal with challenging gendered roles or behaviour before conflict becomes personalised and more difficult to resolve.

Leadership

Although it seems obvious that teams need leadership, research on group performance (Belbin, 1981) indicates that a simple leader/follower dichotomy is much too restrictive. Instead there are a variety of roles which need to be undertaken by the effective team. There are also numerous ways in which different members can carry out these different roles.

Belbin distinguishes eight different team roles. So, for example, the Innovator with creative thinking plays a different role from the Chairman or co-ordinator, or the Completer who looks to the fine detail of the study. All these are different skills which a group needs. Leadership does not have to be fixed permanently: a learning group can allow leadership to be shared according to the particular issue, the expertise of the individual or the stage the study has reached.

Overcoming group problems

There is always a possibility that teams can fail, when the stresses placed on them are too great and when individuals have conflicting perceptions of their group roles and personal interests.

Two reasons which students commonly offer for holding back from wanting to do teamwork are:

1. their fear of being assigned to a team with a person

they have already judged to be less competent or reliable, with the possibility of their own grades being affected adversely; and

2. their categorisation of themselves as individualists, unable or unwilling to work with others.

To the individualists we would say that there is no objection to doing research individually. Doing practical research should be a matter of choice and not compulsion. To those concerned about being teamed with others who cannot be trusted to show suitable competence or endeavour, there are three safeguards.

First, it has to be recognised that practical research is demanding. Only students who have demonstrated reasonable competence in basic research methods training should be encouraged to choose the option of applied research.

Second, by inviting students to enrol in teams of their own choosing, friendship and study groups can form the basis for project teams. However, friendship groups may be tested in new ways by having to work together.

Finally, the supervisor has the important role of being available to help resolve major difficulties, preferably by encouraging and supporting the team to find their own solution wherever possible.

Conclusion

Practical research in the 'real world' offers the opportunity to engage with groups and organisations in the local community to meet their needs. This can be a difficult but rewarding task. The kind of engagement suggested here is collaborative research in partnership with local organisations, which requires an ethical approach based upon openness and voluntary consent. Practical social research also provides the chance to develop personal transferable skills in terms of initiative, communication, problem-solving and responsibility for achievement. Finally, the ability to work in a team is increasingly being seen as an important outcome of students' learning experience and one which is well suited to practical research.

2
Issues in Methodology

Practical social research involves negotiation with a client organisation about the purpose of the research project, its intended outcome and also the research methods to be used. On this last point the supervisor and you the student are the 'experts' who will have to decide how to carry out the research. You can discuss with the client organisation various strategies for obtaining the results, but ultimately you and your supervisor have responsibility for choosing what is appropriate and feasible.

This chapter deals with the ideas behind that choice of research methods. It provides an introduction to the deeper issues concerning the nature of social reality implicit in research practice. Awareness of these issues will help guide your decision, which should be evaluated in your methodology or reflexive report.

Which research method to choose?

The methods for social research which are readily available are fairly few in number: questionnaire survey, interview, observation and use of documents and secondary data. The experiment has been omitted from this book as unlikely to be practicable in the sort of social research project which is here proposed, though for some researchers it still remains 'the scientific method *par excellence* for investigating causal effects' (Singleton *et al.*, 1988, p. 171).

In this chapter, four key issues are discussed:

- the assumptions built into particular methods
- the rationale for employing multiple methods
- the application of these issues within a framework of applied research, evaluation research and social action (Hessler, 1992, p. 293)
- the feminist critique of research methods.

Methods and methodology

It is helpful to distinguish initially between *methodology* as the philosophy or general principles behind research, and *methods* as the practice of research in terms of strategies and techniques. What has to be stressed is that in selecting certain methods you are consciously or unconsciously taking on board their methodological assumptions about the nature of the social world and the principles of social enquiry.

In arguing against an uncritical choice of methods and for an integration of methods with methodology, Bulmer has noted that:

> Unfortunately research methods are sometimes taught as if they were a set of skills, rather like those of cookery or vehicle maintenance, which can be learned and applied regardless of context. (Bulmer, 1977, p. 6)

So what is the context of the practical research being outlined in this book? We can think of context in two ways. First, it is the *needs of the client organisation* which makes your research applied rather than basic or abstract. However, this is not the only context. The second context of your research is the set of *philosophical assumptions* about 'what should pass as warrantable knowledge about the social world' (Bryman, 1988a, p. 5). Pawson (1991) has argued that such philosophical discussion cannot be separated from the real world of research but consists of examining the reasons given for a research design or the rationale for an innovative technique.

Social research is concerned not just with a descriptive 'fact-gathering' exercise, but with understanding the social situation in which the researcher is involved. But as Gilbert points out, even understanding rather than description is not enough. In addition:

> social research has to be located within an academic discipline – sociology, education, management, social work or whatever – which offers perspectives, methods and a 'tradition'. (Gilbert, 1993, p. xi)

At every stage – designing the research, conducting interviews or observations, analysing and interpreting the findings – you are faced with choices and have to make decisions in the light of some criteria. These criteria are the ideas which guide your work and which constantly interplay with what you are doing. These ideas will derive in part from your own academic discipline and represent the connection between theory and data which is central to all research.

Theory and data

According to Gilbert, the three major ingredients in social research are:

> the construction of theory, the collection of data and, no less important, the design of methods for gathering data. All of them have to be right if the research is to yield interesting results.   (Gilbert, 1993, p. 18)

Gilbert suggests that a theory is often an answer to the question 'Why?' A theory provides an answer to puzzling questions because it links together different elements in a causal process to produce a more general explanation of the particulars that have been observed. The 'why' question can be posed by the client organisation or yourself at the initial discussion about the research.

Example 2.1

A client organisation wished to know why some residents from a nearby centre for adults with learning difficulties attended their evening club whereas others did not.

Some explanations were suggested by the key worker of the client organisation and others by the students undertaking the project

- Perhaps some residents did not want to make the journey to the club or did not have adequate transport.
- Perhaps the residents wanted to be accompanied on the journey.
- Perhaps they did not have enough information (or any information) about the club.
- Perhaps the club did not provide the kinds of activities which the residents liked.
- Perhaps the club was not friendly enough.

These explanations are not sufficiently general to warrant the status of theory, but they may point to more general explanations of this kind:

- club attendance is influenced by accessibility
- club attendance is affected by people's information about it
- club attendance is related to people's own needs and expectations.

At this level a theory of attendance at voluntary activities is being explored which should ideally apply both to the situation being observed and to other similar situations. The suggestions offered above are not mutually exclusive – more than one could apply in any particular instance – so our theory of club attendance is *multi-causal*. This might suggest that attendance is dependent on geographical location and the social characteristics of attenders, although other factors such as the potential attenders' values, knowledge and expectations would also have an effect.

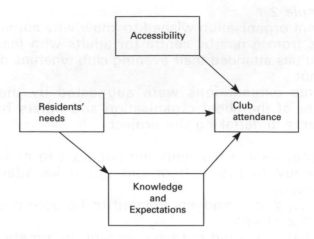

Figure 2.1   Simplified causal model of club attendance

Causal model

The relationship between all these concepts can be shown
by a causal model (Rose, 1982, pp. 93–4), as Figure 2.1
illustrates. Here knowledge and expectations of the club
are shown as intervening concepts which mediate between
the background characteristics of the potential club users
and whether they attend the club.

A research project might therefore try to establish the
range of reasons people give for attendance (or non-
attendance), and the relative priority they give to each
reason, in order to substantiate or disprove such a theoretical model.

Theory provides explanation through a series of general ideas (as above) or abstract statements, and it
may involve prediction. For instance, in Example 2.1 it
might be predicted that attendance at the club would
improve:

- if transport was provided
- if publicity improved
- if the club organised more popular activities, such as
  outings to the seaside.

32

In the research these predictions can be explored through interviews. Are they raised spontaneously by informants as suggestions for change? Or, if you introduce these ideas, is there agreement from informants that these suggestions are relevant and valued?

Induction and deduction

Where do theories come from? They come partly from evidence, and partly from beliefs and ideas. For instance, political parties may hold strenuously to particular theories though they have little evidence to back them up! Philosophers of social science talk about the processes of *induction* and *deduction*. Induction starts from specific observations and uses these to develop a more general theory, deduction starts with theory and uses it to explain observed actions.

Both induction and deduction have been criticised as ways of constructing scientific theories. Induction appears solid because it is grounded in 'facts', and is therefore 'empiricist'. Its assumption is that:

> there is a reality 'out there' with regularities that can be described and explained, and it adopts the epistemological principle that the task of observing this reality is essentially unproblematic as long as the researcher adopts objective procedures.   (Blaikie, 1993, p. 137)

Epistemology refers to what we accept as knowledge – how we know what we know. Inductive reasoning based on observed facts results in theory which, however, can never be totally proved, because of the possible existence of observations running counter to the theory which have not yet been made.

Another telling objection is that observation of facts is not straightforward. It involves subjectivity and interpretation. Anyone who has started out to make a sociological observation of a particular setting – a schoolroom, a hospital ward, a workplace, a church – will have experienced the problem of being poised with pen and notepad, wondering what, of all the activity going on, s/he is to record. Deciding what is to be recorded means making a subjective decision about what is important. That decision must come from ideas or beliefs which are prior to the observation or which develop with it. Even deciding how to describe what is being observed or which category it falls into will require interpretative work by the observer.

As an alternative to inductive explanations of how theory is formed, Popper (1961) has argued that a deductive process takes place so that theoretical notions or hypotheses guide the observations that are made. To make this process rigorous, he argued for the strategy of 'falsification', that is, that hypotheses should be generated which the researcher seeks to *disprove*. If after collecting the evidence the hypothesis cannot be disproved, then it can be provisionally and temporarily accepted – at least until some more evidence is found which does disprove it. If the hypothesis fails, some other more robust hypothesis has to be produced and tested.

Yet it has been argued that even this approach using deduction to select and test theories is not entirely deductive, but involves induction in choosing between competing theories:

> Knowledge concerning the past success of a theory to pass tests is not an adequate basis for future actions based on the theory, except on the basis of inductive assumptions.   (Blaikie, 1993, p. 151)

Another objection takes us back to the issue of where the propositions that form the basis of the deductivist theory come from. Some form of induction seems to operate here, even if dressed up in the language of scientific imagination. So a more convincing explanation of the production of theory is one which uses both induction and deduction in a circular or *iterative* process.

Theory and evidence

Sociologists have come up with different solutions to the relation between theory and evidence. For example, Marxism includes a theory of social class. For Marx, however, understanding society could never be just a matter of collecting evidence in the form of empirical facts. 'Facts' were used by Marx to illustrate his theory, which was designed not just to describe society but, most importantly, to change it. Marx was an ideologist whose theories were devised to show the inevitability of social revolution and to justify that revolution. Marx himself collected very little empirical data, though his colleague Engels did (in the *Condition of the English Working Classes*, 1844) and many subsequent researchers have applied Marxist theory to making sense of data or evidence.

Different solutions to the theory/data relationship have been proposed and the two main general approaches will be considered here:

- the 'scientific' model; and
- the ethnographic model.

To a large extent these two approaches also correspond to differences between quantitative and qualitative research, though nowadays most writers on methodology avoid such a distinction and stress instead the strategy of 'mixing methods' (Brannen, 1992). However, before leaving the discussion of Marx behind, the question needs to be raised whether ideology has any part to play in practical social research.

The role of ideals

It is important to realise that in forming a relationship with a client organisation you are working with people concerned with changing the lives of the service users in their organisation. This concern is based on ideals and all organisations have an 'ethos' or central set of values which they use in formulating policy. For some this may be stated explicitly in a 'mission statement', for others it may be based more on shared informal understandings.

Example 2.2
One organisation working for the welfare of people with mental health problems has devised 'accomplishments' or ideals from which objectives for day-to-day practice can be derived. The service provided can then be evaluated according to whether it meets the objectives or not. The accomplishments include:

- **Community presence** – giving service users a real presence in the community, using local services and sharing community-based activities
- **Choice** – giving service users every possible choice in all aspects of their lives
- **Respect** – giving service users the full respect they deserve as valued adult members of the community, empowering them to have full citizen rights.

Clearly if research were being conducted for this organisation, then it would be necessary to know what its ideals were and how it was working to achieve them. This is why students should familiarise themselves at an early stage with the ethos of the organisation. However, the key methodological issue for the researcher is whether s/he has to share the ideological interests of the client or remain detached.

The philosophy for applied research outlined in Chapter 1 argued that the research is about *partnership* between student and client, and that, where possible, this research should involve empowerment for the service users. Your involvement is to provide a piece of research which meets the needs of the client organisation and is of a high academic standard. You do not therefore have to share your client's ideals, though you do need to be sensitive to them. If you do wish to challenge the client organisation's ideals or practice, it is suggested that you do so in a separate methodology report submitted to your academic department (see Chapter 11). In the chapters on reports you will find discussion of what to do if your informants criticise the client organisation; criticism with which you may or may not have some sympathy, but which needs to be recognised.

Models of research

The issues of theory, evidence and ideology may lead you to consider how 'objective' or 'detached' you should be in your work. Should you aim to be studiously neutral in your interviewing technique, or should you deliberately try to create rapport? What makes research 'valid', and what are the most 'reliable' methods to use? These and many other issues can be related back to a broad divide in the social sciences between research based on the scientific model and research which derives from ethnographic commitments.

The scientific model

In a model derived from how the natural sciences ideally operate, Wallace (1979) has conceptualised the relationship between theory and data as shown in Figure 2.2. This diagram brings together the previously discussed elements of induction and deduction through a process of moving from observation to theory and from theory to observation. It would be possible to enter the scientific cycle at any stage – with hypotheses, observations, empirical generalisations or theories – but each is connected to the others. Thus observations, for example, do not exist in isolation but are linked to the theories which they test.

Though this model of scientific process has achieved a wide degree of support, it is not without its critics. Blaikie, for instance, argues that: 'It is important to recognise, however, that Wallace's scheme ... makes no provision for [the] socially constructed character [of social reality]' (Blaikie, 1993, p. 158). In other words, Wallace argues

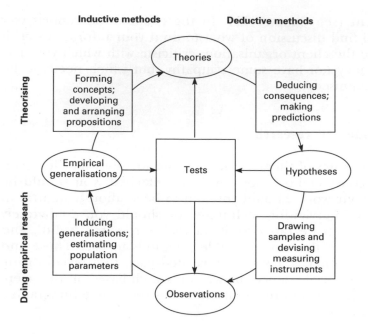

Figure 2.2   The research process

SOURCE: Blaikie, N., *Approaches to Social Enquiry* (Cambridge: Polity) as adapted from Wallace, Walter L., *The Logic of Science in Sociology* (New York: Aldine de Gruyter) Copyright © 1971 Walter L. Wallace, and Wallace, Walter L. *Principles of Scientific Sociology* (New York: Aldine) Copyright © 1983 Walter L. Wallace.

from a positivist standpoint that social reality is open to outside observation and can be objectively studied rather than being constructed by the perceptions and experiences of its members.

   Philosophers of science as well as writers on the methodology of the social sciences have found much to dispute in Wallace's model as an idealisation of the way science really proceeds. They point to examples from the history of science where contrary evidence did not lead to the falsification of hypotheses (as Popper argued for) or to the abandonment of theories.

   For, as Kuhn (1964) demonstrated, the model is based

on the way physics (the 'purest' science) was believed to proceed, yet scientists are subjective in their decisions to accept or reject evidence. In real life they form and work within scientific communities, where scientists share a view of the nature of the reality that they study (called a *paradigm*). The paradigm provides the framework for legitimate scientific activity, so the scientific community tends to act conservatively in defending accepted theories against new evidence – until the evidence becomes so overwhelming that a new paradigm is formed.

But if Wallace's model is not a true description of what happens in the natural sciences, does it apply to how social scientists work? Here the evidence is also not supportive. Increasingly social researchers are providing accounts which reveal the decisions, demands, compromises and sometimes 'messiness' of real life research.

If the scientific model is not descriptive of what takes place, is it (or should it be) *prescriptive*? That is, is it a useful guide for how social research *should* be conducted? Does it set standards which we should aim to achieve?

The survey method, dealt with in greater depth in Part II, does draw on this model, and so adopts a positivistic approach to data collection. For example, in surveys:

1. *deductive reasoning* is used in arguing from the general to the specific – that is, from the wider problem being investigated to specific concepts or *hypotheses* related to one another through causal models;
2. such hypotheses are then *operationalised* into *indicators* – that is, the abstract and unobservable are investigated through variables which are observable and measurable, and again interrelated through causal models;
3. reliable research instruments are designed which reduce *interviewer bias* to produce data which is *standardised*;
4. provided the sample has been correctly drawn according to statistical theory, the results can be *generalised*.

So the scientific model does describe the survey method to some extent. The question raised by many social researchers is, however, the prescriptive issue – is this how social research should be done? Can social reality be comprehended by a focus on objective measurable facts?

Weber and the scientific model

In the late nineteenth century, Weber took issue with the positivism particularly associated with Durkheim – the scientific approach which had emerged earlier in the century. Positivism (Kolakowski, 1993) states that:

1. reality is what is available to the senses;
2. science deals with facts, not values;
3. the natural and social sciences share the same common logic and methodology (the scientific model).

For Weber, the subject matter of sociology was *social action* or social behaviour: 'Action is "social" in so far as its subjective meaning takes account of the behaviour of others and is thereby oriented in its course' (Lee and Newby, 1983, p. 174).

Studying such action involves understanding the meaning of behaviour to those involved. This goes beyond the positivist concern with what is observable to the senses. For Weber any adequate explanation of behaviour has to include an account of the subjective intentions of the actor through using '*Verstehen*', or empathetic understanding. Like Marx, Weber realised that the results of interactions are not always what the actor intended but such intentions are a necessary though not sufficient explanation for understanding social behaviour.

With his concern for the meaning of social action, Weber can be counted within the interpretivist perspective, which recognises that the social world cannot be studied from the 'outside', but is already constituted and reconstituted by social actors as they interpret their own world.

They develop meanings for their activities together, and they have ideas about what is relevant for making sense of these activities. In short, the social world is already interpreted before the social scientist arrives. (Blaikie, 1993, p. 36)

Weber has also become known as the foremost exponent of 'value-free' social science – that is, of social science that is ethically and politically neutral. He did not argue that sociologists should not make value judgements: 'An attitude of moral indifference has no connection with scientific objectivity' (Lee and Newby, 1983, p. 172). Teachers, he believed, should state their values in the classroom – not preach them – and they should make it clear when they are evaluating rather than describing or interpreting an objective fact. Likewise, if sociologists are employed by government, their role is not to say what should be done, but to inform politicians of what can be done – in the light of goals which the politicians have set. The researcher can advise on which means are best and give the different costs involved in different policies.

Weber then drew a distinction between facts and values. Values were judgements about what was right and wrong, desirable and undesirable. Facts were the subject-matter of science.

For Weber, though, science did not just mean collecting quantifiable data to create theory (as inductivists like Durkheim believed) but using rigorous concepts which were derived from criticism, logical rationalisation, exact observation and intuitiveness – as well as from figures. Science also meant looking for causes. Weber argued that causality is never more than a partial view of reality. We select from an infinite diversity and decide how far back our explanation has to go.

Deciding when to stop in the search for causes involves what Weber called 'value orientation'. All scientists make decisions according to their own values:

- in selecting the subject of study
- in sifting the essential from the details

41

- in supplying reasons for establishing a relationship between various elements and the meaning we give them
- in verifying propositions through clear rational thinking,
  not just using personal experience or emotion.

The ethnographic approach

Ethnography can trace its roots to the types of reasoning
highlighted above in the discussion of Weber's work and
also to the practice and methodology of the social anthropologists at the beginning of this century, people such as
Malinowski and Radcliffe-Brown. Ethnography provides an
alternative methodology to the scientific model through:

1. *inductive reasoning* – from the particular to the general – building up cases, letting hypotheses emerge
2. *'grounded theory'* – conceptual schemes arise from the
   data – in a bottom-up, not top-down approach
3. *progressive focusing* – concepts develop and become
   narrower as the work proceeds
4. *theoretical sampling* – with groups selected according
   to age, gender, religion, geographical location or
   other relevant identities and studied at different times
   of the day or week
5. *reflexivity* – the researcher reflects on her/his role
   in the research, dealing with such issues as *reactivity*,
   or how people's behaviour is affected by their awareness of being observed or by the characteristics of
   the researcher.

It is now recognised that researchers should examine the
whole research process and their role in it very carefully,
not only at the end of the research but during the process itself. 'Reflexivity' means the self-awareness researchers
should have developed throughout the study about how
they influenced the results. How did they gain access to
their informants and explain the research? How much
did their gender, race or age affect the way they inter-
acted with their informants?

Data is seen not as something 'out there' to be collected or captured but as something created through a social process. Data is produced or generated through social interaction between the researcher and the informant, so that research itself is a creative process which you will be part of – as you design and negotiate your research, frame your research instruments and carry out your fieldwork.

Validity

With all kinds of research, whether based on the scientific model or the ethnographic, we need to know how much value we should attach to our findings. Are they an accurate representation of what actually exists? In other words, are our findings valid? A common definition of validity is:

> *The extent to which a test, questionnaire or other operationalisation is really measuring what the researcher intends to measure.*

Sociologists assess the validity of their research by looking at evidence, at how the research was carried out, whether anything could have interfered with the research process and confused the results, and the nature of the connection between the evidence and the generalisations. In the past some sociologists have claimed that experiments and surveys are methods with a high validity because they are standardised or controlled. But such methods can be artificial – a finding may be valid in the laboratory, where nothing has interfered with the finding or confounded the results – but it cannot be applied to the real world where social interaction is more complex.

Such research is arguably high on *internal* validity but low on *external* validity (generalisability to a wider population). Small-scale studies using in-depth interviews with a handful of informants, on the other hand, may be criticised for being low on internal validity but high on external validity because they relate to people in everyday settings.

43

Reliability

Researchers are also concerned with whether or not their results can be replicated. A common definition of reliability is:

The extent to which a test would give consistent results if applied by different researchers more than once to the same people under standard conditions.

Teams of interviewers are trained to ask questions in the same way and several surveys may repeat the same questions so that comparisons can be made between samples and over time. Surveys are supposed to rate highly on reliability because each person being studied is asked the same questions. More problematic in terms of reliability are in-depth interviews – would two different researchers get the same data from interviewing the same person using a loosely structured schedule?

Triangulation

Social scientists have gradually realised the advantages of using a variety of research strategies so that the problems associated with one strategy may be compensated for by the strengths of another. This is called triangulation (Denzin, 1970) – using different research methods or sources of data to examine the same problem. The term comes from surveyors who take bearings on the same point from different angles.

Bryman, however, warns that:

In spite of its intuitive appeal, the suggestion that quantitative and qualitative research may be combined for the purposes of triangulation is by no means as unproblematic as it first appears, (Bryman, 1992, p. 63).

If the data from different techniques do not agree, it is not clear which is to be preferred. Nor is it clear that quantitative techniques such as surveys do actually tap the same sort of information that qualitative techniques such as in-depth interviews do. For this reason Brannen (1992) talks in terms of *complementarity* rather than the *integration of methods* recommended by ethnographers such as Whyte (1984).

Different research methods can be used together within combined research strategies in various ways. For instance, qualitative studies can be used to set the scene for a quantitative survey, or to explore in more depth issues thrown up by such a survey. Combined methods which give each type of study equal weight are more rare, though Brannen comments that her study

> drew attention to an advantage of the multi-method approach, namely its ability to confront contradictions and highlight the fragmented and multi-faceted nature of human consciousness. This benefit is one which supersedes the commonly claimed advantage of increasing data validity. (Brannen, 1992, p. 31)

The split between qualitative and quantitative research is no longer as obvious as it used to be. Rather, today the argument tends to be among ethnographers about the best way to handle data – or among survey researchers on, say, sampling design. Perhaps the biggest distinction at present is between those who see multiple strategies as necessary and those who really prefer to use – or to commission – one strategy or a limited range of strategies.

Evaluation research

Many of the projects which voluntary and community organisations would like students to do for them involve an element of evaluation, that is, collecting information on the need for services and how well services are being delivered. Evaluation research, according to Hessler, fits on a continuum between, at the one end, pure basic research, and at the other, social action.

While social action and [basic] research are inherently in-compatible, evaluation research is closer to social action than it is to basic research. Evaluators strive for the best of basic research, that is, carefully designed valid and reliable research, and the best of applied research where research findings ought to really make some impact or difference in the society. (Hessler, 1992, p. 302)

Such research is inevitably value laden, making judgements about how well objectives are met. For Weiss the purpose of evaluation research is defined as follows:

to measure the effects of a program against the goals it sets out to accomplish as a means of contributing to subsequent decision making about the program and improving future programming. (Weiss, 1972, p. 4)

Evaluation research is a form of applied research in which the information has direct relevance to subsequent de-cisions about improvements to, or the continuation of, a particular action programme. It involves a specification of the goals or intended purposes of the programme and collection of data relevant to such goals in a measurable form. It requires some kind of judgement as to whether and to what degree the goals of a programme are being achieved. It is intended for a variety of audiences, such as funding agencies, project directors, project staff, and clients of a programme, as well as scholars – and all of these may require different things from an evaluation study.

Evaluation research is not, then, a specific body of re-search techniques but an approach to research which differs from basic or academic research in its purpose. Though the experimental model of two randomised groups, one using the programme and the other not doing so as a control group, is strongly advocated by some as the best way of doing evaluation research, in practice many other methods have been applied in evaluations – non-randomised comparison groups, case studies, use of extant data and other forms of qualitative research – for what Rossi and Freeman term pragmatic evaluation. For them

Evaluation is an art, and every evaluation represents, or should represent, an idiosyncratic effort to meet the needs of program sponsors and stakeholders. Thus, whereas scientific studies strive to meet a set of research standards set by the investigator's peers, evaluations need to be designed and implemented in ways that recognise the policy and program interests of the sponsors and stakeholders, and that will yield maximally useful information for decision makers given the political circumstances, program constraints, and available resources. (Rossi and Freeman, 1993, p. 30)

Here the term 'stakeholder' is used to refer to everyone involved with the programme – management, practitioners, service users, funding bodies and community members – who have an interest or stake in the organisation and its effective operation.

Evaluators and programme staff

There is often a conflict between the scientific desirability of controlling variables through the experimental method, and practical, political and ethical issues of working in the fluid and changing setting of programme delivery. Weiss (1972, p. 82) identifies a possible conflict of orientations between evaluators' concern for *summative evaluation* (how well different programmes actually worked) and participants' concern for *formative evaluation* (how to make a programme work better). There is also a time-scale difference: summative evaluation has to wait for the end of the research, formative evaluation may be fed back as research progresses.

The different frames of reference of external evaluators and programme staff can lead to real practical problems of co-operation over data collection. Weiss (1972, pp. 102–4) lists a number of potential areas of conflict:

1. *Data collection* – programme staff are too busy to fill out questionnaires or give or arrange interviews;
2. *Record-keeping* – existing records are insufficiently

detailed or accurate to permit use for evaluation; changing or adding to record-keeping provokes resistance from staff;

3. *Selection of participants* – Random selection for experimental or control groups may be felt to negate the professional skills of programme staff;

4. *Feedback* – if staff are not given early feedback they may see the evaluator as uncommitted, and reduce their co-operation;

5. *Status rivalry* – The evaluator goes off to collect the glory while the staff who have made sacrifices to co-operate are unrecognised.

Alternative modes of evaluation

Not only can programme staff feel threatened by external evaluation, they may also reject its findings if they do not recognise the programme as reported by the evaluator as their own. As a result of such problems, which are inherent in evaluation research, alternative strategies have been proposed that:

- use qualitative rather than experimental methods
- involve the evaluator as *partner* in the process of gathering data
- enable programme participants to make their own contribution to evaluation.

So, for example, Posovac and Carey argue that in circumstances where programme goals cannot be clearly identified and measured quantitatively, a radically different approach to evaluation is required.

> One of the central goals of qualitative evaluation is to provide detailed descriptions of programs through the eyes of stakeholders along with the insights of the evaluator. The place of the evaluator is to integrate the views of many stakeholders providing feedback on those views so that every-

one understands the program better than before. (Posovac and Carey, 1989, p. 236)

A more radical approach, presented by Feuerstein (1986) and evolved in community development programmes in many parts of the world, is that of *participatory evaluation.* Here the techniques are tailored to the setting of the programme, and programme participants are involved in gathering information. This may require them to be trained in collecting data, carrying out a survey and writing reports, but the advantages of internal evaluators over external 'experts' is that they already know much about the area, the people and the programme.

Where it is a case of establishing the needs of a community, then another participatory method first used in developing countries, *Rapid Appraisal,* can be applied (Ong, 1993). Rapid Appraisal uses information collected from a variety of 'key informants' (community spokespeople) to identify directly from local people their needs and priorities and then to draw up action plans in collaboration with the community. In this way Rapid Appraisal: 'offers very specific insights: it can tell *what* the problems in a particular community are, but *not how many* people are affected by those problems' (Ong, 1993, p. 75).

Participatory evaluations may be queried concerning their subjectivity, but Lincoln and Guba (1985; also Guba and Lincoln, 1989) address issues of the internal validity or trustworthiness of qualitative evaluation under the concept of *authenticity.* Authentic evaluations are concerned with fairness, and with increasing participants' understanding and involvement to produce empowerment.

> The best evaluations ... will treat all stakeholders and their values with respect and will serve to enlarge their understanding of themselves, the program, and the other stakeholders. According to Lincoln and Guba qualitative evaluation based on intimate knowledge of the program and its stakeholders has the best chance of meeting these authenticity criteria. (Posovac and Carey, 1989, p. 241)

Further developments in methods of research

Social history

History based on *oral* evidence is an important part of social research today. Studies have been based on specific topics such as family, education or work, as well as more general life-history approaches. For example, Belinda Westover's (1986) account of the lives of tailoresses in Colchester in the years 1880–1918 relies heavily on oral evidence. Such studies are important because they give a sense of process and change.

Survey research is a 'snap-shot' of a moment in time, whereas oral history allows the informant to talk about changes in their life and the way attitudes have altered. Oral history provides an important check on documentary history, which often misses out significant but less powerful groups such as working class communities, Black people and women.

Critical methods

Critical theorists such as Jürgen Habermas have argued that science plays a crucial role in controlling people in modern capitalist society and that social research based on the scientific model, particularly quantitative research, is inappropriate for studying human behaviour. Interpretive research such as ethnography is better, but does not go far enough. People need to be emancipated from the forces and ideology which dominate their lives. Ethnography is criticised for describing how people live instead of changing their lives.

> In order to be emancipated from the domination of technical rationality the social theorist must enable people to understand their situation in the social world to help them become emancipated through being competent communicators. (Blaikie, 1993, p. 56)

Action research

Action research seeks to engage the researcher in active involvement in bringing about change, usually in fairly specific projects. In the late 1960s and 1970s action research was used by government sponsored teams tackling social problems in the USA and Great Britain – through such programmes as Headstart, Educational Priority Areas and the Community Development Project. Usually there were two teams, one of professionals who initiated programmes, and one of researchers who monitored and evaluated the programmes as they were being implemented (Bulmer, 1978).

In the mid-1970s action research became identified as a radical way of researching and changing social situations. According to Mies this development came about because the criticism expressed by 'Critical Theory' remained confined to academic institutions.

> It did not reach the working masses and thus reproduced the structural separation of the capitalist mode of production. In the mid-1970s an effort was made to bridge this gap by the proponents of action research, first evolved by Lewin (1948). (Mies, 1993, p. 66)

Today action research is being used in such areas as race issues, health and education and women's rights. The researcher becomes an activist – perhaps in helping local people gain community facilities. The people become part of the research process, learning new skills, and having their awareness raised as part of a conscious empowerment or 'quality enhancement' strategy (Torkington, 1991).

Such instances show that 'detachment' is no longer seen uncritically as a major credential of good social science research. The personal characteristics and perspectives of the researcher are themselves regarded as part of the research, and debate is centring on other issues such as empowerment of the researched, involvement in changing society and commitment to using a variety of methods in any investigation.

Feminist research methods

This most important development in how social research should be conducted and interpreted has been left to the end of the discussion because it incorporates many of the issues listed above. However, feminism goes far beyond being a methodological perspective about how you should carry out research – it is also an *ontology* (way of being).

According to Stanley:

> It is the experience of and acting against perceived oppression that gives rise to a distinctive feminist ontology; and it is the analytic exploration of the parameters of this in the research process that gives expression to a distinctive feminist epistemology. (Stanley, 1990, p. 14)

Here *epistemology* refers to the way a theory is judged to be adequate and how research methods can be assessed. According to Harding (1987), it is this type of judgement that makes feminist research significantly different from 'malestream' research because it focuses on:

1. the alternative origin of problems – raising problems and issues that are of concern to women rather than to men;
2. the alternative explanatory hypotheses that are developed and the evidence that is used;
3. the purpose of the inquiry – to facilitate an understanding of women's views of the world and to play a role in female emancipation;
4. the nature of the relationship between the researcher and the 'subjects' of her inquiry. (Abbott and Wallace, 1990, p. 205)

Feminists are not in total agreement about the way feminist research should be undertaken. Abbott and Wallace point out that no research method is explicitly feminist or anti-feminist: 'it is the ways in which research is carried out and the framework within which the results are interpreted that determine if research is feminist or not'

(Abbott and Wallace, 1990, p. 205). Kelly supports this view, arguing that many of the methods used by feminist researchers are not new: 'What is new are the questions we have asked, the way we locate ourselves within our questions, and the purpose of our work' (Kelly, 1988, p. 6).

However, some feminists have rejected completely the positivism or scientism of quantitative methods identified with malestream research and argued for an increased use of qualitative research (Reinharz, 1979). They argue that those who have been researched have been treated as objects to be worked upon. As Graham proposes, for feminism: 'The commitment is to a sociology in which women are subjects and not objects in the research process; a sociology that enlightens and emancipates' (Graham, 1984, p. 122).

Quantitative research therefore epitomises the exploitation which the Critical Theorists also argue against, an exploitation which has been particularly experienced by women, who have often proved to be compliant and vulnerable sources of information in conventional scientific research. Jayaratne however has provided a reasoned and persuasive argument for retaining quantitative methodology alongside qualitative methods. She states:

> My approach to this issue is political; that is, I believe the appropriate use of *both* quantitative methods and qualitative methods in the social sciences can help the feminist community in achieving its goals more effectively than the use of either qualitative or quantitative methods alone. (Jayaratne, 1993, p. 109)

This position is supported by Maynard and Purvis, who argue that the political potential of research involving enumeration should not be underestimated:

> The challenge to feminists now lies less in the critique of a simplistic qualitative/quantitative polarization and more in how it might be possible to make all methods 'feminist user-friendly'. (Maynard and Purvis, 1994, p. 4)

Much feminist research has been grounded in women's experiences but, as Maynard and Purvis argue, 'there is no such thing as "raw" or authentic experience which is unmediated by interpretation' (Maynard and Purvis, 1994, p. 6). These writers focus then on the place of both experience and interpretation in research.

Feminist research emphasises the importance of accounting for the role of the researcher in what is being researched, not just in interpreting data but in the whole process of creating data. Reflexivity is therefore of vital importance. Stanley and Wise, like others, argue against the artificiality and pretence of orderly research and for recognising the messiness of the research process: '"hygienic research" in which no problems occur, no emotions are involved, is "research as it is described" and not "research as it is experienced"' (Stanley and Wise, 1993, p. 153).

Feminists therefore raise a number of issues relevant to applied social research – concern with the informant as a subject rather than object of the research, the importance of reflexivity in understanding the nature of data generation, and an awareness of the power relationship in conventional scientific research where informants are open to exploitation by those who have career interests at stake rather than the welfare of those they are interviewing.

In addition, feminists are interested in empowerment – in investing the control over the process of the production of knowledge firmly in the hands of their informants. There are important implications for applied research in all these issues, and we shall be returning to them in Part II, particularly in the chapters concerned with ethnography.

Conclusion

Your own research needs to reflect an awareness of the kinds of concerns raised in this chapter which form the context within which you work. As noted earlier, the way you conduct the fieldwork will not be decided simply on technical grounds but on the basis of what you feel is the best way of providing explanation and understanding of the social situation with which you are confronted. In your methodology report you can return to the issues raised in this chapter and illustrate them with examples from your own research practice. This will clarify what you have learned about methodology through your research and help you decide your own position on the different perspectives raised here.

3
Negotiating an Agreement

This chapter deals with a key stage in developing a research project. It is essential that the project is properly set up from the beginning, so that you and the organisation you are working with are clear about what is expected. The aim is to negotiate an agreement which is acceptable to all parties, including the academic supervisor. The agreement will outline the project to be undertaken and define the contributions of yourself and the client organisation respectively.

Introduction

In this chapter suggestions are made about how to get the research project off the ground by working through a sequence of stages. It is assumed that you will be responsible for initiating negotiations directly with a local group or organisation – unless there are already existing arrangements between your academic institution and local organisations that you can draw on.

The points below are based on actual practice and aimed at helping you and your supervisor to hold successful meetings with the client group or organisation. They can be used as an '*aide-mémoire*' or guide for the meetings. The steps are laid out in some detail as an aid to those who have no experience of project negotiations, but can obviously be simplified or adapted to suit local circumstances.

Where institutions of higher education already have some form of link with local community organisations, such as through Work-Based Learning or Research Exchange, this can be extremely helpful in eliciting project opportunities and in making the initial introductions. Such a model of Research Exchange is briefly summarised at the end of this chapter, and covered in detail elsewhere (Hall and Hall, 1995).

To arrive at a project agreement there are five steps to be considered. You may find you should allow for an initial conversation plus at least two face-to-face meetings to conclude this negotiation.

Step 1: Contacting the organisation

Step 2: The initial meeting

Step 3: Negotiating the project

Step 4: Negotiating the research design

Step 5: The outcome – statement of agreement

Step 1: Contacting the organisation

To decide what kind of voluntary or community organisation to contact, first ask yourself why you want to work with a particular type of organisation or with a particular type of client. Is this because you have:

- prior experience of volunteering or working with a specific voluntary organisation?
- an academic interest in a social issue such as youth delinquency or drug abuse?
- aspirations for a future career in the voluntary sector, health, housing or social work?

Consider also whether you prefer working on your own, or would like to work in a team with other students. If you have no particular areas in mind for your project, how would you feel about doing a project in an area selected by another of your team members?

Networking

There is a variety of methods that can be used to select an organisation for initial contact. Personal networks can lead to successful project opportunities. If you are a volunteer with a voluntary group, you may be in a good position to develop a research project with them.

Alternatively, your supervisor or other members of staff in your department may be able to help through their own contacts. Other students who are involved in voluntary work or connected in some way with an organisation may also be able to put you in touch with someone who will be interested in developing a research project with you.

Listings

You may be surprised how many voluntary organisations exist in your local community. The number is likely to be in the hundreds rather than the tens. It has been estimated that there is an average of three local groups and organisations for every 1000 people (Rickford, 1995). In Britain the local Council for Voluntary Service (CVS) or Citizens' Advice Bureau (CAB) or the local authority Community Liaison Officer may be able to supply you with a list. If there are no 'umbrella' organisations covering the voluntary sector, the local library may have a list, or display publicity leaflets for community organisations. Through the phone book, you can look up and contact organisations directly.

Previous projects

Once a programme of applied research becomes established in a department or institution, you may find that organisations that have had experience of a student project in the past come back to suggest further projects, or alert other voluntary organisations to the opportunity. Obviously it helps in negotiating the agreement if the organisation is familiar with dealing with students, though the turnover of staff in voluntary organisations can be such that it cannot be assumed that the same staff will be dealing with subsequent projects – you may have to approach the negotiations as if from the beginning.

First contact

It is probably more effective if your supervisor makes the initial contact, as academics from recognised institutions are more likely to be given a favourable hearing by busy staff. The supervisor can also ensure that the organisation knows that what you will be doing is an officially approved activity and has due academic credibility. In a perfect world students would be able convey this authority too, but this is not always the case!

However, if the supervisor is unable to make the first contact you will have to take the initiative. When telephoning it is a good idea to know the *name* of a worker in the organisation to ask for – especially the manager. If you do not know who this is from a listing, ask the person who answers the phone and make sure you know the official title of the person you will be talking to. This makes the initial conversation much easier.

In your first contact, be clear about what you are proposing to the organisation:

- you are a student who wants to work on a project with the organisation
- the project will be on a topic specified by the organisation and negotiated and agreed with it
- there are no costs involved (except perhaps a small sum for expenses)
- the report will be given to the organisation.

Remember that organisations have lots of requests to deal with, and may already be involved in social work placements or student work experience. Tell them that your research is *not* a placement – you are ready to make a contribution to meeting the organisation's needs. As your request may have to be referred to a management committee, an immediate response may not be possible.

The object of the exercise is to contact a 'gatekeeper' – someone who can give you access to the organisation. Ideally this should be someone who is interested in what you have to offer, and understands what it is like to be a student with a project to complete. The gatekeeper should also be the recipient for your report, who will channel it to others in the organisation.

Step 2: The initial meeting

Experience has shown that a preliminary meeting (or two) is necessary to talk through the possibilities and discuss the organisation's needs before the project can be negotiated. Be prepared for the meeting to last up to an hour or an hour and a half if it is to make progress on defining a suitable project. It is much better if the meeting takes place on the organisation's 'home ground', as this gives you the opportunity to see its work in context, and to meet other staff and possibly service users too.

You will probably have to handle this first meeting on your own without the supervisor present. But, assuming all goes well, when it comes to drawing up an agreed specification for the project your academic supervisor should be involved because your project is part of the assessment for your degree.

At the first meeting you need to introduce yourself – and the other members of your team, if you are working collectively – to the organisation and explain what your objectives are. You also need to pick up background information about the organisation to help you to decide what research will be practicable.

Here are some points you could use to structure the discussion.

1. You want to produce a piece of applied/practical social research and are looking for an organisation to work *with*.
2. The purpose (or commitment) of the project is to do a piece of work for the organisation which it will regard as important, relevant and timely.
3. Your background is in a department which teaches certain skills and has made you interested in certain issues. That is why you are contacting this organisation in particular.
4. The research will be supervised in your institution and forms part of the assessment for your degree.
5. You would like to know about the organisation and what work it does. If there are any pamphlets or leaflets which would be useful you would like to have copies, and also any references to published work which you might follow up in the library. You might also at this stage ask how long the organisation has been running and how it is funded.
6. You would like to know if there are any areas or issues where you could be involved in doing a project. You need to listen carefully to the ideas which your contact is suggesting and make notes to discuss with your supervisor. Feel free to ask questions at this stage and to make suggestions of your own.
7. You might like to ask the organisation to complete a form of the type shown in Figure 3.1, which gives details of its thinking on project opportunities, and to send it to your supervisor.

At the end of your meeting, agree to make further contact after you have seen your supervisor. If the discussion does not seem to be leading to a manageable project, write a letter to the organisation thanking them for their time (you never know when this contact may be useful in the future).

If things are looking hopeful, you are now ready for

The following Organisation Checklist may prove helpful in the first stages of putting together a research project request.

NAME OF ORGANISATION

_____

WHAT IS IT YOU ARE AIMING TO DO/FIND OUT?

_____

_____

_____

WHAT QUESTIONS DO YOU WANT TO ASK/HAVE ANSWERED?

_____

_____

HOW CAN THEY BE ANSWERED?
WHAT INFORMATION/METHODS HAVE YOU GOT IN MIND?

_____

_____

WHAT WOULD YOU LIKE TO PRODUCE AS A RESULT?

_____

HOW DO YOU INTEND TO USE THE RESULTS?

_____

WHO WILL THE PROJECT INVOLVE? (for example, staff/service users and so on)

_____

WHAT COSTS WILL BE INVOLVED? (including staff time/resources and so on)

_____

PROBLEM AREAS IDENTIFIED? (for example, confidentiality/equipment needs)

_____

HOW LONG DO YOU THINK IT MIGHT TAKE TO COMPLETE
THE WORK?

_____ Weeks _____ Months

OTHER COMMENTS (for example, background information on
organisation)

_____

_____

Figure 3.1 Organisation checklist

the negotiation stage, which should be attended by your
supervisor, and again should ideally take place on the
organisation's 'home ground'. Your supervisor will understand the project better if s/he can see what the
organisation does.

Step 3: Negotiating the project

This is a crucial stage for the project, so a set of points is
listed below as a checklist for you and your supervisor to
consider. The list might seem formidable, but some of
the information you may have gathered already and the
other items can be covered through conversation rather
than as a mechanical exercise. The aim is to provide you
with a much clearer understanding of the organisation
and its needs. The first section consists of questions you
need to ask the organisation, the second section concerns
information the organisation needs to know about you
and what you have to offer, while the third section lists
the issues to be negotiated.

In practice your meeting will be a mixture of all three
stages, though it is a good idea to recap at the end on
what has been agreed and confirm that your understanding
is the same as that of the other parties.

Things to ask the organisation about itself and the proposed project

1. Find out about the organisation.
  (a) What is the broad range of its activities?
  (b) Is the organisation national or local?
  (c) Are the staff paid or volunteers, or a mixture of both?
  (d) What is the size of the organisation in this locality? How many staff and clients does it have?

2. Find out about the organisation's ethos and values.
  (a) What are the goals of the organisation?
  (b) Is there a written statement of its mission or philosophy?
  (c) What is the brief history of the organisation – and are there any documents which can be read?

3. Find out how the organisation is funded.
  (a) Is money raised by public donations?
  (b) Is money received by a grant from the local authority, central government, international body (e.g. European Union), or other funding body?
  (c) Is the organisation contracted to the local authority to provide specific services?
  (d) Is fund-raising a particular concern?

4. Find out if the organisation's staff have already identified a project.
  (a) Do they have a clear idea or is it all still to be negotiated?
  (b) Are there alternative suggestions that could be examined?
  (c) What are the organisation's real priorities?
  (d) Are there any deadlines the organisation is working to?

5. Find out about the proposed project.
  (a) Is the activity or programme to be studied new or a continuation of work already in progress?

(b) Is the project to be an evaluation – and if so, is it from the viewpoint of the service users/potential users or the staff?

(c) Is the purpose of the project to collect 'background information'?

(d) Is the project to be mainly concerned with 'hard data' or with attitudes? Does the organisation have a preference or requirement for 'scientific' measurement?

6. **Find out about the audience for your report. Is to be:**
   (a) the staff at local level?
   (b) the local management committee?
   (c) the staff at the organisation's centre?
   (d) the funders of the organisation?
   (e) the users/customers of the organisation?
   (f) some other group?

7. **Find out about how your report will be used. Will it be used:**
   (a) to consider changes at the local level?
   (b) to make recommendations at the national level?
   (c) to make future funding applications?
   (d) as a feasibility study for future developments?

8. **Find out which groups or individuals are to be targeted in the research. What are the implications for the research?**
   (a) Is it 'members of the public'? (for example, market research)
   (b) Residents in a specific locality? (for example, door-to-door survey)
   (c) Past users of the organisation? (Are records of names and addresses available?)
   (d) Present users of the organisation? (Can access be arranged?)
   (e) Potential future users? (How could these be identified and approached?)
   (f) Staff who work for the organisation – paid or voluntary, full time and part time?

(g) Staff in other organisations? (Would these be willing to take part?)

9. **Find out what resources, if any, are available.**
   (a) Is there money for travelling expenses?
   (b) Would there be help with telephone costs (for example, if part of the methodology involves telephone interviewing)?
   (c) Would there be any help with typing or photocopying research schedules?
   (d) Would there be any help with postage for mail questionnaires?

10. **Find out who your contacts are to be.**
    (a) Who is your main contact – for access to the organisation, to service users and so on?
    (b) Who will you present your report to?
    (c) Who are the key workers you will be involved with?
    (d) Are there any secretarial or administrative staff you should be introduced to?

11. **Find out if there are any particular ethical concerns you should be aware of.**
    (a) Are there vulnerable service users who need special consideration?
    (b) What issues of confidentiality are involved?
    (c) Will you require permission to approach informants?
    (d) Will a key worker need to be present as you interview?
    (e) Are there any aspects of your personal safety you need to consider?

Things to tell the organisation about what you have to offer

1. **Explain how this project relates to your degree.**
   (a) It may be a dissertation equivalent.
   (b) It replaces an essay or course assignment.
   (c) Other

2. Explain how much time you have available.
(a) Number of hours per week
(b) Number of weeks involved for fieldwork, and for analysis and report writing
(c) Date your draft and final report has to be submitted to your department
(d) Date the organisation can expect to see a draft and final version of the report

3. Explain what research skills you have to offer.
(a) Interviewing skills
(b) Questionnaire design
(c) Data analysis skills, including computers if applicable
(d) Presentation skills, including word processing

4. Explain what support you have from your department.
(a) Supervisor to act as consultant to the project
(b) Additional research training as part of the course
(c) Institutional facilities for computing, word processing
(d) Possible access to departmental funds for fieldwork expenses (where not paid by the organisation)

5. Explain what your interests are.
(a) How these relate to the work of the organisation
(b) Your previous life experience where relevant
(c) Research interests and preferences
(d) Future career – if known

The outcome of this stage should be that you now know the kinds of issues that the organisation is concerned about, and where some research gathering of information could be helpful. You have met some of the influential members of the organisation, and they have had a chance to size you up. The next stage may follow immediately at the same meeting, or may require a separate meeting – particularly if your organisational contact wishes to bring some other members into the detailed discussion of a project.

Step 4: Negotiating the research design

You now have to 'trade-off' or reconcile the client's interests and needs, your interests and needs and your supervisor's requirements for assessment. If you have worked through the issues above, you will have a clearer picture of what the client wants and they will be clearer about what you can offer them. Now is the time to summarise these points and reach a decision about:

- which project out of those discussed is the highest priority
- how the project will actually proceed.

Remember that you are limited by time and resources. Do not commit yourself to more than you can deliver.
If you are working in a team, you should be able to undertake more than someone working on their own, in terms of any or all of the following:

- using a greater variety of research methods
- contacting a wider variety of informants
- selecting a larger sample of informants.

So, to begin.

Issues to be negotiated

1. **Summarise in your own words what you think the client organisation's priority research need is.**
   Does the client agree with your interpretation?

Example 3.1
One organisation began the discussion by wanting to know what 'the general public' thought of a particular form of learning difficulty. During the negotiation process it began to emerge that the client was actually interested in special cases of this learning difficulty and in particular age groups, and wanted a study focused on an individual institution. This really

emerged towards the end of the meeting when the student and supervisor summarised what they thought the client wanted to be researched.

2. **Make sure the research is 'bounded'.**
   Is the research proposed too wide-ranging or is it specific enough to be completed in the time available?

Example 3.2
Another client began the negotiation by wanting to know the causes of inner-city crime. Through negotiation this was reduced to a manageable scale for a single researcher: interviews with ten workers who helped victims of crime and two interviews with victims in order to evaluate the training programme for volunteer workers.

3. **Decide whether the research is more suited to an individual or to a group project.**
   Does the client require information from a large number of respondents or from a few?

Example 3.3
An organisation was keen to know about levels of public awareness of its services. This implied a survey with a large sample, so a group project was more suitable. As students would be involved in door-step interviewing in a city area, it was also advisable to have pairs of students working together, for safety reasons.

4. **Decide whether the research requires of the researcher special knowledge, maturity or emotional support.**
   Is the research in an area which is sensitive and could be distressing?

Example 3.4
A patients' organisation wanted to find out the needs of the relatives of patients with serious malignancies. Two mature women students, one with nursing qualifications, undertook the research successfully, but

would not have recommended it for younger and less-experienced students.

5. **Check that the proposed research fits in with your own academic timetable.**
   Is the client organisation's proposal realistic, given your other course commitments?

Example 3.5
A community group asked if they could have an interim report on facilities in the area. It was pointed out that the student would not be able to produce this within the time-scale demanded, though the group could look at a draft of the main report before it was submitted for academic assessment.

6. **Clarify that the information required is attainable.**
   If statistics are required, are there known sources of data or a sampling frame which can be readily accessed?

Example 3.6
An organisation wanted a list of all single teenage mothers in a particular city. There was no way of supplying this information and this project was never tackled.

7. **Clarify that access to the informants can be provided.**
   If interviews are required with people not directly connected with the organisation, how easy will it be to involve them in the research?

Example 3.7
A community-based organisation catering for mental illness wished to find out the views of people who would be discharged from hospital into its services. It proved impossible to interview such future service users because health service regulations required ethical approval before interviews could be done with patients, and such approval would take too long a time to obtain.

Negotiating an Agreement

8. Agree on the methodology to be used.
Various methods are discussed in brief in Chapter 2,
and at more length in Chapters 5 to 9. Make sure that
you have read through these chapters and considered
the issues they raise before committing yourself to your
project. The method(s) chosen will depend on:

- what is most *appropriate* for the study
- the *time* and *resources* you have available
- your own *interests* and
- your *philosophy* of research (using quantitative or
  qualitative methods or a mixture of both, for
  instance).

The client organisation may have some ideas of its own
about the preferred methods to use, but you should
try not to be swayed into doing something you are not
happy with. You may choose from:

- *ethnographic research*: in-depth interviews, observation,
  diaries, or case studies
- *survey research*: postal questionnaires/telephone
  interviews, face-to-face structured interviews
- *documentary sources*: client's records, published statistics,
  literature review.

As noted in Chapter 2, it is accepted nowadays that a
combination of methods should be used (triangulation)
so that the weaknesses of one method are balanced by
the strengths of another.

A client often initially wants a survey conducted with
a very large number of respondents (or even a complete census) because this is felt to be more 'scientific' and what 'real research' is like. However, when
in-depth 'exploratory' research is explained, the client
is often attracted to this type of research instead, because informants' views can be probed in some depth
and a greater understanding gained of why, for instance,
they are or are not satisfied with an aspect of the organisation's work.

71

Example 3.8
In the project on patients' relatives mentioned in
Example 3.4, the client initially proposed a large sample questionnaire study with relatively few questions,
as this fitted the medical pattern. Neither the students
nor the supervisor felt this would provide the necessary
depth or be appropriate to administer to relatives,
some of whom would be recently bereaved. What
was eventually negotiated was a smaller, substantial
interview study with a mixture of closed and open-
ended questions.

Step 5: The outcome – a negotiated agreement

It is a good idea to produce a short written agreement
which all parties can sign. This could be called a 'contract',
as 'placement contracts' are used for social work students,
for instance, who work in various agencies. But contract
sounds somewhat legalistic and the term 'agreement' is
preferable.

In the agreement we suggest you cover the issues listed
below.

- Parties to the agreement, and date of meeting
- Contact names, addresses and telephone numbers
- Description of the client organisation
- Project outline and methodology
- Ethical standards and confidentiality
- Duration and timing of project
- Student's contribution in terms of workload
- Arrangements for academic supervision
- Arrangements for access to the organisation and
  its service users
- Payment of expenses (wherever possible)
- Date of submission of draft and final reports
- Ownership and use of report

It should also be stipulated that all parties may comment on the agreement and that if any section needs to be altered, this can be negotiated and a fresh agreement issued. At the initial meeting you or your supervisor should spell out that the completion of the research cannot be guaranteed, because of unforeseen circumstances that could affect either the organisation or yourself. It has been found that organisations appreciate this point, and it provides a safeguard – which you hope will not be needed.

Preliminary discussions with some organisations may reveal that the needs for research are too diffuse to allow agreement on a project, or that the organisation has no control over access to the informants it wishes to have details on. In such cases it is prudent to close negotiations at this stage and try elsewhere.

In other cases, what has been negotiated as a potentially viable project may face unforeseen difficulties when it comes to collecting the research information. The focus of the project may then have to be changed – in consultation with the client.

Specification of the amount of fieldwork to be completed should not be too precise in the project agreement. It is helpful to leave some latitude at this stage. Details will be worked up afterwards in the Research Brief (Chapter 4).

Example 3.9
One student 'contracted' to do sixteen interviews for an organisation working with single parents, but in the event was only able to complete half this number, because of problems of contacting informants. It is preferable therefore for a student to agree to 'conduct in-depth unstructured interviews with a small representative sample' without too many details being prescribed.

Conclusion

This chapter has outlined the steps involved in setting up a practical research project with a client organisation.

It can be used as a guide for your own negotiations. Remember you are in *partnership* with your client. You and the client should both feel happy about the proposed project – it should meet the organisation's needs and be a piece of work you feel satisfied can be accomplished.

Through the written agreement the client organisation is reassured that the research is being conducted in a professional manner and the student is clearer about their commitments. The supervisor might like to be responsible for completing this agreement form; at any rate it should be signed by the student(s), client organisation, and supervisor, who should all retain their own copies. An example of a completed agreement is given in Appendix B (with identifying details omitted).

Research Exchange

If the steps given above are followed, then you should end up with a project negotiated with a local community organisation. However, we do not underestimate the difficulties of this process or the time it will take. Also it becomes inefficient for each student to set up their own contacts with organisations when this step could be done more effectively at an institutional level.

For these reasons the Research Exchange concept is beneficial. A Research Exchange is a link organisation which can:

- make initial contacts with local voluntary community organisations
- respond to their requests by finding suitable students for projects
- help organisations refine their original ideas into potential projects
- permit students in a variety of departments and higher education institutions in the locality to take advantage of this opportunity.

Negotiating an Agreement

Most higher education institutions these days have mission statements about making contributions to the community. So ask if your institution has such a link organisation on the Research Exchange model – and if not, ask why not.

4
From Agreement to Research Brief

This chapter takes the research agreement one step further by showing how it is expanded into a research brief. To do this, decisions have to be made on research strategy, and methods must be elaborated in greater detail. The research brief is a document which proves to the organisation that you have a clear view of the research objectives and how the project will be carried out. It also demonstrates your commitment to sound ethical practice. Frequently, the kind of applied research which voluntary organisations require is evaluation of their activities. How this can affect the choice of methods and schedule of research is discussed.

Finally, the research brief is developed into a research action plan. The action plan serves to guide you in organising your time, and in completing the project as effectively as possible. Unlike the research brief, which is likely to remain unchanged once formulated and agreed with your organisation, the research plan should from the outset be regarded as a provisional statement, which will need to be updated at regular intervals as the project proceeds.

Purpose of the research brief

After reaching agreement with a client organisation over the topic of research, you may well be asked by the organisation to submit a research brief for its consideration. The *research brief* – or *research proposal* or *research protocol* (the name differs but the meaning stays the same) – is a short but detailed statement of:

- *what* you are going to do
- *how* you are going to do it
- *who* will be your informants
- *when* and
- *where* the research will be done, and
- *what* the expected *benefits* of the project will be.

The research brief has two purposes:

1. to show other people (your organisational contacts, and your academic supervisor) that you have a clear and workable idea of what the project will include, and how it will proceed; and
2. to provide you with an initial outline strategy to guide the research.

As has already been seen, the agreement negotiated with the organisation outlines the general areas to be looked at and clarifies expectations about your contribution to the research and the organisation's support. It is suggested that the agreement should not be too specific about details, because you may not yet have had time to consider these in depth, and you do not want to be tied to a specification, for example about sample size, which turns out to be impracticable.

The research brief goes beyond these generalities to document the research strategy in finer detail. To do this you will now have to take some early decisions about the methods to be used, and the nature and number of your informants. As these decisions will remain more or less fixed for the rest of the project, it is important to come up with a viable strategy at this point. The different methods of research and their implications have been discussed in Chapter 2; the application of these methods will be explained in detail in Part II. Here we concentrate on the format of the research brief.

Format

A useful format for a research brief can be borrowed from the types of application form used by grant-awarding bodies for social research. These require research proposals to be structured in such a way as to allow easy identification of objectives and methods, while imposing strict limits on length, detail and supporting papers. The research brief must be informative but concise.

If the format presented below is followed, the research brief need not take up more than two or three pages (plus appendix) when completed.

Title of research
Name(s) of investigator(s)
Name of organisation
Abstract of research
Research outline

- methods
- sample
- questions

Timescale
Costs and Expenses
Access and Confidentiality
Report
Appendix

Contents

The *title* of the research provides a focus for what you will be doing, and signals to the organisation that you understand its requirements. The title will subsequently appear at the front of the project reports. It should not be longer than eight words.

Although the *names* (and contact addresses and telephone numbers) of yourself as investigator and the organisation concerned appear at the head of the research agreement, it is worth repeating the information here because each document should stand alone. The project brief may be referred onwards for information or comment to other parties such as the organisation's management committee or field workers.

It is essential that the *abstract* of research is written in non-technical language. Its purpose is to summarise succinctly the purpose of the research and what you intend to do. This is the part of the research brief where you are communicating directly with someone who may be a non-specialist, and hoping to enlist their interest and support. It should not be longer than 150 to 200 words.

The main detail of the project is covered in the *research outline*. This should enlarge on the abstract by showing the kinds of research you will be undertaking, giving details of the methods to be used – for example, interview and/or questionnaire and/or observation. Try to think of using more than one technique for data collection.

You should show why the research you propose is appropriate for the purposes required by the organisation, and also give an indication of who will be questioned, and how many; and whether this is intended to be a sample or a complete census of all relevant people. Again, think of covering many or all of the different groups of people who could provide information on the topic.

Practical considerations for evaluation

If you are asked to do an evaluation study, then a major methodological question will be, what kind of an evaluation should it be? We have already discussed in Chapter 2 different views on how research methods should relate to the world. Should these methods quantify, describe or try to effect change? In addition, the methods chosen need to be appropriate for the task in hand. Evaluation means understanding the client organisation's programme and considering how abstract goals and concrete action can be empirically studied. The following issues therefore need to be thought through.

1. What are the client's programme goals? Can they be specified clearly?
2. Where there are multiple goals, which are the priorities for evaluation?
3. Is the programme likely to produce any unanticipated consequences?
4. How can the goals be translated into empirical measurements, questions or observations on outcomes?
5. How can information be collected to describe what the programme is actually doing?
6. How can what the programme intends to achieve (the goals) be compared with its practice (the outcomes)? (adapted from Weiss, 1972, pp. 24–53)

Writers on evaluative research point out that a variety of 'stakeholders' need to be covered during the course of the research. Guba and Lincoln (1989, p. 40), for instance, identify three main classes:

- *agents* producing, using or implementing the programme
- *beneficiaries* of the programme, direct and indirect
- *victims*, who are negatively affected by the programme.

Here it is worth noting that service users can benefit from a programme – or be adversely affected by it. A structured approach to gathering data would need to identify and question representatives from all three of the above groups. It is possible – indeed probable – that such questioning would reveal that the groups have different views about the programme under consideration. An evaluator taking an 'outsider' role might just report and comment on such differences.

However, this role of the outside expert, who can supposedly be objective in their assessment, is in itself controversial. Can reliable judgements be made, especially on the limited acquaintance provided by a project? Guba and Lincoln argue that if there are doubts on this score, then the purpose of evaluation might be to allow the different groups to become aware of and respond to the views of the other stakeholders, in which they state their claims for the programme under evaluation and also their concerns. Such 'responsive evaluation' (Guba and Lincoln, 1989, pp. 38–9) requires time for the involvement of representatives of the stakeholders and for feedback from each others' views. The advantage is that: 'final conclusions and recommendations . . . are thus arrived at jointly; they are never the unique or sole province of the evaluator or the client' (Guba and Lincoln, 1989, p. 42).

In this way questions about the style of research feed back in to details of how the research will be conducted. In drawing up a time schedule for research, you would need to build in meetings to review the emerging information, certainly with your organisational contact and possibly with other stakeholders too. Research then becomes iterative – as information is fed back, some issues become resolved but others then emerge for further investigation. The end to this process is the limit of time available, rather than the exhaustion of topics for enquiry. And as a student project is likely to be tightly limited by time constraints, evaluation may have to compromise on the suggested involvement of all groups in the client organisation's programme, as outlined above.

How specific should you be on numbers and methods?

The question of how many people you should contact (either by interview or questionnaire) is always a difficult one. Where only a handful of people are involved it makes sense to try to contact them all, but when greater numbers are involved, some form of sampling will be needed. Issues of sample size are considered in Chapter 5. For the purposes of the research brief, it may be sufficient to come up with an approximate figure which is acceptable to the organisation, and which you feel is manageable in the time available. As a rough guide, students on projects described in this book have conducted in-depth interviews with between 8 and 20 people each. Survey interviewing using structured schedules may involve students interviewing 50–150 respondents, although this is dependent on ease of access to the sample.

You may have to resist pressure from the organisation to achieve impossibly high numbers of returns, and allow your own enthusiasm to be tempered with caution. Your supervisor can be helpful here, as s/he will have an idea about what is feasible as well as academically sound. The problem arises from the common perception that research has to include everyone to be valid, and that large numbers of responses give better information than smaller numbers. Neither of these two ideas is correct in itself, for random sampling permits you to spend your time more fruitfully getting detailed information from a proportion of your population of interest, rather than trying to cover everyone in lesser detail (Moser and Kalton, 1971, p. 57).

In any case, it should be acknowledged that the numbers you come up with in the research brief are those you *expect* to be able to survey, and are not a hard commitment to a definite figure that will necessarily be achieved. Any number of problems may intervene between plan and fulfilment. This point is best made in discussion with the organisation as the brief is presented. Organisational members usually recognise the problems in trying to contact others for research (and may already have experienced these problems for themselves in earlier attempts at gathering information).

In planning the work to be done, it may be helpful to divide the project work into five sections:

- preliminary interviews with key informants
- development of research methods
- the main fieldwork
- further investigations (or increased numbers in the survey) if time permits
- data analysis and report writing.

Organisations usually want to be consulted about the questions to be asked in interviews or by questionnaire, and it makes good sense to check with them that none of their important concerns has been omitted, and that they approve of the way you will go about handling sensitive issues. However, at the stage of this research brief it is unlikely that you will have a completed questionnaire or interview schedule to present.

The best strategy, therefore, is to list the areas or topics you want to cover, and regard this as the beginning of a dialogue to be continued as the questions are refined. Of course, if you do have a questionnaire ready, or are replicating work conducted elsewhere, then that can be included in the appendix to the research brief.

Practical considerations for undertaking research

It is important to have an idea at this early stage about the *timescale* for the project. The start and finish dates are given by your academic timetable; what goes in between clarifies to yourself, to the other members of your team (if appropriate), and to the organisation when the fieldwork can be done, given the sequences of activities listed above, and foreseeable contingencies such as holiday periods when informants will be unable to be contacted.

You may already be aware from earlier negotiation with your organisation of any time constraints they may be under – for example, if they need to have a report available by a certain date to meet deadlines for funding applications or other external requirements. This could present a problem, as the main determinant of your timescale will be the academic timetable laying down dates for the submission of assessed work. You should check that your academic timescale will be acceptable to the organisation, and if necessary negotiate to produce some interim findings to meet their requirements, with the full report coming later. Assuming a full-year or two semester course, then a draft timescale may look like Figure 4.1 (overleaf).

The issue of *costs and expenses* for the research has already been raised as part of the negotiated research agreement. In the research brief it may now be possible to quantify

May/Jun.	Preliminary contacts with organisation
	Summer Vacation
Sep./Oct.	Negotiate agreement with organisation
Oct.	Prepare research brief
Oct./Nov.	Preliminary interviews with key informants
Nov./Dec.	Main period of fieldwork
	Christmas Vacation
Jan.	Supplementary fieldwork
Feb./Mar.	Analysis of data
Mar./Apr.	Draft client report written
	Easter Vacation
Apr./May.	Final version submitted to client and institution

Figure 4.1   Timescale of research

this element roughly in terms of numbers of visits to research sites, and other expenses of research such as photocopying interview schedules or questionnaires, and postage (out and return) if a mailed questionnaire is planned.

If the total sum for expenses is going to be greater than the organisation can bear, it is better to find out now rather than later. You have a choice, either to look for alternative sources of support from your academic department's fund for student expenses, or to renegotiate the fieldwork towards less-costly methods or less-extensive data gathering ('trading down', see Hakim, 1992, pp. 120–2).

Access and confidentiality arrangements are essential, for the organisation will want to be assured that its members' privacy will be respected before it is willing to allow access to them. You should make it plain that individuals will be asked to give their consent to being interviewed, and that they have the right to refuse. Furthermore, you should offer guarantees of anonymity and confidentiality so that:

- individuals will not be named in any report unless they agree to this, and
- only the researchers will have access to individual information. Replies from individuals will be gathered together, or reported under a pseudonym so that no individual person is identifiable.

Particularly where voluntary organisations have service users who are dependent in some way, with special needs (disabilities) or stigmatised conditions, organisations may be reluctant to grant access until the gatekeepers are confident that the integrity of their clients will be respected.

In addition to adherence to ethical guidelines such as those of the British Sociological Association (see Appendix A), it is also important to gain the trust of the organisation. One way this can be done is to understand and accept the language the organisation uses in its practice: thus 'learning difficulties' or 'learning disabilities' have replaced many of the earlier terms for mental retardation or mental handicap, while the term 'clients' may be replaced by other phrases, such as 'service users' (or even 'members'). (The Glossary [pp. xv–xvi] contains a fuller list of the terms you are likely to encounter.)

As to the eventual *report*, there is not a lot that can be said about it at this stage, other than restating the agreement that the report is to be written for the client organisation, and that it is hoped that a draft report will be ready for the organisation to comment on before the final version is produced.

Complications of access in health care settings

The two to three pages of detail in the research brief should be sufficient to demonstrate that you have clear ideas about the research process, and to enable the organisation to judge whether your project proposal meets its requirements. However, access to informants may be further complicated if they are medical patients or their relatives, and if data will be gathered in a health care setting. In such a case it will be necessary to obtain the approval of the appropriate *research ethics committee*.

Research ethics committees are established in Britain under the guidance of the Department of Health to ensure that all research on patients is conducted in the best interests of the patient, and that any harm is minimised, in proportion to the benefit expected from such research (Hall, 1991). Institutional Review Boards perform a similar function in the USA. Particular difficulties arise with patients who are not able to give valid consent themselves for research, such as children (minors) and those with learning difficulties (non-competent). In such cases the proxy consent of parents or guardians is usually required (Nicholson, 1986).

Harm and benefit, and voluntary informed consent

Social research on health care premises also comes under the jurisdiction of research ethics committees, even though, in contrast to medical research, it is *non-invasive* and does not involve any physical contact with the bodies of the patients as in administering drugs or other treatments. The issues of any harm to the patient caused by the research, and the potential benefit must still be weighed, however, and arrangements must be specified for the valid administration of voluntary and informed consent. This applies even to the use of questionnaires or interviews, where the most likely source of harm is upsetting or disturbing the informant because of the intrusiveness or insensitivity of the questions.

86

Because of the administrative difficulties and delays which will be encountered when a research brief is put to a research ethics committee for approval, the simplest advice must be not to attempt research in health care settings. However, such research is not impossible. One successful student project investigated the needs of patients and their relatives. This was done through semi-structured interviews in the hospital wards and in the relatives' homes. From this experience we offer the following tips.

- Identify the appropriate research ethics committee, and find out if it requires applications to be on a standard form.
- If at all possible, see that your application is submitted with a medical professional as co-researcher.
- Be prepared to give as much information as possible about the purpose of the research, the methods to be used, and the means of informing patients and obtaining their consent.
- If a questionnaire is to be used, list all questions to be asked at this stage, and be prepared to revise these in the light of comments from the committee.
- Give details of how many patients you will be contacting, and how you propose to select them.
- Specify what patients you will *exclude* from the study – for example, severely ill people, children, the elderly and confused.
- Include a draft of the explanation of the research you will be giving to the patients, and a form which they can sign to signify consent.
- Specify that you will curtail an interview if a patient appears to become distressed.
- Show that the proposed research has been discussed with and has the approval of the medical and nursing staff involved.
- Submit the application early – you should allow for a delay of *at least eight weeks* for a reply, and for having to revise the brief to meet ethical objections from the committee.

This topic has been dealt with at some length because the exercise of preparing a brief for submission to a research ethics committee is actually good practice in making you think about the issues of the harm and benefit that could arise from your research. It also requires you to make explicit how you will achieve the full consent of your informants, by giving them information about what you are doing and what you want their views for.

Moreover, as Chapter 5 argues, *all* informants have rights concerning the way the research project treats them. They have rights to information about the purposes of the research, and a consent form for vulnerable service users may well be advisable. Certainly the client organisation should be alerted in the research brief to your sensitivity to these issues.

The research action plan

The research brief is mainly for the client organisation, to show what you intend to do and to legitimate your claim for access to the organisation and its members. The *action plan* extends this by sketching in an orderly sequence for your work.

The research plan is an internal document for yourself, your supervisor, and your team of colleagues (if working in a group). It turns the things you have committed yourself to doing for the project into a *schedule of events*. It sets out a priority for concentrating your efforts on the various stages of the research, and acts as a reminder of things that remain to be done. It provides a *checklist of actions*, which can be ticked off on completion.

Flexibility

Things rarely go according to plan. So be prepared to regard the action plan as provisional and changeable. Some changes may be brought about because of things you or your team were unable to do at the time – perhaps because other urgent priorities, such as having to complete an assessed essay on a particular date, intervened. More changes will be brought about by other people not being able to fit into the timetable. Other changes will be because what you originally planned to do no longer seems feasible when you actually get down to the mechanics of doing it.

So it is important to stay flexible, while not losing sight of the agreed objective. On occasion you may need to be assertive – other people will not know of your time constraints unless you tell them, and if you let them know your problem they may be able to suggest alternatives.

Time management

The project takes place against a defined timescale, outlined in the research brief and spelled out in more detail in the action plan. So effective time management is vital. Time management involves two things (Northledge, 1990, p. 8):

- finding enough time, and
- using it effectively.

To complete the project it will be necessary to block off time fairly regularly and in decent-sized chunks. If working in groups, you need to co-ordinate some of that time with your team members so that you meet regularly at least once a week. Your supervisor will also want regular contact, and you should endeavour to keep the supervisor up to date with what you are doing at weekly or fortnightly intervals – even if you do not require formal supervision each time.

Using the time effectively is more difficult. But it helps to break down a large task, such as designing a questionnaire, into a set of smaller tasks, setting yourself a target for deciding when enough time has been spent on each item.

Using meetings

If working in a team, then group meetings are essential. Meetings can increase the sense of togetherness, but unless there is a clear *agenda* the time can be frittered away without much progress being made. Each team member should go prepared with a set of objectives for the meeting and the group can begin the meeting by deciding what the agenda should be. It is helpful if one member keeps a record. If this is felt to be too formal, then each member should take notes of the meeting – and these can be used as part of the research diary (see below).

At the end of the meeting, make sure that you are all agreed on:

- what has been decided
- what each person is to do next
- when you will meet again.

Summarise the discussion in your own words, for the benefit of yourself and the other participants, perhaps saying something like:

> So we've now agreed to do X, Y and Z . . .
> Can I check that you want me to do . . .
> Am I right in assuming that A will be doing . . .

Getting people to agree a date for the next meeting is much easier to do at the time than it is to do afterwards through a series of phone calls or letters.

The points being made about meetings with other students on the project also apply to meetings with the client organisation. You also need to check on what has been agreed and when the next meeting will be held. Remember to take your diary with you to the meetings.

Research diary or log

It is important that you keep a complete record of your activities on the project. The research diary should be started at the beginning of the project, and record details of whom you meet, phone or interview, together with an outline of the topics discussed. Use it also to jot down any issues requiring further investigation as and when they occur to you. Some students also find it helpful to record their feelings about the work – both the high points and the low points.

The diary or log can eventually be quoted in the appendix to your methodology report, when it provides evidence about what you have done, how you have gone about it, and if in a team, how you have contributed to the team effort. The diary therefore serves a number of purposes, as:

- a report of meetings you have been involved in
- a record of your contribution to the research
- an address list of the people you have contacted or tried to contact
- a notebook of the development of the research and the origin of insights and questions
- a memoir of your feelings at the time.

Practically, it will also come in useful as evidence for submitting claims for reimbursement of travelling expenses to your organisation or department.

Task management

Task management turns attention away from the input of effort – how many hours the being spent on the project – to the output, what are you trying to achieve. The aim is to avoid becoming distracted and wasting the time on minor details, and instead to press on with the major items. Because these are the more demanding and difficult tasks, it is all too easy for them to be pushed to the back of the queue as simpler and more easily accomplished items are given priority. The sense of achievement which comes from tackling these may prove false if the major difficulties remain.

Yet task management has to be tempered with time management, otherwise in the search for perfection the task may never be completed. In writing a questionnaire, for example, and revising successive drafts, it is easy to let the task drag on too long. Further redrafting will only achieve marginal improvements. At some stage, preferably decided well in advance, you have to commit yourself to action. Be aware too of the balance of time available for the different aspects of the research – negotiation, preparation, fieldwork, analysis and writing the report. Above all, leave plenty of time for the analysis, which can take longer than the data collection to do satisfactorily (Stacey, 1969, p. 108).

Task and time schedule

The research brief gives the broad outlines of the tasks to be undertaken and the time constraints for doing them. Now is the time to flesh out the details in your own action plan. One way of doing this is to rule a sheet of paper into five columns, labelled Task, Resources, Contact, Date started and Date ended, as shown in Figure 4.2.

- In the first column you break down the research task into component elements – design questionnaire; select sample; arrange interviews; interview key informants, and so on.
- In the second column you list the resources that are required to allow you to do the task – books on questionnaire design and sampling; questionnaires and reports from studies of similar topics.
- In the third column you list the people you could contact to get the resources you require – your supervisor; college librarian; research centre on voluntary organisations, and so on. This could be extended to become an address list with phone numbers.

Task	Resources	Contact	Date started	Date ended
1.				
2.				
3.				

Figure 4.2   Task and time schedule

- The final two columns allow you to pencil in a sequence of activities, and to check them off when completed.

Some tasks can be undertaken concurrently – for example, searching the library, drafting interview questions, and deciding on a sample of informants. Others are sequential, and have to follow one another – drafting a questionnaire, piloting it, and using it for real. Diagrams can be used to identify potential bottlenecks – things that must be done before subsequent activity can be started (Torrington *et al.*, 1989, pp. 103–5).

Whichever method you choose, the action plan presents a checklist of activities, and their expected time of completion. Add in the actual time of completion as you go along. Remember, the plan is there to help you find time for the activities you need to do to complete the project, not to make you feel guilty about not keeping strictly to it. Expect that revisions will be required, be prepared to review your progress frequently, and revise the plan when necessary. You may need to do this every month or so.

Finally, think of the balance in your research. We have suggested already, in Chapter 2, that a mixed methods strategy has advantages in gathering different types of information. Should you find when implementing the plan that some methods are just not working as anticipated –

perhaps because of difficulties in contacting informants –
then other methods and other samples may be adopted
more readily if you have thought about alternatives beforehand in your action plan.

Example 4.1
Two students intended to interview former residents
at a young person's hostel, but contact letters sent
to the addresses supplied by hostel staff were often
returned by the Post Office marked 'no longer at that
address', leaving few to interview. As the students
were already spending time at the hostel organising
the survey of those who did reply, the project was
refocused to concentrate on the experiences of current residents.

Conclusion

The research brief is a short document allowing you to
put down on paper the strategy you wish to adopt for
your project. It enables the client organisation to see how
you will study their programme by outlining the research
methods to be used, indicating timescale and likely costs.
The brief also provides an opportunity to show your awareness of the ethical issues which are involved and should
reassure the organisation of your 'professional' approach
to the work. Above all, the brief clarifies the tasks which
need to be completed and helps to flesh out the ideas
which have been discussed at the negotiation stage. A
research action plan is a development from this which is
for your use and which enables you to itemise the key
stages in the project and their likely timescale for completion. Both the brief and the action plan should help
you feel in control of the work to be done, although, as
this chapter has indicated, real life research does not always
run to plan and you should be prepared to accept changes
as necessary.

PART II

PART II

5
Producing Data: the Questionnaire

In this and the next three chapters you will learn
about using research methods from the scientific
and ethnographic traditions, beginning with the
questionnaire. The questionnaire is a tried and tested
method of generating information. This chapter looks
at the issues involved in creating a questionnaire,
and at the various forms that structured questioning may take and considers how to select a sample
of informants. The importance of the data matrix
is discussed as a means of investigating, summarising and comparing responses across the totality
of those interviewed. Although there is no guaranteed way of devising a trouble-free questionnaire,
the chapter offers suggestions for good practice and
indicates some obvious sources of poor design.

Introduction

The social survey using questionnaires is widely recognised
as a standard method of collecting information. Its purpose is to generate information in a systematic fashion
by presenting all informants with questions in a similar
manner, and recording their responses in a methodical
way. It thus exemplifies the scientific approach to data
collection. It addresses the issue of *reliability* of information by reducing and eliminating differences in the way
in which questions are asked, and how they are presented.

97

For example, interviewers might be instructed that if their informant asks what is meant by a particular question, they are not allowed to offer any explanation of their own, but must simply repeat the question as worded (McCrossan, 1991, p. 34). Contrast this with the much freer use of prompts and probes in in-depth interviews (see Chapter 7).

This emphasis on maximising reliability has given rise to concerns about the positivistic assumptions underlying the questionnaire – that data are only what can be measured in an objective and 'scientific' manner. It is argued that this may affect the *validity* of the data so obtained. Responses to set questions may be reliable, but do they adequately cover the concept that the researcher is interested in? For example, how far can questions on whether or not an informant is a member of wildlife and conservation groups really be used to measure the degree of 'green' environmental awareness (Young, 1991, p. 117)?

As we shall see later, one way round this problem in structured questionnaires is the use of 'open-ended' questions, which allow the informants to speak for themselves, without being forced into the interviewer's predetermined categories. This is particularly the case in exploratory surveys, while unstructured interviews often have a part to play in developing ideas and indicators for use in questionnaires at a later date.

What is a questionnaire?

The answer to this turns on the method of use. A narrow definition of a questionnaire is a set of questions for respondents to complete *themselves* (Newell, 1993, p. 96). Typically such questionnaires will be sent by mail. A broader definition includes any set of questions used in a research study, such as an *interview schedule* used by an interviewer to question a respondent directly (Oppenheim, 1992, p. 100). This may be done face to face or, increasingly these days, by telephone.

Here we are concerned with all forms of structured questioning, whether at a distance or face to face, and so we use the broader definition of questionnaires. It is the precision, detail and order of the questions, leaving little discretion for the interviewer, which distinguishes the interview schedule from the interview guide for in-depth interviews.

What form can questions take?

Open-ended questions leave informants with a space to write in their answer just as they like, or for the interviewer to record the exact response given. *Closed or pre-coded* questions are those which ask the informant to choose one (or more) from a set of pre-selected answers. These can range from the simplest Yes/No through 5-point rating or ranking scales to a choice from a checklist of alternatives.

As indicated above, questionnaires can be used in a variety of ways:

- for self-completion with no researcher present
- for self-completion in a group setting, with the researcher present
- as an interview schedule face to face with the informant
- as an interview schedule by telephone.

The key differences are:

- who controls the situation by reading the questions?
- how much interaction does the researcher have with the informant?

Advantages and disadvantages of the different uses of questionnaires

1. Self-completion, no researcher present

The costs of administering a postal questionnaire for self-completion are mailing charges for sending and return, plus the cost of envelopes, plus the cost of sending reminders to those who do not reply. There is no cost for an interviewer's time and travel, which is particularly significant where informants are widely scattered. Informants can complete the questionnaire in their own time and, provided they are willing and able to reply, a large number of responses can be received in a relatively short period of time. *Time* and *cost* are strong reasons in favour.

However, *response rates* are likely to be lower than in interview surveys (de Vaus, 1991, p. 107). Although response rates for well-conducted mail questionnaires of between 60 and 75 per cent have been reported, it is not uncommon for response rates to fall below 50 per cent. This certainly would raise questions of possible bias. Are the people who have replied significantly different from those who have not? Will this, in turn, affect the validity of the findings?

Though the self-completion questionnaire avoids any bias due to the characteristics or manner of the interviewer, there is no control over how the questionnaire is answered. You cannot be sure who in the household actually filled it in, or in what order the questions were answered. There is no way of ensuring that the informant answers all the questions. However, some kinds of questions – particularly on sensitive or controversial issues – may be more truthfully answered by self-completion rather than by interview (Wellings *et al.*, 1994, pp. 16–17).

2. Self-completion in group, with researcher present

Self-completion in the presence of a researcher is a very useful alternative to the postal questionnaire, particularly if you

- are working with a specific organisation
- wish to question its members or clients, and
- can find a time when your informants are already gathered together as a 'captive audience'.

Handing out questionnaires to the assembled people allows you to keep a guarantee of anonymity of response –

nobody's name is recorded on the form – while ensuring a high response rate through control of the situation. The key here is, if at all possible, to ask your informants not to leave without putting their questionnaire form in an envelope or posting the questionnaire in a 'return box' to ensure anonymity. If informants take the questionnaire away, then the chance of getting it back again, even with a supplied envelope, is much reduced.

The questions themselves can be explained before you ask people to fill in the questionnaire, so that everyone has a clear idea what is being asked of them. However, if informants are able to discuss their answers with others, then the answers that they give may not be truly their own.

Example 5.1
A Well Woman Centre wanted to know how much 12 and 14 year olds thought about their health, and whether there were any barriers in the way of their seeking advice on health matters. In co-operation with school teachers, a student made a presentation during classes to talk around the issues, and handed out questionnaires to be completed anonymously in class.

3. Interview, face to face

For interviews the advantages and disadvantages are the reverse of those applying to postal questionnaires. The interviewer guides the informant through the questions, and (if the instructions permit) is able to prompt the informant for further information or explain misunderstandings. Response rates to interviews are generally much higher – de Vaus suggests they are of the order of 80 per cent. Once the door is open, the interviewer stands a good chance of going on to complete the questionnaire.

Interviews depend on developing some kind of 'rapport' with the informant. Perceived characteristics of the interviewer – sex, ethnic group, age, social class – may bias the information given, as informants provide the answers they think the interviewer wants to hear (sometimes referred to as the 'acquiescence effect'), or gloss over less reputable aspects of their own behaviour, or refuse to answer.

Interviews take time, as well as requiring the full concentration of the interviewer. There is a limit to how many interviews can be done in a day. Obviously this depends on the length of the questionnaire and the amount of detail required, but it is equally important to remember that finding people who are at home and willing to answer is not a trivial undertaking. Where a number of different interviewers are used in a study, it is important to spend time on briefing beforehand, so that each understands the questions and uses them in the same way. This increases the reliability of the survey, by reducing the likelihood of individual interviewers asking questions in differing ways.

One main advantage of interviews is being able to use more *open-ended* questions, where the answers are not precoded, and the interviewer writes down the responses verbatim. However, these questions will require more time to be spent at the analysis stage.

4. Interview by telephone

The telephone survey is becoming more widely used, because it keeps some of the advantages of the interview in terms of personal contact and the ability to interpret questions and answers, while saving on the cost of an interviewer's travel. Interviews can also be completed in the evenings when it might be less safe for an interviewer to conduct doorstep interviews and when elderly informants might be unwilling to open their doors.

However, unlike the face-to-face interview, it is not possible to give visual information on 'show cards' (Oppenheim, 1992, p. 90) for people to check off their answers, so long or complex questions have to be simplified. A schedule with pre-coded answers to closed questions is easier to administer over the telephone than open-ended questions.

Example 5.2
A student was asked to evaluate a 'parish links' programme whereby city churches in inner-city areas were
linked to parishes in other parts of the country, usually rural or suburban. The student conducted in-depth
interviews with a small sample of city clergy and sent
out postal questionnaires to a sample of city and rural
parishes. She also decided to conduct telephone interviews with those in parishes some distance from the
city which she could not afford to travel to. In her
methodology report, she notes this was problematic:

> There were diffioulties in recording the information
> since it was quite tricky to keep the conversation
> going and at the same time take notes. However
> brief notes were used to write up the interview
> immediately after the telephone conversation.
> (Callaghan, 1993)

The main point against telephone surveys is that not everyone has a phone. The disadvantaged are less likely to have
a phone, and so results may be biased in favour of the
more advantaged. Even when people do have a phone,
their numbers may be ex-directory, so obtaining a random sample from published sources may be difficult. To
get round this problem computer-aided dialling has been
used to select randomly for different areas (Lavrakas, 1987),
but this technique is well beyond the bounds of a student project as well as raising ethical issues concerning
access to private information. As in the example above,
you are more likely to be negotiating with an organisation for access to their list of phone numbers of members, volunteers, service users or contacts from which to
draw a sample.

Choice of method

For your project the choice of method should be guided
by its appropriateness to the problem, to the selected

informants, and to the quality of data you are seeking. For example, when a client organisation is concerned about public attitudes, then a structured interview on the door-step or in a shopping centre may allow you to acquire a selected range of information from a reasonably large number of local residents. If an organisation wants you to evaluate its services to its members, a more wide-ranging interview with relatively fewer informants may usefully collect similar information from each, but using open-ended questions to explore individual responses. Postal questionnaires or telephone interviews could be used to contact individuals who have used the services of an organisation but are no longer in everyday contact with it, or are widely dispersed.

What to ask?

Whichever method of questioning is chosen, you still have to decide what to ask. In this you will be guided by:

- the requirements of your research brief
- other similar research
- your own provisional understanding of the situation and influences on people's actions and attitudes

Your client organisation generally has a pressing problem – for example, how to attract more volunteers; how to improve publicity for the services on offer; how to find out what users really think of these services. Your questionnaire must meet these requirements through specific questions about your informants' behaviour and attitudes. Usually you will want not just to present a catalogue of informants' responses, but also to make comparisons to show how people's views differ and why.

Comparisons can be made between different categories of informants – male and female; young and old; new or long-standing users of the service; and so on – using categories which you believe are relevant to their experiences and attitudes. In each case you have to collect the appropriate classification items (McCrossan, 1991, p. 48) or *background information* on your informants. Such comparisons help provide reasons to explain the differences in attitudes.

There may be other matters too, of a more general nature, on which it would be helpful to have information. Beyond the question of the attitudes of volunteers on a particular project lies the issue of volunteering in general – why do people do it, what kind of people are involved, and what kinds of things are they likely to volunteer for?

To help with writing questions on these broader topics, you could look up library information, and see what has been written in relevant journals. Depending on your library resources, you may have access to key word abstracting services on CD-ROM which can provide some comparative material. However, remember the client organisation will have considerable expertise and information and can contribute a great deal of the understanding needed to help decide on wider as well as specific issues.

The data matrix

With all surveys the answers need to be collated to allow comparisons between different groups and categories. By this it is hoped to shed light on the reasons why people respond as they do. The data matrix lies at the heart of the questionnaire method (Marsh, 1982). de Vaus (1991, p. 3) explains that information is collected about the same variables or characteristics from each of the cases or informants. This creates a matrix of information. In the data matrix, there is an array of *rows* and *columns* (the rows running *horizontally*, and the columns *vertically*). The rows represent each different informant, and the columns represent each different question topic or variable, as in Figure 5.1.

Information given by one person can now be compared with that given by others; there are no blank spaces caused by individuals failing to be asked the questions that others

Informants	Questions				
	1	2	3	4	etc.
A					
B					
C					
D					
etc.					

Figure 5.1   The data matrix

have answered. Should a person actually not give an answer to a question, then that should be coded as 'non-response'.

Thinking about the questionnaire in terms of producing a data matrix is useful because:

- visualisation of the matrix helps you understand the process of data analysis
- questions are judged worth asking only by the use that will be made of the answers
- having 'cases' as the other dimension of the matrix shows the importance of careful selection of informants at the outset.

Sampling

While you are outlining the topics to be covered by the survey questionnaire, you should also be considering who exactly are going to be your informants – the second dimension of the data matrix. When the number of people falling into your category of interest is small, it may be possible to question them all – in which case you have a *census* or complete enumeration of the target population. (The term 'population' is used here in a restricted sense, not of the population of a country, but of all the individuals who fall into the category of interest [de Vaus, 1991, p. 60]). But in most cases, there are more people in the target population than you can possibly contact, so sampling is required as a form of selection.

Rose (1982, pp. 56–9) explains the logic of sampling by contrasting three overlapping entities:

- the general universe
- the working universe
- the sample.

The *general universe* or survey population refers to the broad category of people about whom the research is concerned. These could be 'volunteers', 'people with special needs', 'students' and so on. Findings from research done in one place on one particular set of people is often generalised to this larger universe of 'volunteers in general', for example.

The *working universe* or target population is much smaller. It consists of all those in the category of interest who *could* actually be selected for the sample in your particular survey (the population). So, it might be 'volunteers working with a specific local organisation' or 'undergraduate students at a named higher education institution'.

The *sample* is smaller still. It is those who are *in fact* selected for inclusion in your study. These are the only people you will have information on, but you want to use them to stand in for the working universe, and possibly to begin to generalise to the general universe. Diagrammatically this can be represented as in Figure 5.2.

Representativeness

To provide a sound basis for generalisation, the sample has to be *representative* and must be chosen carefully to mirror the characteristics of the target population. In addition, the sample needs to be large enough to inspire confidence in the results.

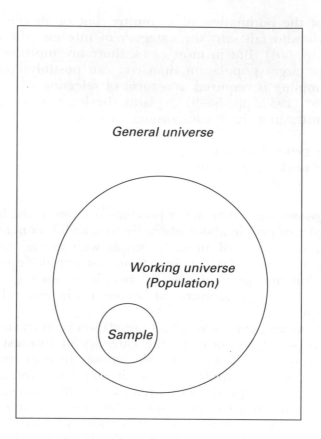

General universe

Working universe
(Population)

Sample

Figure 5.2   Sampling diagram

Relying on the researcher's own judgement as to who to include in the sample is unfortunately not the best way of ensuring representativeness, as this can introduce all kinds of unsuspected bias. Nor is a large sample size by itself any guarantee of its representativeness either. If the sample is biased in selection so that some groups are under-represented, then merely having more people in the sample will not correct that.

The best way of ensuring that the sample is representative of the population concerned is to use random methods in selection. In fact some statistics books will say this is the only valid method of selection. But practical research goes on in the real world, where

> representative sampling should be looked on as an ideal-type which, for a variety of reasons, is unlikely to be achieved in the majority of studies ... wherever typicality is the *aim*, we should contrast the real situation with this ideal-type, so that possible biases may be analysed and the problems of generalisation from sample to population can be assessed realistically. (Rose, 1982, p. 59)

The basic distinction in sampling methods is between random or probability samples and purposive or non-probability samples (Arber, 1993, p. 71). The most common types of sampling are:

Random
- Simple random sampling
- Quasi-random sampling
- Stratified sampling
- Multi-stage cluster sampling

Purposive
- Quota sampling
- Snowball sampling
- Judgemental sampling
- Accidental or convenience sampling

Random sampling

Simple random sampling (SRS) is based on the use of chance in selection. *Everyone in the population has the same chance of selection*, and the choice is made objectively by random means. In practice, this means you first need a list of all people who could be selected (the sampling frame). Then a table of random numbers can be used to select a sample (de Vaus, 1991, p. 63). These random numbers are computer-generated and lists can be found in the back of many statistics textbooks.

Example 5.3
Three students wanted to conduct a door-to-door questionnaire survey of local attitudes towards a proposed community centre. They had first to define the local area in terms of streets of houses, then they had to find out how many houses were in each street in order to draw up a sampling frame of houses. Having set a sample size of 150 from the 1619 houses in the area, they then used random numbers to select their sample of houses.

> *Technical note* This is a sample of houses, not of people: some houses had one inhabitant, others had many more, and only one person per house was to be interviewed. So people living in families stood a lesser chance of being selected than single people. In a larger and more technical survey this would require a correction factor (Hoinville *et al.*, 1977).

Quasi-random sample

A quicker method of choosing the sample from a sampling frame, which still preserves an element of randomness, is the quasi-random or systematic sampling method. In this you decide how many you want in your sample, and divide this number into the total in the sampling frame to give the sampling fraction. So for a sample of 150 from 1619 (as in Example 5.3 above), the sampling fraction would be 11 (to the nearest whole number).

Choose the first number at random from between 1 and the sampling fraction (for example, 8), then at intervals of the sampling fraction (11) throughout the rest of the sampling frame. Again, this is not entirely random because not everyone has the same chance of inclusion in the sample, but in practice it does not seem to make that much difference – provided the list itself is not ordered in such a way that certain groups will always be passed over (de Vaus, 1991, p. 65).

This kind of quasi-random sampling can be applied to time periods as well as to a list of individuals, which may be useful if you are doing an observational study (see Chapter 9) and want to investigate what goes on at particular locations throughout the day.

Stratified random sample

Often it is preferable to order the population into different groups or *strata*, such as gender, age and social class. You would then select informants randomly within each stratum, usually by quasi-random sampling. The stratification results in obtaining a sample *proportionate* to the size of the stratum in the target population, so that if 60 per cent of a population were male, then 60 per cent of the sample would be also. This has the advantage over SRS that the numbers of men and women in the sample are controlled and not left to chance.

On occasions *disproportionate* stratified sampling (Moser and Kalton, 1971) is used. For instance, in a survey of mature students there may be far fewer in science disciplines than in arts and social science, so you would select very few mature science students by proportionate sampling. In such cases you might want to increase their sample size, in order to have enough people for analysis in your tables.

Random multi-stage cluster sample

Large national surveys, such as the British Social Attitudes Survey, use multi-stage clustering to retain the advantages of random selection while taking informants from specific areas to reduce the costs of interviewing. This type of sampling first selects large areas (such as parliamentary constituencies) by stratified random sampling. Next, a sample of districts (such as electoral wards) within those areas is selected. Then households within those districts are selected. The interviewer on the doorstep will finally use predetermined random methods to choose one person from the household to interview (de Vaus, 1991, p. 67).

This method is mentioned for completeness, but

obviously is beyond the scope of a student project. It is much more likely that a project will have to rely on some form of purposive sampling, at the cost of the ability to generalise validly from the sample.

Non-random sampling

Quota sample

Market research provides the example of non-random sampling through its use of *quota sampling*, where interviewers are instructed to find people to interview who meet the target numbers for the relevant characteristics of gender, age and social class (the 'quota'). This at least ensures that all sectors of the population are covered, and in larger surveys quota sampling may be employed in a multi-stage strategy, with random selection of geographical districts such as parliamentary constituencies being used as the clusters from which informants are drawn.

The final selection of informants is left in the hands of the interviewer, and crucially the availability of those who are ready for interview – in the street at the time – excludes a large percentage of the population, whose attitudes, opinions and behaviour could be quite different from those asked.

Quota samples are therefore looked on askance by academic social scientists, because the representativeness of the sample is seriously compromised. However, despite these faults quota samples have the advantage of being quick and cheap to administer, and may be your only choice on limited resources for finding out the opinions of a broad section of the population of an area. Provided you use the information as a guide and clearly state that it must not be taken to be representative of the population at large, you may produce some interesting results.

The quota should break down your intended sample size by the categories for which you want to control. Usually these will be age and sex (and possibly social class), as any more detailed specification will make it difficult to find people who match all the desired characteristics. Census statistics for the local area will tell you what proportion of each category there is in that area, and your quota should ideally reflect this distribution, or at least give you enough respondents in each category for meaningful analysis later.

Example 5.4
Three students were asked by a client organisation which aimed to recruit volunteers for a variety of projects to discover how the public in a certain locality felt about community volunteering. The survey aimed at achieving a sample of 120 informants contacted through a quota sample in the shopping area. Table 5.1 shows the categories of the sample aimed at (with those actually obtained in brackets).

Table 5.1 Quota sample

Age	Male	Female	Total
25–40	20 (19)	20 (20)	40 (39)
41–55	20 (16)	20 (17)	40 (33)
56 and over	20 (23)	20 (16)	40 (39)
Total	*60 (58)*	*60 (53)*	*120 (111)*

SOURCE: Caldwell, Crotty and Meehan (1993).

Snowball sampling

A *snowball sample* is often useful in exploratory research, when it is impossible to identify beforehand all those who might fall into your category of interest. Instead, you start with one or two informants, and get them to refer you on to others whom they think you should talk to as well. Like rolling a snowball, the sample gets bigger the more interviewing you do.

When you do not have a sampling frame to go on, this can be a useful expedient. But remember that your sample could be biased (Davidson and Layder, 1994, pp. 95–6).

Talking to other people might have given a different impression. In Figure 5.3 the procedure is shown in diagram form, from a study of illicit drug use.

Example 5.5
On the project for a proposed community centre (Example 5.3), the students wished to supplement their questionnaire administered to a random selection of houses by interviewing people already involved in youth activities. Starting with a few names of contacts from the client, they were referred on to others, and in fact ended up with more names of potential informants than they eventually had time to interview.

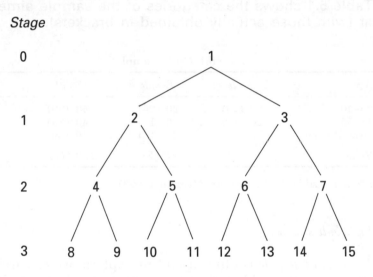

Figure 5.3   Snowball sample

Source: H. Parker *et al.* (1988), *Living with Heroin.*

Judgement sample

Less detailed than a quota sample, a judgement sample (Oppenheim, 1992, p. 43) relies on the researcher to try to obtain as wide a representation of individuals as possible, taking account of likely sources of difference in their views and experiences. This may be the only feasible method in certain circumstances, when access to the population is difficult or restricted.

Example 5.6
A project investigating the feasibility of a respite care house for people with HIV wished to interview 'positive' people who might make use of the service. Working with a support group, the students did not have access for ethical reasons to names and addresses of people with HIV/AIDS. Instead they asked the support group activists to contact a sample of informants to see if they would be willing to be interviewed. It was agreed that the sample should ideally include people of different ages, gender, occupational and family circumstances.

Accidental or convenience sample

A *sample of convenience* is the polite way of saying that you chose for your sample whoever happened to be around at the time. This sample is hardly representative of anyone else. 'Persons met at random, that is accidentally, do not comprise a random sample' (Dixon *et al.*, 1987, p. 137). All you can report are the views of the informants. The more there are of them, the more weight these views might appear to have. But, as we have noted already, if the sample is biased in some way, getting more numbers does not correct that bias. It is not possible to generalise from these informants to any wider universe, because you do not have any information about how well your chosen sample matches up with the rest of the population.

Sample size

How big should the sample be? That is probably the first question people ask when they are thinking of doing a survey. It has been left until last because the method of selecting the sample needs to be tackled first.

Where the aim is to use the results to generalise to the population, and you have a random sample, statistical methods can be used to choose the size of the sample for given levels of accuracy in making generalisations. de Vaus (1991, pp. 72–3) presents tables of calculations showing that, for instance, with a sample size of 400 the sample value of a variable is likely to be within plus or minus 5 per cent of the true population value (at the 95 per cent confidence level). In other words, if a sample of 400 service users produces an average of 70 per cent satisfaction with the facilities, then the true average satisfaction level for *all* the organisation's service users (the population) is very likely to be somewhere within a range of 65 per cent to 75 per cent. de Vaus also shows that to double the accuracy, to within plus or minus 2.5 per cent, would require the sample size to be quadrupled to 1600. In terms of practical research, even a small survey is going to have to be quite sizeable if you want to generalise from it: 100 is pretty much the minimum, and 400 would be better – but this is likely to be too ambitious for a student project.

So is there another way of tackling the question? Your sample is unlikely to be large enough to allow valid generalisations to the population. But in practice much of what you will be doing is gathering exploratory data on a topic where there is little known for sure.

Assuming that in your report you will be presenting tables to make comparisons between different groups on different variables, then Dixon *et al.* (1987, p. 149) suggest two basic rules, from which to choose the one that gives the larger number:

1. a minimum sample size of around thirty, and
2. a minimum of five in each 'cell' of a table.

This second point refers to the combinations produced when different variables are cross-tabulated. For example, a question might ask men and women if they had used a day centre within the last week. Cross-tabulating use by gender would produce four possible combinations: Men Users, Men Non-users, Women Users, Women Non-users. You would need to ensure that there were five or more people in each of these combinations in your sample.

The conclusion is:

- be realistic about the size of sample that is actually achievable within the time and resources available
- prefer random methods, but consider other methods of sampling if random methods cannot be used
- do not claim more for your findings than is warranted by the method of selecting the sample and its size
- employ mixed methods and do not rely entirely upon a single sample.

We can now move on to the intricacies of questionnaire design.

Stage 1: Consult similar research and questionnaires

If a questionnaire around your topic already exists, then this could well save a lot of time designing questions. Check out what has been published on the topic. Though this does not absolve you from examining whether such questions 'work' in terms of providing valid answers, there is often some merit in using the same or similar questions for comparative purposes. Reports sometimes do not give the questions actually used, but you may be able to re-interpret how they were phrased from information in the tables of findings.

Do not neglect the information your client organisation may be able to provide. They are likely to have access to relevant national reports, as well as to internal documents. The organisation may even have tried a survey before. That is the cue for you to find out what was

117

done, and if there were any problems. Then you can try to do something better.

Stage 2: Identify topic areas and use brainstorming

This preliminary activity is to identify the issues you need to build into the questionnaire. It is often useful to get some help from others, by throwing a few ideas together in a brainstorming session. What you hope to end up with is a set of topics, and maybe some actual questions, but the main thing is to cover the whole area of investigation fully.

Example 5.7
A group of students agreed to carry out a survey of mature students at a university. Discussion with the sponsors of the research, the research workers and a small number of mature students identified the main areas of concern as the following: applications and the admissions process; careers advice; finance and care of dependents; evaluation of courses and departments' teaching and learning practices; background information on age, sex, and prior occupation. These topics were then used to work up specific questions.

Stage 3: Work up each area into a set of questions

As you begin to devise questions there are some important points for you to consider about the wording and layout of questions.

- *Questions should be clear and readily understandable.*
  Consider the question from your informants' point of view. Would they understand the language? Is the question too long or convoluted? Could it be simplified?
- *Questions should avoid bias or presuming a certain answer.*
  It has been said that with the 'right' form of words you can get any result you want from a survey. You need to

demonstrate that the questions are fair and can stand external scrutiny. If you are presenting alternatives for people to choose from, are they each given the same emphasis?

- *Questions can be about matters of fact or opinion.*
  It might appear that matters of fact are easier to ask about, as there should be a definite answer. Opinions, on the other hand, are less easy to pin down because the variety and intensity of possible answers is far broader, and because you are asking for a person's evaluation of what may be an emotionally laden topic.

- *Questions can be open or closed.*
  The choice between open and closed questions may well be guided by the type of research you are conducting: *exploratory* research on a relatively little known topic can make good use of open-ended questions to develop knowledge of an area, while pre-coded questions are more suitable for *confirmatory* or hypothesis testing research, where you already have a clear idea of the subject, and wish to provide quantifiable information (Oppenheim, 1992, pp. 112–15).

- *Closed questions can often be turned into rating or ranking scales.*
  One general issue with which many organisations may be concerned is users' satisfaction with their services. The simple question:

Are you satisfied with the services you receive from X?

Yes [ ]

No [ ]

---

is unlikely to give useful results because it lacks *discrimination*. First, most people tend to report they are satisfied with what they are getting most of the time. Secondly, one general question about satisfaction is unable to reveal any specific items of high satisfaction (or dissatisfaction).

You will get more from your questions if you ask about different items of service, facilities and personnel, and use a *rating scale* to determine the level of satisfaction or dissatisfaction. Comparison between the scores for different items can then show up issues for further consideration. So one might ask instead:

How satisfied are you with service A that you receive from X?

Very satisfied [ ]
Quite satisfied [ ]
Neither satisfied nor dissatisfied [ ]
Quite dissatisfied [ ]
Very dissatisfied [ ]

There is some debate about whether or not to include a neutral middle point – include it and you give your informant the opportunity to avoid declaring an opinion one way or the other, omit it and you may be forcing your informant to choose an option on which she is really indifferent. The practice of most questionnaires seems to be to include the neutral option, and unless you have strong reasons not to do so then this seems preferable.

Avoid known pitfalls

Designing questions is more of an art than a science, and Moser and Kalton (1971, p. 348) suggest that it is 'a matter of commonsense and experience, and of avoiding known pitfalls'.

They provide a helpful list of such pitfalls, including the following:

- *double questions* – where two ideas are linked in the question.

These can often be identified by the use of 'and' or 'or' in the question. When your informant answers 'Yes', you do not know if they are agreeing to the first part of the question, or the second part, or both.

- *hypothetical questions* – where you present a future state of affairs without going into alternatives or the cost of provision.

People are quite likely to say they would like more of a service, especially if they do not have to worry about its cost. Response to a hypothetical question is not therefore a good guide to what people would actually do in the future.

- *vague measures of time* – such as 'frequently', 'usually', 'often', and so on.

What is frequent to one person may not be to another. If you really do want to find out how often people take a particular action, it is better to frame an exact question, for example asking 'How many times a week . . . ?' Questionnaires on health behaviour and lifestyle seeking information on diet, exercise, alcohol use and smoking rely on specific measures, for example in terms of units of alcohol to quantify drinking.

- *questions which may be perceived as intrusive* – because they deal with matters which 'are surrounded by strong social conventions' (Moser and Kalton, 1971, p. 311).

These are questions where changes in wording may produce the biggest changes in responses. The advice then is to *pre-test* such questions, and to consider their place in the questionnaire as a whole. If placed towards the end, you stand a chance of having most of the questionnaire completed, even if this particular question is not answered.

With such cautions in mind, you can set about creating your questions.

Stage 4: Type out the questions and assemble in order, for scrutiny

We assume that you will be word-processing your reports, so it is well worth doing the same for your questionnaire. It makes it so much easier to alter the order of questions, and to set out standard responses for the questions.

At this stage your questionnaire may be quite long, and growing in length as you see it as a whole and think of new items to ask about. Scrutiny of the questionnaire at this point is required to justify each question:

• Does this question really need to be asked?
• How will the responses be used in the final report?
• Will an informant understand what the question is really asking for?

Each question has to be examined to see if it is:

• essential to the report, or
• desirable but not essential, or
• merely there to satisfy curiosity – in which case, omit.

Next, scrutinising the questionnaire as a whole, you should address a different set of problems.

1. Is there a *logical order* to the questions?
   It is good practice to introduce your questionnaire with a statement about its purpose. You should keep to an order which begins with questions on that topic which informants will enjoy answering (de Vaus, 1991, p. 94). Group together questions on similar topics, rather than darting around from one topic to another and back again. Lead into a change of topic with a few introductory words, such as 'Now I'd like to ask you a few questions about . . .' (Converse and Presser, 1994, p. 142).

2. Do *filter* questions provide clear directions for answers?
   Filter questions direct informants to different sup-

plementary questions depending on their initial answer. Make sure that explicit directions are given in the questionnaire, so that informants (or interviewers) are clear which questions are relevant and should be answered next, and which questions can be skipped over.

3. Are the *instructions* for response *consistent?*
   It matters little whether you ask your informants to tick the relevant box or ring the appropriate response number – but it should be one or the other throughout, not a mixture of both. Similarly, rating scales should be consistent from question to question. If you want your informants to make complex judgements, like ranking a list of items in order of importance, then do make this clear in the instructions – but it might be safer to rely on simpler questions.

4. *How long* is the questionnaire?
   The urge to add more and more questions has to be resisted. Long questionnaires can be off-putting. Long questionnaires will also take more time to analyse. On the other hand, a short, one-page questionnaire may not provide the detail you need. It is a question of balance, where you have to be guided by what you will need to write the report. If it takes more than 6–8 pages of questions, then you are probably attempting a subject which is beyond the scope of a student project.

5. Have you *budgeted* for the cost?
   Photocopying the requisite number of questionnaires, with postage on top for mail return, can be quite costly. Telephone charges also have to be considered. You need to check that your organisation or institution is willing to cover such costs. As part of your project brief you should already have thought about how to meet these research costs.

Information for informants

You should tell your informant the purpose of your survey, and the name of organisation it is being done for. Letter-headed paper can be useful here in conveying authorship of the survey. You can mention that you are a student if you think this will gain you sympathy, but remember that you are working on behalf of an organisation which is going to take action on the basis of the results.

You could tell your informants the expected benefits that will come from the questionnaire responses: for example, in terms of the better service the organisation hopes it will be able to provide – though avoid raising expectations about the likely outcomes.

You must give your informants a guarantee of *confidentiality*: that information gathered in the survey will not be disclosed to other people, except to the organisation which will receive the final report – without, however, identifying individual informants. So you are also giving your informants a guarantee of *anonymity*: that no individuals will be identified by name in the report and that nothing they say (or write) will be attributed to them personally.

With a postal questionnaire you need to include a code number on the questionnaire, so that you can check who has returned the questionnaires, and who requires a reminder letter. It is good practice to explain that the code number is only needed for administrative purposes, and does not compromise the guarantee of anonymity.

Finally, you should give a name, address and telephone number for people to contact if they would like any further information about the survey, or if they have any comments they want to make. Most probably this will be the name and address of your supervisor. Hopefully this will not be needed, but it is as well to offer.

Motivation and consent

It is an obvious point, but a questionnaire assumes that your informant is *able* and *willing* to respond. Some people may have disabilities that prevent them responding adequately. Questions about past events that rely on memory assume people can remember accurately. The presentation and content of the questionnaire will also affect people's willingness to respond. They may be more likely to respond if they:

- approve of the purpose of the questionnaire
- can see some advantages to themselves or those like them from the use the replies will be put to
- approve of the body sponsoring the questionnaire or are impressed by its prestige
- feel important because their opinions are valued
- are able to complete it quickly
- are rewarded for completion (This last point is not really applicable to student projects, though commercial questionnaires do dangle the opportunity of entry into prize draws and suchlike).

People are less likely to respond if they:

- are inconvenienced by the time it takes to answer
- think the questions are intrusive
- have other more urgent priorities
- are suspicious of the questioner's motives.

It has to be accepted that some people, particularly in inner-city areas, are suspicious of others coming round seeking out information. You have to establish quickly that you are not connected with 'authority'.

Informal consent

In handing out a questionnaire you are trying to make an informal agreement with your informants such that they will be motivated to answer fully and truthfully. So the introductory letter accompanying the questionnaire is extremely important as the only method of persuasion you have in the case of postal surveys. With structured

125

interviews you can introduce yourself at the doorstep; however, it is good practice to reinforce your words with a written introduction as well.

Formal consent

In addition, you may like to consider using an 'informed consent' agreement with your informants for survey and ethnographic interviews. It is particularly important that vulnerable service users are aware of the reasons for the interview and are happy to take part. A sheet of paper should contain short paragraphs explaining the *purpose* of the interview, the *requirements* – such as a 15-minute chat, and a sentence clarifying the *consent* given; for example, 'I understand the explanation and agree to take part in this research. Signed . . .'.

Stage 5: Pre-test and pilot

With the questionnaire assembled, it is time to go through it carefully once more to make sure that you feel all the necessary questions have been asked, all the unnecessary questions omitted, and the layout and design is straight-forward and consistent so that it is clear what the inform-ant is being asked to do.

Use your friends and colleagues and academic super-visor for the pre-test to see if they understand the ques-tions: what seems obvious to you may not be so to other people. And make sure you find the time to take the questionnaire to your organisation and check with the people there that it meets their objectives.

These consultations may throw up further revisions to the draft. Assuming it passes scrutiny, your questionnaire is now ready for *piloting*. This is the stage where you try out the questionnaire on a small number of people from the same population as the one you wish to survey. The aim is to reveal any further *unanticipated problems* with the questionnaire before you commit your time and effort to the fieldwork proper. Even if you have decided to use a mail questionnaire for self-completion, you could get more useful feedback from your pilot if you do this stage as an interview. If you have closed questions, have you thought of all the options or do your informants raise options you have not considered? If you have open-ended questions, do they need to be reworded?

How many people should be included in your pilot sample? It is difficult to be precise – enough to cover the variability in your expected answers, so select informants who are not all the same age or gender. Given the scope of your survey and the limited time available, around half a dozen or so should be enough to reveal any problems with your questionnaire. Any problems, of course, will necessitate a rewrite of the offending questions, and ideally a retest – though this is a counsel of excellence when you may find time against you.

One final point: as you look at questionnaires produced by others you will often find a ruled column at the right hand margin of the questionnaire 'for office use only'. This is where replies to closed (pre-coded) questions are assigned numbers for the eventual computerised data file. So at this stage you should already be thinking of how the data will be coded for later analysis. This is dealt with in Chapter 6, on analysing the questionnaire, which also needs to be read at the survey design stage.

Stage 6: Administer the questionnaire

For postal surveys you will have a list of names and addresses from the sampling frame from which to send out your questionnaires. You need to keep a *record of returns*, and send out a *reminder letter* (with another copy of the questionnaire) when returns begin to tail off. Usually you should allow a couple of weeks before sending a reminder. As your aim is to achieve as high a return rate as possible, and certainly over 50 per cent of those dispatched, a second reminder may also be used if you think it worth while, and you have the time to do so.

If because of problems of access you are relying on other people such as your contacts in the organisation to hand out the questionnaires, your control over this process is much weaker. Again, it is important to keep reminding your contacts that you need their help – the survey depends on getting an adequate response rate.

If response rates stay low even despite reminders, you have to consider alternatives. Is there some reason why your informants are unwilling to respond at this time? Would it be better to try to get the information some other way? At this stage the advantages of a mixed strategy of research methods become apparent.

When conducting interviews in a neighbourhood survey, you must consider your own personal safety. If at all possible, work in teams of two or more and do all the interviewing in daylight.

Remember to carry identification with you and a letter of authorisation from your supervisor on institute-headed notepaper. For door-to-door interviews it is also a wise precaution to inform the local police station of your work. Interviews in shopping malls are likely to require authorisation from the shopping centre's management beforehand.

Conclusion

This chapter has covered the issues of data collection using the survey method. Sampling is a crucial element of the process, both in terms of the size of the sample and the way in which it is selected. Drafting questions has also been covered in terms of what to aim for and what to avoid. This is best seen as a collaborative enterprise. Even if you are doing a project on your own, you need to try out your questions on others. They are bound to spot problems which you have missed. When administering a questionnaire, ensure your informants are clear about who you are, why you are asking questions and that the responses will be treated confidentially. Yet all of this is only the first step. You now have a pile of completed questionnaires. How do you begin to analyse these? This is what the next chapter is concerned with – so read on!

6
Data Analysis: the Questionnaire

The aim of this chapter is to enable you to handle data efficiently and to 'tell a story' with the data that has been produced. It deals primarily with survey information which can be counted and measured, summarised in terms of averages and percentages and displayed in graphs and tables. The level of statistical knowledge covered here is quite basic, with the emphasis on *describing* variables and *comparing* the characteristics and experiences of different groups. For those unfamiliar with the language of statistics, suggestions for further reading are included at the end of this chapter.

In the beginning

Data analysis marks a stage in the project work where you begin to draw back from the field and concentrate on making sense of what has been discovered. It is important to leave enough time for this stage, even if it means keeping to a strict cut-off limit for data collection.

Once the data have been collected it is tempting to rush off to start the analysis. But the first stage is the less interesting one of checking and filing the responses. So, as the questionnaires arrive in the post, or as you finish an interview, make sure that the questionnaire or interview form is marked with its unique identification number, and

129

the date. It helps to keep a separate log so that you can keep an up-to-date count of all the work you have done.

Response rates

There comes a point when the time and effort of arranging one more interview, or calling back for one more questionnaire return would be better spent in sifting through the data already collected. Only you know when that point is reached. You know how many informants you originally planned to contact, and how many you have achieved. If the gap between these two is large, consider what is causing the problem and what can be done about it.

- If the problem is catching people in at home, then try calling on different days and at different times.
- If the problem is that you are relying on other people to hand out questionnaires, try to enlist their co-operation by persuading them of the value of the information to be gathered. Remember, though, that what is vitally important to you can just seem to be another burden to them.
- If the problem is that very few people want to be interviewed, or to fill in your questionnaire, think of alternative methods of obtaining the information – for example, by talking with a group of informants, or by observation.

The difficulty with *non-response* is that if the number of informants not replying to a questionnaire is large, then the information from those who do reply may be biased because they differ in some significant way from those who did not reply. The information then becomes unreliable, and may lead to invalid generalisations.

In the previous chapter various suggestions were made for maximising response rates to surveys by presenting questions in a clear and logical order, by offering explanations of the survey and by thinking about how to enlist the informant's motivation to respond (see also, de Vaus,

1991, pp. 114–22; Oppenheim, 1992, pp. 103–6). Call-backs and follow-ups will boost the initial response rate at the expense of extra cost, time and effort.

When you have achieved all that can be done, and if a sizeable non-response rate remains, it may be possible to check for bias in the responses you have achieved by comparing those who replied with those who did not in terms of known characteristics, such as gender or area of residence. It is unlikely you will ever achieve a 100 per cent response rate, but what you are looking for is to achieve a reasonable one – well over 50 per cent – which does not contain any obvious sources of bias; so that, for example, men and women are represented in proportion to the known population figures.

Should this prove impossible despite your best efforts, do not despair. You still have the data that has been gathered from those who did reply. But you will need to make it clear to the client organisation that the responses relate only to those who were surveyed, and that it may be unwise to generalise from this information because of possible bias.

Frequency counts – closed questions

Analysing the data that has been produced is largely a matter of counting and summarising the replies, and comparing the results for different groups of people. Closed questions where the informants have ticked boxes or circled answers are the easiest to deal with, as the categorisation of answers has already been done in the format of the questions. So for simple Yes/No questions it is merely a matter of going through the replies and counting up the different responses.

The only difficulty comes from *missing data* (Bourque and Clark, 1994, p. 60). In contrast to non-response, where there is no information at all from an informant, with missing data just some of the questions have not been answered. Actually, getting incomplete information on a questionnaire is quite common and could be due to a

131

Table 6.1 Tally count – Have you ever been a volunteer?'

Response		No.
Yes	~~IIII~~ ~~IIII~~ III	13
No	~~IIII~~ II	7
No answer	III	3
Total		23

number of reasons such as poor layout and instructions, a page being skipped by mistake, or loss of interest in completing the form.

Missing data also differ from a 'Don't Know' response that is ticked as part of the question. 'Don't Know' is a definite and valid response, whereas missing data is a lack of any response to the question. In counting up responses it is necessary to add a line for missing data. The tally system of counting in groups of five works well with a limited number of questionnaires, but when the numbers start to become unmanageable by hand – that is surveys of around fifty people or more (depending on the number of questions asked), then it is going to be worth while spending some time learning a computer package for data analysis. This is considered at the end of the chapter.

But for now, with a small number of questionnaires, you can produce a count something like Table 6.1.

Percentages

When it comes to presenting the results of such questions in a report, it becomes difficult to compare the actual numbers of people saying 'Yes' to different questions if the number of people with missing data varies from question to question. So percentages are used to allow easy comparison. Percentages are calculated *after excluding missing data,* so the example given in Table 6.1 would become as shown in Table 6.2.

Table 6.2 Tally count with percentages – 'Have you ever been a volunteer?'

Response		*No.*	*(%)*
Yes	卌 卌 Ⅲ	13	65
No	卌 Ⅱ	7	35
No Answer	Ⅲ	3	
Total		23	
Total valid replies		20	100

Percentages on their own can be misleading if the total number of informants is low (fewer than 40) because:

- percentages magnify the actual differences between categories – for instance, in a sample of 40, each individual accounts for 2.5 per cent of the total;
- when percentages are quoted to one or more decimal points (for example, 7 out of 11 = 63.64 per cent), the impression of accuracy is spurious.

With small samples (fewer than 20) it is always better to give the actual numbers, and in any case rounding up percentages to the nearest whole number provides sufficient accuracy. In writing the report you may find that your audience relates more easily to words rather than percentage figures, and that the level of accuracy is not compromised by substituting, for example, 'around a third of the sample' for 30–35 per cent, and 'three out of every four people questioned' for 75 per cent.

Frequency counts – open-ended questions

Open-ended questions, where the informant writes in the answer or the interviewer takes down verbatim what the informant says, require more attention at the analysis stage. What is required is some form of *content analysis,* in which the various responses to the question are grouped into a

133

logical and orderly set of discrete categories. It is worth noting that although we are discussing quantitative analysis here, regarded as the hallmark of the 'scientific' approach, this process of categorisation is quite subjective.

The answers from each question have to be written out, so that all the answers to that question can be viewed together. After about twenty or so responses have been transcribed in this way, there will be enough to develop a provisional set of categories to describe the responses.

Where the same words appear in different people's responses, you can be fairly confident in grouping the replies together. Where the words are similar but different, you have to exercise your judgement about whether to put them together or keep them separate. You will be losing some of the richness of the information – in order to simplify the task of analysis.

Example 6.1

If the open-ended question: 'Why do you think people volunteer?' had been asked, possible answers might include:

'to give them something to do'
'maybe they're at a loose end'
'stops them getting bored'
'don't have a paid job'
'gives experience for getting work'
'want to help other people'
'way of making friends'

For analysis you might prefer to merge the first three answers under the heading 'alleviation of boredom' although it could be argued this notion is really too negative to express the first answer, which is positive rather than negative. This is where subjective judgement comes in. With open-ended questions like this it is also likely that responses will vary from some informants giving no reply at all (missing data), to others writing in a long response containing many different points which could be coded into separate categories (multiple responses).

Pragmatically, the aim is to end up with a manageable set of categories (no more than a dozen) which encapsulate the variety of responses found. In fact, for initial analysis and presentation in tables in the report you may wish later on to collapse your dozen categories into a much smaller number – two, three or four at the most.

But for now it would be better to keep a reasonable number of categories. These can always be simplified later, but if only two or three categories are chosen at this stage, you cannot expand the number later without going through all the responses again from the beginning. Remember that your categorisation is provisional: further questionnaires may reveal different responses not already catered for in your content analysis. You then have to decide whether to add a new category – for example, by splitting off a more precisely defined category from a miscellaneous or 'other' category – or to broaden one of the existing categories to include this new response.

Once this provisional categorisation has been applied to all the questionnaires and you have produced a frequency count for the question, it is then time finally to review your coding for this question to see if:

- it makes good sense (face validity)
- it is comprehensive (covers all responses)
- it discriminates between responses (the majority do not end up in the same category because that has been drawn too broadly, or there is a category into which only very few responses fall).

Multiple responses

Some questions allow the informant to offer more than one response. This would be the case with the open-ended question of Example 6.1, where more than one option is valid, or in a similar but closed question such as that in Example 6.2.

Example 6.2

Why do you think people volunteer?
(Tick all that apply.)

```
Because they [1] Are  Bored               [  ]
             [2] Are  Unemployed          [  ]
             [3] Have Spare Time          [  ]
             [4] Want To Help Others      [  ]
             [5] Other (explain what)     [  ]
             [6] Don't know               [  ]
```

With multiple-choice questions the simplest way of dealing with the data is to treat each category as a separate variable (boredom, unemployment, spare time and so on) which the informant ticks or mentions (Yes) or leaves blank (No). The only problem occurs in presenting percentage tables of the composite responses where informants can specify multiple answers, as percentages of responses may add up to more than 100 per cent when you divide the number of different answers by the number of informants.

So, for example, you might end up with something like Table 6.3.

Forced-choice and ranking questions

When one clear and succinct response is required or as a follow-up to a multiple response question it can be useful to use *forced-choice* questions. For instance, after the question in Example 6.2, 'Why do you think people volunteer?' the informant could be asked 'What is the most important reason for people volunteering?' This reduces the many alternatives to one – the most important one. An alternative is the *ranking* question, which asks informants to rank a set of alternative answers in order of importance. This preserves all the alternatives, but is quite a complex question to answer. Informants may be able to pick out the more important or less important alterna-

Table 6.3 Multiple response question – 'Why do you think people volunteer?'

Response	No.	(%)
To Help Others	92	87
To Fill Spare Time	40	38
To Alleviate Boredom	21	20
Because of Unemployment	20	19
To Gain Work Experience	15	14
Don't Know	3	3
No Answer	5	
Total of informants with valid answers	106	*

* Responses total more than 100 per cent because some people gave more than one response.

SOURCE: Adapted from Caldwell *et al.*, 1993.

tives but be relatively indifferent to many answers of middling importance.

Measurement scales

To extend analysis beyond frequency counts, it is important to understand how data are measured. Walsh points out that

> information comes to us from the real world in many forms, ranging from crude to very refined. The statistics we use in our research depend greatly on the relative crudity or refinement of our measures. (Walsh, 1990, p. 8)

The three types of scales of measurement for variables are:

- nominal scale
- ordinal scale
- interval (or ratio) scale.

Yes/No questions as well as questions about marital status, area of residence, ethnicity or religious affiliation, where the aim is to place the informant into one of a variety of mutually exclusive categories, are all examples of *nominal scales* of measurement. These are 'the crudest form of measurement' (Walsh, 1990, p. 8). The categories in nominal scales are not better or greater than each other – they are just different. So for the variable marital status, the categories are single, married, widowed, divorced and separated. The categories are *exhaustive* (everyone in the sample is included) and *discrete* (no one is in more than one category) but there is no implication that one category is better than another.

Other questions may also offer a choice, but from categories which stand in a definite relationship to each other, as in the case of occupationally-based social class (for example, professional, intermediate, skilled non-manual, skilled manual, semi-skilled manual, unskilled manual) or attitude scales (strongly agree, agree, neither agree nor disagree, disagree, strongly disagree). These are examples of *ordinal scales*, where there is a definite implication that each category represents a point on a continuum from highest to lowest, or most favourable to least favourable. However, there is no precise measurement of the difference between any two points on the scale, so that the difference between professional and intermediate cannot be equated to the difference between semi-skilled and unskilled manual).

The most refined form of measurement comes in the form of numbers with precisely defined intervals (*interval scale*) and with an absolute zero point (*ratio scale*). Examples would be age, income, number of children or the number of hours spent on voluntary activities each week. With ratio scales precise comparisons can be made: a person aged twenty is half as old as a person aged forty, and someone earning £30 000 a year is three times better off than someone on £10 000. In theory there is an exact value for each informant on such questions – though in practice informants may provide you with an approximation rather than the exact figure, some more approximate than others.

An assumption is often made by social scientists that attitude scales which are formally ordinal scales can be measured on the interval scale by assigning the numbers 1 to 5 to points on the agree/disagree scale. This is debateable, as it assumes that there is an equal interval between each attitude item: for example, that the difference between 'strongly agree' and 'agree' is the same as the difference between 'agree' and 'neither agree/disagree'. However, it does permit the ready summarisation of attitudes in terms of average scores. As we shall see, the scale on which your data is measured has implications for the statistics you can use to summarise and describe your findings.

Averages

Averages are measures of 'central tendency', that is, they can be used as a single value in the middle of a set of numbers which represents or stands in for all the values of that variable. However, there is a choice as to which 'average' is the best to represent any particular set of data:

- **Mean** (technically, the arithmetic mean)

- **Median**

- **Mode**

When dealing with nominal scales, analysis of data takes the form of counting the number of people falling into each category and noting the category with the largest number of responses (the *mode*). This is the only average which is meaningful here; it gives the 'typical' response to a question.

With interval scales, however, exact calculations of the average are possible. The *arithmetic mean* is what people usually understand as the 'average'. Its calculation is straightforward: for a specific variable such as age, add together all the values reported by each informant, and

139

divide the total by the number of informants (excluding those for whom no information was available).

How well the mean actually represents all the values in a set of numbers depends on two things:

- how spread out or dispersed the values are around the mean
- whether there are any extremely large or small values in the data set.

Where the range (difference between the highest and lowest value of a data set) is large the calculation of the mean may produce a value quite different from any actually reported by informants. And when there are several extremely low or extremely high values, as is often the case with income distribution, the mean is affected by these extreme values and the distribution is said to be *skewed*.

With skewed data an alternative measure of the centre of the distribution may be preferred. This is the *median*, which is defined as the middle value of a variable, when the values are arranged in order of size. Half the values fall on one side of the median, half on the other. For this reason official statistics on income usually present the average in terms of the median. A few untypically high incomes distort the mean, pulling it up so the mean does not give an accurate summary of what is representative of most incomes, whereas the median is unaffected by extreme values.

Where there is an odd number of cases, the median is easily identifiable – it is the one in the centre; where there is an even number of cases, the median falls between the two 'middle' numbers of the distribution, and is conventionally taken to be the mean of these two numbers.

The median is also the appropriate average for *ordinal scales*, though, as we have noted, for 5-point attitude scales it is quite common to treat these as interval scales and calculate the *mean* level of agreement with each item. This seems to work in practice, and then permits comparison between items with higher or lower average agreement scores.

Data Analysis: the Questionnaire

Grouped data

As we have seen, questions which produce answers in terms of numbers on an interval scale lend themselves to a calculation of the mean. But usually you will also want to show how the different values are arranged around the mean. This can be done quite readily using a grouped frequency count, and is particularly appropriate when the actual responses take on a wide variety of values.

For example, if the ages of your informants ranged from 16 to 85, it would be tedious to construct a table with each year of age represented separately. Instead the replies could be grouped into discrete age groups (for example, under 21, 21 to 44, 45 to 64, over 65) and frequency counts performed for each age group. By doing this an interval scale would be reduced to an ordinal scale. And if you further reduced the data to two categories, 44 and under ('young') and 45 and above ('old') the data would now be on the nominal scale (different). By transforming data in this way you alter which average is appropriate to describe the data, because the measurement scale has been changed.

If a closed question for age is used, asking informants to tick their age group (and this is the most common way of asking people their age), then a frequency count can be done on the numbers in each group. However, without information on people's exact age it is impossible to calculate new age groups should you decide, for example, that what is really needed is the number of people in the sample under 40 years of age. For this you would require the actual ages on dates of birth.

If your survey has yielded only grouped data, the mean can still be calculated by multiplying the midpoint of each group interval by the number in each group, adding these subtotals and dividing by the total number in the sample (Walsh, 1990, pp. 37–8). However, this is an estimated mean as some precision is lost in the grouping. Statisticians talk about *data transformation* (putting ages into groups, for instance) as involving *data degradation* – loss of information.

141

Dichotomies

Reducing the number of categories in the data to simplify complex information (data transformation) involves regrouping or recoding the original data. The most extreme form of recoding of scales of measurement is the creation of a *dichotomy* (literally, cut into two), where the data are reduced to just two categories (for example, young/old, or high income/low income).

Data on interval, ordinal or nominal scales can be recoded into dichotomies. With interval scales, you can use the mean (or median for skewed distributions) to divide the range into two approximately equal halves, or use some other reasonable rule, such as the top 20 per cent in income terms if you are particularly interested in the rich rather than the poor. With ordinal and nominal scales, you need to group the categories according to some logical shared identity so that the two resulting categories have at least face validity as different entities, for example 'satisfied' and 'not satisfied'. Try to avoid one of the two resultant categories being very small (fewer than ten cases), as this will cause problems with low frequencies when you come to compare this variable with others.

Although it may seem extreme to reduce the diversity of information available by recoding a variable into just two categories and thereby to produce data degradation, for preliminary analysis the gain in simplicity and ease of understanding when it comes to producing tables may well outweigh the loss of detail. The disadvantage is that in losing the detail you are also losing the opportunity of using the more powerful statistical techniques which apply to ratio scales. However, many of the variables sociologists are interested in are only measured on ordinal and nominal scales, so techniques which depend on ratio scales are often inapplicable.

Univariate analysis

Univariate analysis means taking each variable in turn and looking at the pattern of response. The discussion above on frequency counts, averages, and grouped data from closed and open questions provides the basis on which to work through each set of answers. If this is done systematically you should be able to produce a summary table of each question.

A full discussion of descriptive statistics would also cover measures of dispersion and the normal distribution, for in order to describe properly a set of values for a variable measured on an interval scale, it would be necessary to know the

- mean
- standard deviation (measure of spread around the mean)
- shape of distribution (normal, skewed or other)
- outliers or extreme values, if any.

However, in practical research you need to have before you the requirements of your intended audience in the client organisation. Detailed statistical breakdowns are not going to be understood by everybody. Nor will a simple presentation of the results of one question after another be satisfactory. Now is the time to think about how to select and prioritise the information which is most salient to the organisation. The original research brief will be a guide in presenting particular themes, and you will want to flag up any findings which strike you as interesting, unexpected or otherwise unusual. You should try to explain in words what you have calculated in figures, but do not need to give each finding equal prominence.

Graphical representation: bar charts and pie charts

Tables such as Table 6.3 above are in a sense a graphical representation of the data, in that the data are not simply reported in plain text. But usually graphical representations mean bar charts and pie charts. The bar chart expresses frequencies by the length of the bars, and is well suited to representing frequency counts, whether there are two categories or more in a set of answers. The bar chart conveniently sums up data from nominal, ordinal and grouped

143

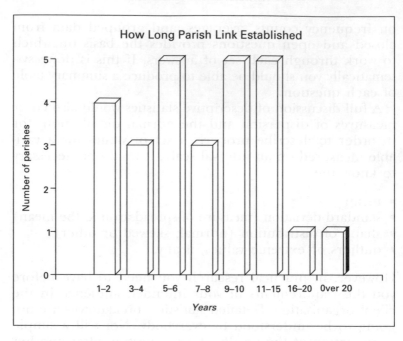

Figure 6.1   Bar chart

Parish Links are not new; they were established in response to perceived inequality and injustice in the geographical and social divides between Christians. Parish Links were, however, given considerable impetus by the publication of *Faith in the City* (1985).

It can be seen from the chart that some Parish Links have been in existence for over 20 years, while others are relatively recent. However, over half the Links have been in existence for over 6 years. Since 1985 there has been an average of two Parish Links a year being established in this diocese. (Adapted from Callaghan, 1993.)

ratio scales. In the last case, when the bars are joined together side by side the chart is technically called a histogram. However, computer programs tend not to maintain this distinction from bar charts, so with Robson (1993, p. 319) we agree there is little point in insisting on it.

Pie charts are used to show how the categories make up different *proportions* of the whole (rather than showing absolute frequencies as in bar charts). These charts

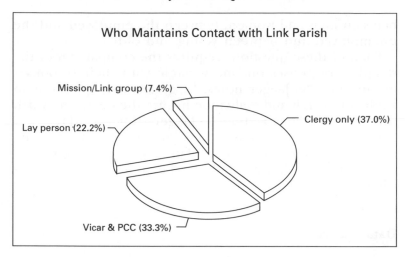

Figure 6.2   Pie chart

The chart shows that the clergy, either on their own or together with the Parochial Church Council, held the responsibility for maintaining contact with the Link Parish in two-thirds of the sample. Lay people or mission groups were responsible in only one-third of parishes.

However, these broad figures may be misleading. Interviews with clergy showed that many would like other members of the congregation to take on the responsibility of maintaining contact with the Parish Link, but felt unable to impose any more responsibility on 'the willing few' in small parishes. (Adapted from Callaghan, 1993.)

can be drawn by hand with ruler and compasses, but word-processing packages and spreadsheet packages have computer graphics facilities to produce charts easily, which can then be imported into a word-processed report.

Comparing variables: bivariate analysis

So far the responses to questions taken one at a time have been considered. However, the information from one question can be tied in with other variables. For example, do the attitudes to volunteering shown in Table 6.3 differ between men and women, between the employed and the unemployed and between young and old?

Each of these questions requires the comparison of the sample's responses on one variable with their responses on another. As Jaeger notes, 'A great many questions in applied research and evaluation involve the degree to which two variables "go together"' (Jaeger, 1990, p. 61).

Univariate analysis has to be supplemented by bivariate analysis if we are to try to explain the patterning of attitudes and why they are held, rather than just document what the attitudes are.

Data matrix

The data matrix discussed in Chapter 5 is important at this stage. It provides a composite view of all the data, so you can pick out any pair of variables and then see how each individual person responds on both variables together, on age and attitude, for instance. With just a few questionnaires or interviews, a data matrix can be constructed simply by transferring the information from questionnaires on to a large sheet of paper ruled off into boxes. This saves having to go through all the questionnaires afresh each time you want to compare another two variables. With a larger data set, the use of computers becomes more advisable.

Causal model

When comparing two variables, there is an implicit *causal model* (see Chapter 2) in our thinking: a person's attitudes are influenced by (or dependent on) the social group to which s/he belongs. The variables of gender, age or employment status can each be thought of as independent variables which may affect or influence the dependent variable of attitude. It makes no sense logically to suggest that the causal relationship is the other way round, that a person's attitude affects their gender, age, or em-

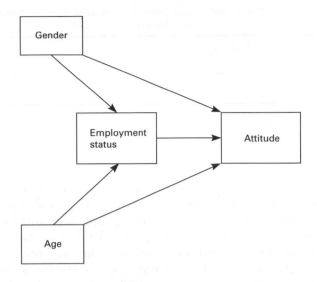

Figure 6.3   Simplified causal model to explain attitude

ployment status. The causal relationship can be represented diagrammatically as shown in Figure 6.3.

However, it is important to note that in a strict sense the survey can never show causality – that A causes B. This is because there are so many factors in the real world which interact with each other and are impossible to separate out. There may be factors X, Y and Z which also affect B and may also affect A. Moreover, these factors will interrelate with each other in a variety of ways. And it may not always be the case that there is a simple one-way relationship between A and B – both variables may affect each other to some extent. *Surveys show correlation rather than causation.* The causal model helps us sort out our ideas logically and aids in making sense of data, but only the experiment can exert the kind of rigorous control of variables which enables conclusions about causality to be drawn.

Table 6.4 2 x 2 table: opinions of men and women about volunteering

People volunteer in order to fill their spare time:	Gender: Men	Women
Yes	26	14
No	30	33

Tables

To test out a causal model some way of comparing two variables together is required. For initial exploration of relationships between variables, *cross-tabulation* is a convenient way of displaying and analysing data from questionnaires and surveys. Variables are related to each other on tables and this is particularly useful when the variables are measured on nominal and ordinal scales and statistical techniques appropriate to ratio scales cannot be used.

The simplest form of table is the 2 by 2 table which shows how two variables relate to each other, with each variable broken down into two categories (dichotomies). This produces four different combinations of response which are entered into the four cells of Table 6.4.

The data matrix is used to identify how many informants fit into each of these four cells. Informants with missing data on one or both variables are omitted.

Tables with more than two categories for each variable obviously produce more combinations and have more cells – and may be harder to interpret. That is why for initial analysis the practice of dichotomising variables has something to recommend it in terms of ease of interpretation, although there is some loss of precision.

Cross-tabulations are used to answer the questions:

- Is there any association or relationship between two variables?
- If there is, how strong is the relationship between the variables?

148

- Is the relationship statistically significant, or just the product of chance?

When comparing one variable with another, you should refer to the causal model to decide which variables should be chosen for the tables, and, for each pair of variables, which is the independent and which the dependent variable. The dependent variable is the one whose information you are trying to explain by reference to the (prior) independent variable. In the example of Figure 6.4 the dependent variable (belief that people volunteer to fill their spare time) is explained in terms of the independent variable (gender of the informants).

With even a moderate number of variables (twenty to thirty) produced by a simple questionnaire, the number of different tables that could be produced for each pair of variables quickly becomes unmanageable, so selection is necessary – and it should be done *before* the analysis on theoretical grounds. When it comes to writing the report, further selection may be needed to make the report readable. Where some significant difference or relationship has been found then you will want to present tables to show this. However, you may also need to show tables where *no* relationship has been shown – for instance, between age and volunteering. This is also a finding and may confound the preconceptions which the client organisation has previously held, and which have influenced the groups which they have targeted in the past.

Percentages

Tables should show the actual number of informants who fall into the different categories of response, and the relevant percentages for comparison between groups. If you can identify on logical grounds the independent and dependent variables, that will help in deciding which percentage figures to display (row percentages and column percentages give different results). A standard approach to setting out tables is to use the *column variable* as the

Table 6.5 2 x 2 table with percentages: opinions of men and women about volunteering

People volunteer in order to fill their spare time:	Gender: Men	Women	Total
Yes	26 (46%)	14 (30%)	40 (39%)
No	30 (54%)	33 (70%)	63 (61%)
Total	56 (100%)	47 (100%)	103 (100%)

independent variable, and the *row variable* as the *dependent variable.* If you follow this practice, then percentages should be calculated for the columns, as in Table 6.5.

Table 6.5 also includes the marginal totals round the four cells giving the breakdown of opinion by gender, and the actual numbers of informants are reported as well as percentages.

For a table to be readily understood by readers it is important that it is laid out with all the necessary information.

1. A *table number* should be included, for reference and to locate it in the sequence of the text.
2. There should be a *title,* to explain the variables, which may be continued with a subtitle if necessary.
3. The *column variable* should be named, and its categories or values should also be identified by name (as here: Gender – Men/Women).
4. The *row variable* (to the left of the table, reading across) should be named, and its categories or values should also be identified by name (as here: Fill Spare Time – Yes/No).
5. The *actual number* of informants who fall into the relevant categories of each variable should appear in the four main 'cells' of the table.
6. The *marginal totals* should be included, to the right of the column variable and below the row variable. Where the margins meet at the bottom right of the table is the grand total, the number of informants with valid (non-missing) responses to both variables.
7. The *percentage* figures for categories of the indepen-

dent variable should appear alongside the actual number of informants. If you set out your table as suggested, with the independent variable as the column variable, then it is the *column percentages* that are required.

8. *Statistical information* such as the Chi-square value, degrees of freedom and associated probability value (see below) may be included where your informants have come from a random sample.

Interpreting tables

As Table 6.5 showed, the simplest form of table is the 2 by 2 table. In analysing such a table, the question is whether particular categories of the independent variable are associated with particular categories of the dependent variable – for example, whether women are more likely (or less likely) to agree with a particular opinion.

The column percentages allow you to compare the categories of the independent variable even if there are different numbers of people in each category. In Table 6.5 men are 16 per cent more likely than women to agree that volunteering fills spare time (46–30 per cent). This 'percentage difference' is a useful figure for estimating the size of the association between two variables. The stronger the relationship between the variables, the larger the percentage difference. Marsh (1988, p. 149) refers to the percentage difference as d, Rose and Sullivan (1993, p. 111) refer to it as epsilon, but whatever the name the percentage difference is a simple measure that is easy to understand.

Percentage differences can vary from 0 per cent (no association between the two variables) to a maximum of 100 per cent (complete association). In practice you are unlikely to find percentage differences as extreme as this. As a very broad rule of thumb, anything over about 40 per cent is likely to indicate a strong association, and anything under 5 per cent suggests no real association (Erickson and Nosanchuk, 1992, p. 237). However, it is

151

important to note that an association between two variables does not necessarily indicate a causal relationship. As was argued above, the survey can only show correlation rather than causality, and terming one variable 'independent' and the other 'dependent' is best understood as a logical process which aids in making sense of data, rather than as a test of what 'causes' what.

Statistical tests

A variety of statistical tests exist to test the strength of a relationship and to answer the question:

Could the results I have found in my table have arisen purely by chance through the selection of the sample?

If a random sample has been used to select your informants, then the Chi-square test is a useful statistical test to apply to a table. It shows whether a relationship or association exists between the variables, and because the results can be compared with statistical probability distributions, it also shows whether the results could be chance findings or not. However, the Chi-square test becomes unreliable when the numbers in the cells are small (less than 5). It is also sensitive to sample size – a small sample may indicate no relationship between variables at a given level of probability whereas a larger sample from the same population might show a relationship exists – albeit a weak one.

For this reason a correlation statistic which is not influenced by sample size is also useful. The Phi coefficient provides such a measure and varies from 0 (no association) to 1 (complete association). It is suitable for 2 by 2 tables (with data measured on the nominal scale) and is based on Chi-square but takes account of sample size. For tables with more than four cells, then Cramer's V provides an alternative measure of association which, like Phi, has the useful property of varying between 0 (no association) and 1 (strong association).

Details of the calculation of these measures have not been

included here because they go beyond the scope of most client reports, which are designed for a 'lay' or non-statistical audience. The calculations can be found in most statistical textbooks, and they are implemented in most statistical computer packages. Some useful introductory statistics texts are listed at the end of this chapter. For students who have facility with statistics and who would like to extend the statistical analysis of their data, it is important to ensure that an explanation of the statistics used is provided for the client. A report which 'blinds with science' is not going to communicate your findings well.

Putting it all together

The techniques outlined in this chapter should be sufficient to give you a feel for what the data are telling you. Counts, percentages and averages, especially when linked to bar charts or pie charts, can be used to summarise the information you have collected for each variable – and to present it to your audience.

But as mentioned earlier, simply to list the results variable by variable is not the best way of presenting your data in a report. Instead, consider what questions are most important to your contacts in the organisation you are working with: what is their most pressing problem, what do they want to know, what will be most useful to them? Sometimes negative information (for example, that people are not using their services) will be as important as the evaluation of the services they do use.

Inevitably in the process of analysis you will be prioritising the information you have gathered, highlighting the most relevant and pushing other information into the background. The quantitative information has to fit into the themes for the report which you have already outlined while drawing up your questionnaires and interview schedules. New themes may arise at this stage as you consider unanticipated leads or outcomes arising from your information, but in many essentials the structure of the report will already have been established.

Tables should be used to explore the most interesting or relevant findings, by breaking down the results into different categories of respondent and by comparing answers to one question with answers to other questions. The percentage difference is suggested as an easily calculated and easily explained measure for investigating such effects – though, as noted, for a more technically minded audience you may prefer to use alternatives like Phi and Chi-square.

Conclusion

In this chapter we have concentrated on providing some guidelines on handling the information which your data gathering will produce. Much of the emphasis has been upon simple descriptive statistics and graphical representation of data. Tables can also be used to present information relating to two variables, choosing these according to your causal model.

Data analysis is a lengthy procedure: it will take twice as long as you first thought, so it is important to allow sufficient time for this stage. A lot of hard work will already have been spent gathering the data, but this may be wasted unless you have time to interpret that data and communicate it effectively to your audience.

The task of data analysis is potentially never-ending, so you will have to be selective. Even if there were time to do it all, there would be no point in overloading your audience with all the fine detail of what you have collected. So, here is a recommended strategy for analysis.

- Keep it simple, even if this involves recoding and losing the fine detail.
- Keep it as non-technical as possible.
- Do not claim more for your data than is justified by the sample size and method of selection.
- Use graphs and charts for single variables.
- Use tables for two or more variables.
- Use statistics sparingly and with caution.

154

- Above all, think of who will read the report and what they would expect to find in it.

Data analysis by computer

Data analysis by computer offers the advantage of being able to construct frequency counts, tables and charts quickly and easily once the mechanics of operating the computer have been learned.

If you decide to use a computer, you will need to turn the written information on the questionnaires into numbers representing the various responses the informants have made to each question. So the first task is to produce a *codebook* (sometimes called the *coding frame*), which gives the rules you have adopted for turning written answers into numerical values. The question responses for each informant can then be put into a data file and read into your computer.

Computer analysis of data still follows the logic of the processes outlined above, but for information on using specialist packages such as Minitab or SPSS/PC+ the following references are useful: Bryman and Cramer (1990); Cramer (1994); Nolan (1994); Norušis (1988); and Rose and Sullivan (1993).

For introductory statistics the following can also be recommended: Clegg (1989); Erickson and Nosanchuk (1992); Freedman *et al.* (1991); Jaeger (1990); Malec (1993); and Walsh (1990).

7

Recording Data: Ethnography

The last two chapters have dealt with research based on the questionnaire survey. Data can also be collected using the techniques of in-depth interviewing. This chapter considers the issues and practical steps you need to understand to conduct your research. You will learn about 'semi-structured' interviews as a general method, as well as specific types of research which use this and more 'unstructured' approaches such as the life history and oral history. Feminist concerns about the practice and use of interviews are important contributions to the debate on research methods.

Introduction

One major methodological text begins with the startling (if hopeful) statement that 'qualitative data are sexy'. The writers go on to explain more realistically: 'They are a source of well-grounded, rich descriptions and explanations of processes in identifiable local contexts' (Miles and Huberman, 1994, p. 1).

Interviews designed to yield rich or in-depth data can be very useful in practical social research projects. For instance, your client organisation may want to evaluate a service by discovering its effect on the people who use it. The survey can produce quantifiable information but it does have defects deriving from the rigid form of questioning. In-depth interviews provide data which give fuller expression to the informant's views. This method can be used on its own or in combination with the survey method.

The alternative to the survey is therefore a methodology which originates in the ethnographic concerns discussed in Chapter 2. It is more 'humanist' and the informant's voice is more clearly heard than in data generated by the survey. However, opinions vary about how this research should be done and feminist researchers have raised particular concerns which will be dealt with as we work through the issues. How you decide to conduct interviews is a matter to be thought about, discussed with your supervisor and possibly consulted on with your client. This chapter intends to make you aware of the opportunities as well as a few pitfalls.

Interviews

May (1993, p. 92) distinguishes four types of interview: the structured interview, the semi-structured interview, the group interview and the unstructured or focused interview.

Structured

The survey uses a tightly structured form of questionnaire, or in the case of interviews a structured schedule. This type of interview has been covered in Chapter 5.

Semi-structured

In-depth interviews use a less-structured approach which is sometimes referred to as *semi-standardised* or *semi-struc-tured*. As Fielding puts it: 'the interviewer asks certain, major questions the same way each time, but is free to alter their sequence and to probe for more information' (Fielding, 1993, p. 136).

Questions are open-ended so that informants can discuss

157

the issues more freely than they could with the closed or forced-choice questions of the structured questionnaire.

Example 7.1
A student was asked by an organisation concerned with the needs of lone parents to investigate a possible link between dependence on state benefits and inadequate or non-existent childcare facilities available for one parent families. The student interviewed twelve lone parents with or without childcare facilities. The in-depth interviews lasted about one and a half hours each and explored themes including finances, ambitions, hopes for the future and what it really means to be a lone parent in the 1990s. The student approached each interview with a list of topics or open-ended questions, such as:

• number and ages of children
• the circumstances regarding lone parenthood
• what successes or disappointments have there been in trying to get childcare facilities?

Often these questions were not answered in the order on the schedule and the student simply made sure that the questions *were* answered so that comparative analysis could be made. Informants were also free to add information which the interviewer had not thought about asking.

By taking advantage of the flexibility of this method, the interview comes closer to a conversation and is more natural than a formal interview with a highly structured schedule.

Group

Group interviews can be conducted with the interviewer acting as a facilitator or moderator of the research. A special example of this is the *focus group*, defined as a carefully planned discussion designed to obtain perceptions on a defined area of interest in a permissive non-threatening environment. (Krueger, 1994, p. 6)

A project using this approach (along with other methods) was one where single parents discussed their use of fuel as part of a fuel poverty survey, providing a lot of useful information in a short period of time. However, Krueger notes that:

> people who regularly interact, either socially or at work, present special difficulties for the focus group discussion because they may be responding more on past experience, events or discussions than on the immediate topic of concern. Moreover familiarity tends to inhibit disclosure. (Krueger, 1994, p. 18)

In another project students interviewed adults with learning difficulties in an informal group setting to find out their satisfaction with facilities in their club. They discovered that informants tended to agree with the dominant view being expressed, whereas when they were interviewed separately they tended to differ more in their opinions.

This latter example shows how group and individual interviews can produce different results. As May argues, it does not follow that one result is 'true' and another 'false':

> As most of our lives are spent interacting with others, it comes as no surprise that our actions and opinions are modified according to the social situation in which we find ourselves. (May, 1993, p. 95)

Unstructured

The final type of interview is *unstructured* or *focused*, and is distinguished from the other types of interview by its open-ended character. The interviewer uses a *guide* or *aide-mémoire* which lists the topics to be covered. Informants are allowed greater scope to develop their contribution in the direction they wish and the interviewer may join in with his/her own views.

Choice of approach

For the purposes of practical social research where you will be exploring areas of interest to your client organisation it is most likely that you will have to use the semi-structured or semi-standardised approach rather than unstructured interviews. You will have negotiated and agreed the topics – and perhaps the questions – which you are going to ask.

Example 7.2
The lone parent organisation of Example 7.1 wanted to know whether the student could provide evidence to support the probable positive effects of a childcare centre. This evidence (if it were found) would be used to support the organisation's application for funding from a government programme designed to combat urban poverty. The questions asked therefore focused on whether childcare would provide an avenue of escape from dependency on state benefits, and enabled the student to reach conclusions about her informants' circumstances. She was then able to make recommendations which included ideas about the type and cost of the childcare needed, the hours when it should be available and its likely benefits.

A further reason for using a semi-structured rather than unstructured approach is also illustrated by this example. The student could have conducted a series of 'life-histories' (see below) which would have explored the informants' lives using the categories, ideas and areas which they themselves raised. However, she wanted to be able to *compare* the responses given by lone parents within and between the sub-sample groups she was interviewing. Standardisation of the questions was necessary to produce comparability, although she often had to be flexible about the order in which the questions were asked. If the informant had already answered a question in the course of discussing a different topic, then it was not asked a second time.

Recording the interview – audio-tape recorder or notes?

Interviews have to be recorded in some form. The decision about how to record data is an important one. There are two choices, to take notes or to use a tape recorder, and both techniques have advantages and disadvantages.

Note-taking

Advantages Note-taking has an appeal, as it is straightforward and does not involve any technology which might go wrong, while informants might be expected to be less anxious faced with a notepad than with a piece of machinery. When taking notes the interviewer needs to be seated in a position facing the person being interviewed so that they do not read everything being written down. This can be off-putting for the informant and for the interviewer and can lead to constraint in what is being said.

The interviewer should aim to maintain as relaxed and normal an exchange as possible, so should only jot down key words and phrases – otherwise the interview becomes stilted, with long pauses as the researcher writes furiously. The interview notes should be written up as soon as possible so that recall is maximised. With practice a surprising amount of information will be remembered.

The main advantage of taking notes is that it reduces the amount of information to sift through which is generated by the tape recorder. Given that you will be working to a tight schedule, you may feel that this form of data recording is adequate for your purposes and enables you to control the volume of information to be analysed.

Disadvantages Note-taking does, however, make the interview more artificial and less natural than is desirable

161

for an ethnographic method. Even if the minimum is recorded, you are likely to have your head down for long periods and eye-contact will be lost. As some silences are inevitable as you write, rapport is difficult to maintain. The tone of the speaker is not recorded, and although it may be possible to write up the interview straight away, recall will still be partial and so the data will be biased. The longer the delay between interviewing and writing up, the more data will be lost.

Tape recording

Advantages Using an audio-tape recorder means that the interview is more like a conversation, and all exchanges are recorded. There will be a full record of what the informant said and how they said it. Importantly, there will also be a record of the interviewer's own questions and interjections. Students are often surprised at the extent to which they asked leading questions unwittingly and this can provide a useful guide for conducting further interviews.

Disadvantages The main problem with using a tape recorder is that it does produce a mass of data which has to be transcribed into written form before it can be analysed. With video-tape the problem is multiplied, taking this technique beyond the bounds of small-scale projects. For practical research, it is usually sufficient to transcribe only the information of direct relevance to the analysis rather than producing a lengthy and time-consuming verbatim report. If you wish to follow up other issues at a later date, perhaps in the light of further interviews and fresh directions which unfold, at least the data is available to work from.

Remember that data transcription is a very long process. Allow at least six times the length of the interview – that is, 3 hours to transcribe a 30-minute tape. You will need to make sure this is timetabled when you plan your work. It will affect the number of interviews which can be conducted and so influence the sample. It will impose limits on the interview schedule, so you should only collect information which you will be able to work with.

Ethical and practical considerations

Tape recording creates a record which appears more formal and permanent than the handwritten note. Therefore it is important always to ask the permission of the informant before using a tape recorder. Covert recording is unethical. Nowadays most people are sufficiently used to technology to find the tape recorder acceptable. However, if they are suspicious you can demonstrate what is being recorded in a short practice session at the beginning and offer them a copy of the tape.

One student who had obtained agreement to use a tape recorder found that it became intrusive. The informant's eyes were fixed on it and the interview was not flowing freely. She covered the recorder with a chiffon scarf which did not affect the recording but did stop the informant being mesmerised.

Before conducting an interview, it is vital to try out the equipment in different settings and with different types of background noise. Passing traffic, lawn-mowers and even ticking clocks can drown out speech. You may need to experiment with how close a microphone needs to be to the informant's mouth for an audible recording and you may need to use a microphone attachment to get sufficient clarity.

Use new, good quality tape and check that the tape recorder batteries are working. Also try out the equipment before beginning the interview, whether the informant is suspicious or not. It is important to check that everything is working and perhaps the person being interviewed will be impressed with your expertise. Above all, remember to switch on the recorder, and the microphone if it has a separate switch, and check at intervals that the tape has not run out. It is a good idea to speak an introduction on to the tape as a record, which details:

- the date
- the time
- the place
- the initials or pseudonym of the person being interviewed.

Notes and *tape*

Perhaps the best solution to recording data is to use a combination of tape recording and note-taking. Jotting down key phrases can help the interviewer maintain control of the interview by reminding the informant that there is an agenda being followed. In a lengthy interview, it is also possible to forget the questions raised earlier and so notes can be useful to refer to. Finally, you may want to note down reflective remarks about how you feel the interview is going, and any points you are uncertain about.

Producing the interview guide

In drawing up the research brief you will have clarified the aims of the research which emerged at the negotiation stage of the research. These aims now need to be translated into topics to be explored and then questions to be asked. As a preliminary exercise it may be useful to talk to someone who is associated with the client group to clarify the topics.

The client organisation may want to see a copy of the resultant guide and may have a list of questions they specifically wish to have included. Some clients have very clear ideas and know exactly the information they are after. As this can sometimes be rather technical, students can find themselves feeling grateful for the input the client puts into the guide. Other clients are less clear about their objectives and may wish the questions to be more 'exploratory' in nature. They will be happy to give you a free rein.

Ultimately, however, the guide is *your* responsibility. You will want to take the advice of the client and your academic supervisor on whether the questions are aimed correctly and framed adequately. But once the research starts, only the student as researcher will know which questions work and which need to be altered because they are unclear or ambiguous.

As with survey research, it is strongly recommended that the guide is tested by conducting a *pilot* interview. This can be with someone similar to the sample group. Not only will this reveal whether the questions are on the right lines, but it will help you gain confidence. Most students feel nervous about interviewing and having a trial run-through is extremely valuable.

The introduction

When it comes to contacting people for interview, the client organisation will often want to circulate its service users to inform them of the research and your role in it, and to find out whether they wish to be involved. This is an important ethical consideration, as the client has responsibility for releasing confidential information such as names and addresses. Such an introduction, whether by letter or phone, also establishes your *bona fides* as a legitimate researcher.

For in-depth interviewing it is vital that the interview is as 'natural' as possible and that informants feel free to express their views without constraint. The initial introduction is therefore highly important in terms of getting off to a good start. You should tell the informant briefly what you hope to gain from the information and how it will be used, and ensure they have no objections. This establishes a basic groundwork of agreement for the interview to go ahead.

The introduction is important also in terms of establishing rapport. A friendly and confident approach will help set the tone for the interview, which is after all a type of interaction with which the informant may not be familiar – and about which they may be anxious.

Benney and Hughes note a general assumption that in

the research interview information is more valid the more freely it is given. However, for this sense of freedom to exist, the informant as well as the interviewer must understand the nature of the social roles which they are playing. They state:

> unlike most other encounters the interview is a role-playing situation in which one person is much more an expert than the other, and while the conventions governing the interviewer's behaviour are already beginning in some professional circles to harden into standards, the conventions regarding the informant's behaviour are much less clearly articulated and known.   (Benney and Hughes, 1977, p. 236)

Informants act out their roles using knowledge from previous situations and in response to the conduct of the interviewer. The introduction sets the scene and can reassure the informant about the purpose of the interview and how the material will be used. The interviewer should clarify the confidential nature of the work and stress either that everyone interviewed will be anonymous or that their names will not be used without permission.

A particular need to introduce yourself in a sensitive way as a researcher arises when the informants are part of a 'vulnerable' group such as people with learning difficulties or mental health problems. In these situations it is good practice to get to know the informants first in an informal and non-threatening way. For example, two students who were investigating the use of an evening club for adults with learning difficulties attended the club for a couple of nights before beginning the interviews. Another student who was asked to research the feasibility of using volunteers in community homes for people released from large mental hospitals used the summer to visit the homes and become familiar with the residents and their routines. Not only did the informants gain confidence from this, the students did too.

Briefing the informant

In addition to the introduction, it is a good idea at the outset to brief informants on the sorts of questions which will be asked, as well as any issues which will be excluded. This should reassure them that the questions will not be intrusive and give them the opportunity to state whether there are areas they would prefer not to discuss. The briefing can also be used to state that the informant has the right at any time not to answer any questions they are unhappy about, and that nothing will be recorded if they do not want it to be. The briefing can be in written form, with informants being given time to read it carefully. Such sensitivity has been particularly important when students have interviewed vulnerable service users.

Example 7.3
A pair of students interviewed women from a support group for partners of men in prison. One of the ground-rules of the group was that the offences of the men were never mentioned – they were irrelevant to the experiences and needs of the women. The students had to show awareness of this principle, and in the briefing before the interviews they were able to make it clear that no questions about why the men were in prison were included.

The setting

Where the interview is conducted has a noticeable effect on the sort of information which is given. Informants interviewed in their own homes are more at ease than those interviewed in a more formal setting. The former are on familiar ground and are therefore more likely to answer at length and in a more 'conversational' style. Those interviewed in the workplace tend to give shorter, 'to the point' answers, partly because this is felt to be more appropriate for a business setting, and partly because they may be under time constraints (for example, the lunch

167

break) or in a room where others might enter and disturb their privacy.

If interviewing vulnerable service users, then it may be necessary to have a professional worker present. Ethical issues need to be respected here, as well as the professional code and judgement of those in the client organisation concerning the rights of the service users. The presence of a third person will inevitably create a different interview situation which may inhibit certain kinds of responses such as complaints about the service or comments about staff members. However, the professional may also be useful in interpreting responses if the informant has difficulty with communication and there may be other benefits to the student.

Example 7.4
A student was asked to evaluate a training centre for autistic adults. She interviewed the staff individually in a quiet room in the centre and interviewed the service users less formally as they went about their tasks. This was done to avoid the anxiety of a formal interview situation and the interviews were conducted in the presence of a staff member (for reasons of personal safety for the student). Although the work was done in the centre and not in private homes, the student was sensitive in her approach, notes were written up after the interviews and as far as possible everything was done in a non-threatening and reassuring manner. As with the other students who dealt with people with learning difficulties, this student also attended the centre to socialise before she started asking questions for the evaluation.

Ethnography and sampling

Survey research is concerned with generalisability – how representative the findings are to a wider population. Does ethnographic research share the same concern?

In the 1960s ethnographic methodology was a major

concern of sociologists who wanted to develop a rationale for research to counter the emphasis on enumeration in survey methodology with its statistical approach to sampling. Glaser and Strauss (1967), the exponents of 'grounded theory', provided the argument for what they termed *theoretical sampling* in ethnographic research. The ethnographer, according to this approach, is concerned with sampling through developing a theoretical framework. This is produced through the researcher giving thorough consideration to the data (gathered from observation and interviews). From this consideration analysis develops. A conceptual scheme is produced which becomes increasingly focused or narrowed to explain the processes being researched. The researcher then gathers fresh data to cover areas which they have not previously sampled – because the emergent analysis reveals gaps in knowledge. The researcher moves between data collection and conceptual analysis, seeking to refine the way different categories fit together to provide explanation. As Bryman explains:

> the researcher observes only as many activities, or interviews as many people, as are needed in order to 'saturate' the categories being developed, and then turns to the next theoretical issue and carries out the same process over again. (Bryman, 1988a, p. 117)

Bryman adds, however, that although Glaser and Strauss's view of sampling exemplifies the disinclination of qualitative researchers to emulate the approach of quantitative researchers, this particular view of the sampling process is 'probably cited far more frequently than it is used'.

In practice, ethnographers are usually concerned with sampling for the same reasons that survey researchers are – they want to know how 'typical' their results are. Sampling tends to be purposive rather than random (see Chapter 5) and cannot therefore be submitted to statistical probability testing. And, unlike survey research, sampling in qualitative research cannot always be pre-specified but may evolve once fieldwork begins. Miles and Huberman comment:

Initial choices of informants lead you to similar and different ones; observing one class of events invites comparison with another; and understanding one key relationship in the setting reveals facets to be studied in others. (Miles and Huberman, 1994, p. 27)

In addition to the non-random samples mentioned in Chapter 5 (quota sampling, convenience sampling and snowball sampling), Robson adds the following examples of sampling, appropriate for ethnographic research.

- *Time samples* – that is, sampling across time, for example in a study of characteristics of the persons who use a particular space at different times of the day or week
- *Extreme case samples* – that is, concentration on extreme values when sampling, perhaps where it is considered that they will throw a particularly strong light on the phenomenon of interest
- *Rare element samples* – where values with low frequencies in the population are over-represented in the sample; similar rationale to the previous approach. (Robson, 1993, p. 142)

Time sampling can be useful when observing and interviewing in a particular setting. One student who conducted an evaluation of a 'drop-in' centre for the mentally-ill found that her attendance at weekends yielded few informants, whereas attending mid-week gave her more informants and a completely different impression of the usage of the facilities. Sampling at both times was valuable – both were 'typical' of usage at different times of the week.

The 'extreme case' and 'rare element' samples mentioned above may be helpful in formulating case studies. If presenting data in this way, you would have to state that the cases had been chosen because they were atypical rather than representative, but that they illustrated genuine problems or needs in the group under study.

Many other types of sampling are employed in ethnographic research, and Miles and Huberman (1993, pp. 27–34) provide an exhaustive discussion. One further type relevant for our purposes is *reputational case selection* – where instances are chosen on the recommendation of an 'expert' or 'key informant'. Sometimes it is useful for the key worker in a client organisation you are working with to draw up a sample for you, based on the categories which they are familiar with in their organisation.

Example 7.5
Two students were asked by a community organisation which acted as an 'umbrella' for various local charities to estimate the training needs of the charities. The organiser wanted a cross-section of large national charities with neighbourhood offices, plus locally-based, well-funded groups, and tiny 'grassroots' movements. Because the organiser knew which groups in her directory fell into which category, she devised the sample for the students and they were then able to interview the groups, asking about the training they required, where the training should be provided and how much they could afford to pay for it. These results enabled the community organisation to put together a package of activities for a newly-appointed training officer to run.

The role of the interviewer

Most textbooks stress the importance of minimising the effect the interviewer has on the data gathered. At the same time, however, the ethnographic interviewer is supposed to be able to put the informant at ease, to be friendly and encouraging, and to create and maintain rapport. This probably sounds a tall order! Although it is a technique which gets easier with practice, some writers in recent years have pointed out that it is an inherently contradictory approach. Such criticisms are considered later in the light of feminist methodology.

1. *'Uh-huh'*, a nod of the head, or 'That's interesting'.

2. *Reflection* – Let us say the informant concludes his or her statement with these words: 'So I didn't feel too good about the job.' The interviewer then says: 'You didn't feel too good about the job?'

3. *Probe the informant's last remark* – The interviewer raises some question about the last remark or makes a statement about it.

4. *Probe an idea* – an informant may go over half-a-dozen ideas. The interviewer probes on an idea expressed in the informant's last statement.

5. *Probe an idea* expressed by the informant or interviewer in a much earlier part of the interview. This gives the interviewer a broader choice and consequently he or she exercises more control than is the case in limiting choice to immediately preceding remarks.

6. *Introduction of new topic* – Here the interviewer raises a question on a topic that has not been referred to before.

Figure 7.1   Interviewer directiveness scale

Directiveness

A number of writers have developed *scales* to indicate how much the interviewer contributes to influencing the responses given. William Foote Whyte, writing from many years of experience, offers a 6-point scale from low to high directiveness which was developed for use with unstructured interviewing. The scale is reproduced in Figure 7.1 in abbreviated form (Whyte, 1984, p. 99).

Probing and prompting

Probes and *prompts* are used with open-ended questions to clarify what the informant's answer means without biasing the response. The original answer may be too brief to be intelligible, so a neutral probe can be used, such as:

Can you tell me more about what you mean by . . .?

Or the informant may give an ambiguous response, in which case the interviewer should clarify what is meant and not assume the answer. A probe might be phrased like this:

When you say 'not convenient', what do you mean by this?

Sometimes an informant may query the question. The interviewer should not offer a response which might bias the result. For instance, if someone is being asked to say what is most important to them about a service, they might ask:

What do you mean 'important'?

The standard solution to this is to feed the words back, as in:

Whatever *you* think is important. Whatever 'important' means to you.

Prompts seek specific information and are often used when the question is initially completely open-ended so that the reply is spontaneous. However, if the sought-after information is not forthcoming, a prompt may be used to elicit it.

Example 7.6
Two students evaluated a day centre for adults with mental health problems by talking to the staff and the members. The staff interview guide began as follows:

1. How long have you worked here?
2. What is good or bad about this day centre?

The first question could be answered in a straightforward manner, but the second may well have required both probing such as:

What is good about that?
Why do you think that's such a bad thing?

and prompting:

What about the activities here, how do you feel about them?

Probes and prompts may be necessary if the informant is not too articulate or forthcoming. Or it may be that in the course of the interview issues are raised which were not previously thought of, and the interviewer wants to explore these areas with other informants. This is the value of this method – it has a flexibility which the survey lacks.

Clearly though, if you depart too much from the guide and probe more deeply with some informants than with others, then some of the comparability discussed earlier is lost. This would really have to be 'traded off' with the value of the information being gained from going more deeply into a question with one or two informants – which might yield material for use as case studies or to illustrate a point with a vivid example.

Withdrawal from the field

In projects where vulnerable clients have been interviewed or observed or where relationships have been built up with grassroots organisations, you need to think about how to withdraw sensitively from the research. The two students in Example 7.6 visited the centre after the fieldwork, bought the members a Christmas tree and helped out at a Christmas fund-raising fair. Other students have revisited the organisation after their exams were over, one student visiting a summer fair with her family, and others 'dropping in' for a casual chat. In addition to revisiting service users, delivering the client report directly to the organisation provides the opportunity of a final visit.

174

Reactivity

Though the ideal of traditional social research has been to produce data uncontaminated by the interviewer's effect on the interview, it is now recognised that this is impossible to achieve. There will always be a reaction between the interviewer and the informant stemming from:

- the method of research used (*procedural* reactivity) and
- the personal characteristics of the researcher (*personal* reactivity).

Whether the researcher is young or old, male or female, Black or White, middle class or working class will have an effect on the informants according to their own age, gender, ethnicity and social class.

The interview is a form of social interaction. Both the interviewer and the informant are playing out different roles according to their experiences and expectations of others. Awareness of this process, of how the researcher has been influenced in her or his work, and how their personal characteristics may have influenced the data, is termed *reflexivity*.

Reflective remarks

During the course of the interview you may operate reflexively by noting remarks which are unclear and need to be checked further. Or you may record the emotional response to a question – for example, 'didn't seem too keen to pursue' or 'very enthusiastic'. If you are using a tape recorder, these remarks could also be added to the transcript as the tape is written up – remembering to leave margins wide enough for this.

Reflective remarks can also be made just after completing the interview when the interviewer notes whether he or she felt comfortable, if the informant was relaxed and so on. Fieldwork notes can also be used for this purpose. Wherever you record reflective remarks, it is important

175

- what the relationship with informants feels like, now that you are off the site
- second thoughts on the meaning of what a key informant was 'really' saying during an exchange that seemed somehow important
- doubts about the quality of some of the data; second thoughts about some of the interview questions and observation protocols
- a new hypothesis that might explain some puzzlilng observations
- a mental note to pursue an issue further in the next contact
- cross-allusions to material in another part of the data set
- personal reactions to some informants' remarks or actions
- elaboration or clarification of a prior incident or event that now seems of possible significance

(Miles and Huberman, 1994, p. 66)

Figure 7.2   Reflective remarks

that a clear distinction is made between the researcher's comments and those made by the informant.

Miles and Huberman suggest a useful list of reflections after the interview has been completed: see Figure 7.2.

If working in a team, team members need to standardise how they record the reflective remarks and why. It is useful to have a sheet for 'remarks' which can be photocopied and circulated.

Throughout the project you should therefore reflect upon what is happening in terms of the *process* taking place. This leads to greater sensitivity about the issues and topics being discussed and whether these are central to the concerns of the informants or not. In Chapter 11 you will be introduced to the idea of recording reflexive accounts in the Methodology Report.

Feminist concerns

The influence of researchers on research and on their informants has been a major concern of feminist researchers.

Feminist research has gone through three stages, the first being deconstructionalist, exposing the male-centred nature of sociological knowledge and the neglect of women in research. The second stage concentrated on research by women on women in developing theories based on an understanding of women's experience. The third stage has been to include studies of men and masculinity by feminists (Abbott and Wallace, 1990, p. 206).

Feminist researchers have raised many issues of importance to research practice. In a now well-known article, Ann Oakley challenged the conventional approach to the interview as a guided conversation dependent on the achievement of 'rapport' for good results. She comments that rapport in research methodology does not mean the 'sympathetic relationship' of the dictionary definition

> but the acceptance by the interviewee of the interviewer's research goals and the interviewee's active search to help the interviewer in providing the relevant information. (Oakley, 1981, p. 35)

This results in a passive role for the person being interviewed rather than the interview being what a conversation normally is – interaction with give and take.

The interview takes place within a power situation and is not an exchange between equals. If it is conducted according to the kind of scale recommended by Whyte in Figure 7.1, then it is undoubtedly hierarchical, with in-formation passing only from the interviewee to the researcher.

For Oakley, conducting research on the transition to motherhood, a long-term relationship developed with many of her informants over the ten-year period of the research. Rather than being neutral or detached about herself, she answered 'all personal questions and questions about the research as fully as was required' (Oakley, 1981, p. 47). She also gave advice when asked and was careful to treat her women informants as subjects rather than objects to be exploited for academic purposes.

Janet Finch (1984) commented that Oakley's article heightened her awareness of the issues involved in

177

interviewing women. Finch was pleased to see that the common practice of those being interviewed providing hospitality was mentioned, though this is often missing from textbooks. But she noted another important issue arising in two studies she conducted with clergymen's wives and with playgroup mothers. The women treated her as a friendly guest in their homes and willingly trusted her with intimate details of their lives. She concluded:

> There is therefore a real exploitative potential in the easily established trust between women, which makes women especially vulnerable as subjects of research. (Finch, 1984, p. 81)

Liz Kelly, who conducted research with women who had been the victims of domestic violence, has commented on how she was unable to retain the 'aloofness' traditionally regarded as the proper style for an interviewer to adopt. Interviewing women who were greatly shaken as a result of sharing distressing accounts altered her interviewing style, and led to the interview including the sharing of information.

> I often spent as much time talking with these women informally as in recording the interviews. These conversations ranged from specific requests for information, to reflections on aspects of the interview, to discussion of preliminary research findings. (Kelly, 1988, p. 11)

What are the implications of these feminist concerns for practical social research?

First, be aware of the ethical and political context within which you are working. The context of practical social research will often be the client organisation and the aims which have been negotiated, perhaps in terms of evaluating a service to improve life for the service users. Ethically, as a researcher, you have a commitment both to the client organisation and to the service users who have been interviewed to produce 'honest' research which allows the informants' views to be clearly heard. Politically, the client report may contain recommendations for action based on the views which have been recorded and also perhaps on your own observations as an 'informed outsider'.

For writers such as Margaret Mies (1993), the Weberian distinction about separating science and politics, discussed in Chapter 2, is not in the interests of liberating women from oppression. Instead she advocates an action research model with 'the integration of research into social and political action' which was the guiding principle of her work with battered women in Cologne (Mies, 1993, p. 70). Practical social research can be about changing social conditions. This will commonly take the form of influencing those who make policy and decisions (as Weber advocated), but there are projects where the informants are being changed through the research process, as are the student researchers. For instance, the project evaluating a support group for prisoners' partners has already been mentioned (Example 7.3). In documenting the work of the group and in recording the experiences of the women, a process of awareness and empowerment was achieved. Mies writes of a similar process occurring with the battered women in her study:

> For the women concerned, the systematic documentation of their life histories has the effect that their own subjective biography assumes an objective character. It becomes something at which they can look from a certain distance. They are not only prisoners of their own past and present sufferings and mistakes, but they can, if they want to, draw lessons for the future from their own past history.   (Mies, 1993, p. 78)

In the project with the partners of prisoners, the students made sure that the women could read the transcripts of the interviews and the draft report before it was submitted to the client organisation (in this case the probation service which funded the group). The principle of involving informants in analysis is often advocated by feminist researchers (Skeggs, 1994, p. 84). However, the attempt to democratise research practice is problematic and may require feminist researchers to be involved in a denial of their own skills and knowledge (Kelly, 1988, p. 7). In

179

practice, therefore, feminist researchers find it hard to maintain the demands of their methodology because they are often given little alternative but to produce research according to the traditional academic (malestream) model (Abbott and Wallace, 1990, p. 206).

The concern with women's experiences highlighted by feminists, is central to understanding rapport and sharing information, which is a two-way process.

Example 7.7
A student working with a 'grassroots' community housing movement had to be accepted as an individual rather than just a student researcher. She developed what anthropologists have called a 'joking relationship' with her group – they played a practical joke on her which she took in good part, and was later able to reciprocate to the chief perpetrator. She worked as an equal with this group and continually fed back the results of her work as tenants moved into their new houses and expressed various anxieties and problems to her.

Feminist research goes beyond the concerns outlined here to the ontological and ideological dimensions noted in Chapter 2. However, the issues raised by feminists are of vital concern to anyone undertaking research and need to be considered when planning a practical social research project. Feminist concerns enhance the research practice in such projects, fostering sensitivity about relationships with informants and above all setting out clearly the aims which practical social research also shares – to conducting non-exploitative and empowering research.

Life history and oral history

Life history and oral history methods are not readily associated with applied research. However, such methods can be successfully employed in projects where individual students and teams interview informants about their past to meet a specific need of the client organisation. According to Ken Plummer:

> in oral history the aim is to gain information about the past; in the biographical life history to gain information about a person's development; and in the sociological life history, to grasp the ways in which a particular person constructs and makes sense of his or her life at a given moment . . . the oral historian's goal – of recapturing the past – is altogether more ambitious than the sociologist's goal, who is in a sense merely concerned with getting at the way a person sees his or her life history at the moment of the interview. (Plummer, 1983, p. 105)

Life history

The life history document is typically a full-length book giving the account of one person's life in his or her own words. Usually the data will be gathered over a number of years with what Plummer calls 'gentle guidance from the social scientist', as the informant writes down episodes of life or tape records them. It may also be backed up with observation of the informant's life, interviews with friends, photographs and extracts from letters and diaries which all act as validity checks to the interview material. In sum, it is a detailed and purely subjective view of the world primarily through the informant's eyes.

The life history was developed during the 1920s and 1930s in the 'Chicago School', the Department of Sociology at the University of Chicago, as an approach to understanding the social world of the city. 'The Jack-Roller' by Clifford Shaw is one of the most famous of these studies and tells the story of one delinquent boy, Stanley, from his own perspective. In his introduction to the book, Howard Becker notes the value of Shaw's type of study:

> This perspective differs from that of some other social scientists in assigning major importance to the interpretations people place on their experience as an explanation of behaviour. (Shaw, 1968)

Becker argues that a life history document performs useful functions:

- as a 'touchstone' with which to evaluate theories – if the theory is not consistent with the facts of the detailed case history then we may be forced to find it inadequate;
- as a means of giving insight into the subjective side of institutional processes (For example, Stanley's story describes the degradation of 'stripping' associated with socialisation into rehabilitative institutions such as mental hospitals and prisons);
- as a way of throwing up new variables and new questions when an area of study has become stagnant;
- as a way of giving meaning to the notion of process – which the 'snapshot' approach of the survey cannot encompass;
- as a way of putting over a message to those who are not social scientists but who will be touched by the description of a way of life with which they may never have come into contact.

The life history in practical social research

Obviously students do not have the time or resources to produce a book based on years of interviewing. However, you can produce a report giving the detailed biography of an individual for a client group. The methodology could be used to provide a case study (or series of studies) of clients such as drug users to inform the organisations which are working with them and devising policies to meet their needs. The rich data of life history can tell a story and provide an input into the programme based on the participant's views and experiences.

Such material can be useful in providing support in funding applications. Funding bodies may find it easier to relate to and harder to dismiss the 'human' experience than the tables and graphs which quantify the need.

Oral history

Oral history has affinities with life history, although its emphasis is less on understanding the social world from the individual's perspective than with gaining insights into the past. The information you are given is obviously highly subjective and will be affected by memory and by the sorts of constraints discussed earlier in the chapter. But Lummis argues against critics who maintain that current experience so distorts recollections that the information is seriously devalued:

> The drawback lies less in distorting those memories, however, than in denying them a role in history, and part of the constructive role of the oral historian lies precisely in seeking-out people who would not otherwise record their historical experience.   (Lummis, 1987, p. 149)

Oral history as part of practical social research

Increasingly organisations and community groups are realising the importance of collecting information about their past as a way of recognising their identity as a group and establishing the status of their members. 'The people's history' is about the value of ordinary individuals who may have an extraordinary story to tell to those who have no other way of knowing about their way of life. In the context of practical social research, oral history can be *empowering* – used not simply by a researcher to illustrate theoretical concerns, but used to benefit the people who have shared their reminiscences.

Example 7.8
A long-established community was faced with a new building development which most local residents regarded as intrusive. The local amenity group which was fighting the development wanted an oral history conducted in the area to raise morale and to emphasise the very important history of the community. The

research helped the amenity group to feel their work was not simply negative – a rearguard action against developers – but also positive – concerned with pre-serving not just the physical features of the com-munity but a way of life. The research was also useful in publicising the residents' attachment to their lo-cality. A special lunch was held to thank those who had participated in the research and a local radio station was invited to attend. In the subsequent pro-gramme which was broadcast, the residents aired their 'story' directly on the air to a wide audience.

Oral history has some special considerations:

1. Because oral history is not based on a client defin-ing the 'problem' to be studied, you may need to inform yourself of the background to the research before interviewing. There is, however, some debate about how informed an interviewer needs to be – as oral history is intended to be non-elitist, related to the ideal of something ordinary people can do for themselves.

   Lummis argues that the problem of expertise can be met by using a team to undertake research. Knowl-edge and expertise can be pooled. In Example 7.8, a team of students divided up the work into topics such as childhood and education, women's work and men's work and concentrated their attention on these specific areas. This was particularly important when the report was being written. When the interviews were being conducted informants often moved from one topic to another, so students had to 'swap' material at the analytical stage.

2. As Lummis points out, tape recording is part of the methodology of oral history – it is not an optional extra: 'An interview should be on a system of repro-ducible sound so preserving the spoken word as the original source' (Lummis, 1987, p. 23). Such tapes become a resource in themselves – for the organisa-tion to keep, perhaps, or at least for future researchers

to consult. For this reason it is especially important that good quality equipment and new tapes are used.

3. It is also important that the tape is accompanied by a face sheet and information sheet to identify its contents. Yow advises:

> The interviewer's comments go on an information sheet that accompanies the tape. At the top is the information any listener will need to know: the title of the project, the general topic of the interview, the narrator's name (or pseudonym if required), birthplace, date of birth, occupation, and family members if you are using the narrator's real name.
>
> In addition, there is the interviewer's name, the date, and the place of the interview. A face sheet is placed over this as a title page. All of this gives information necessary to orient the listener to the situation of the interview.   (Yow, 1994: 222)

4. Ethical issues arise when informants are clearly identifiable. It is essential to establish whether people wish their names to be used or not. The researcher may have to go to some lengths to disguise the identity of people who do not wish to be identified. A pseudonym may not be enough – information they have given may have to be left out. Informants may also state at various points in the interview that what they are about to share is confidential and, of course, this must be respected.

As with all interviews, it is important to be sensitive to the informants and not probe areas of their lives about which they are reticent. However, with elderly people the interviewing experience, far from

Should you wish the information to be used for other purposes – educational, broadcasting or publication – then you would need to get the consent of the informant at the end of the interview. An example of a consent form for establishing uses to which the material may be put is reproduced in Appendix C.

being damaging, can be therapeutic. Reminiscence therapy is in fact growing in popularity as a way of mentally stimulating elderly people and exercising their long term memory which is often surprisingly good.

Mies, whose research with battered women in Germany has been referred to earlier, lists a variety of ways in which the research was beneficial for the women. As well as providing the sense of detachment and perspective mentioned earlier, it also had a practical purpose in providing the documentation and hard data these women needed to reorganise their lives. Interviewing in a group, Mies found that the women began to understand their common destiny as: 'most of the women, when they listened to the stories of others, were struck by the similarity of their experiences, i.e. the commonness and monotony of the everyday violence'   (Mies, 1993, p. 79).

Oral history and feminist research

In recent years feminist researchers like Mies have shown considerable interest in women's life history and oral history as a way of telling the story of women whose lives have been invisible in traditional *HIStory*. Such researchers point to the necessity of providing a full account of feelings as well as 'factual' data. 'Oral historians should explore emotional and subjective experience as well as facts and activities' (Anderson *et al.*, 1990, p. 101).

Oral history is seen as more than a description of women's lives, it can help to change them. As Jennifer Scanlon notes:

> Oral histories are empowering for all those involved. They provide a voice for women whose stories would otherwise go unrecorded and offer readers personal stories of and insights about groups of women they might not otherwise meet. They provide feminist researchers with a way to uncover significant information about women and to further political causes by weaving women's stories into a narrative.   (Scanlon, 1993)

Scanlon's article is concerned with the ethical issue of exploitation. The imbalance of power between the researcher and subject must be recognised and something given back – something more measurable and direct than 'scholarship'. For Scanlon this meant practical involvement in the welfare of the immigrant women she was studying.

In oral history the informants gain indirectly as the work is being done for their community group and so for their benefit rather than simply for academic purposes. In one oral history project, for example, the community organisation has arranged a meal for the informants as a tangible way of thanking them for their participation. It has also been a celebration of what they as individuals and as a group have contributed through their lives. Local radio has also been invited to these meals and the informants have been very happy to be interviewed and hear themselves on the air.

Another way of giving something back to the community has been through exhibitions in schools and colleges using photographs and documents collected during oral history projects, along with extracts from the interviews. Educational packs of materials have been produced for use in local schools. You may be able to realise other ways in which the oral history project can be developed with your informants and for their benefit.

Conclusion

This chapter has considered different types of interviewing, the practical issues of recording interview material and the place of sampling in ethnography. The role of the interviewer requires careful consideration, in how to make an introduction and what the effects of the interview setting may be on the data gathered. In addition to these 'nuts and bolts' concerns there are deeper and more philosophical issues to deal with. Ethical issues have been raised in how to deal sensitively with vulnerable informants and how oral and life history can empower those who are interviewed rather than exploit them. Feminist writers have highlighted these concerns and made awareness of the researcher's own characteristics and approach a key area for methodological debate. Reflexivity is seen as an essential part of the ethnographic process of research, revealing as it does how data are created through a process of social interaction. Such commitments and concerns carry over into the way ethnographic data are analysed and this is the topic of the next chapter.

8
Analysing Ethnographic Data

This chapter deals mainly with how to handle material generated by semi-structured, in-depth interviews focused on the particular topics required by the client. The analysis of qualitative data from interviews, case studies, oral and life histories will be considered, as well as how it can be presented in a report and still retain the richness or depth which is its main value.

Time constraints: a cautionary note

Interviews which use open-ended questions can yield copious amounts of data and their analysis can be very time-consuming. As you only have limited time at your disposal, you may have to make some realistic decisions about how much of your material you can afford to analyse in detail. Much of the rest of this chapter is concerned with those choices.

Data reduction

According to Miles and Huberman (1994, p. 10–12) qualitative analysis involves three activities:

- data reduction
- data display, and

- conclusion drawing and verification.

All three activities will be dealt with here, though conclusions are further considered in Chapter 10, on writing the client report. Data reduction refers to:

> the process of selecting, focusing, simplifying, abstracting, and transforming the data that appear in written-up fieldnotes or transcriptions. (Miles and Huberman, 1994, p. 10)

A pragmatic decision may well be to concentrate on information which is directly relevant to the client report in terms of the aims which have been negotiated. Other data can be left for future analysis, provided that tapes or notes are retained.

As Miles and Huberman indicate, this process of data reduction occurs throughout a research project – when questions are being formulated, when data collection methods are chosen, when fieldwork notes are being taken – as well as after the fieldwork stage. The decisions on which data to use and how to summarise and display them are all part of an ongoing process of analytic choice – 'reducing' data before, during and after it has been collected.

Form of data record

Notepad

If you have taken notes during the interviews rather than using a tape recorder, then (as Chapter 7 indicated) you should amplify these notes immediately afterwards and use the full notes for analysis. Remember to include in your analysis any reflective notes you may have taken during fieldwork.

Tape recorder

Much the same applies to tape recordings. It is a good idea to listen to the tape soon afterwards, checking that the tape is audible and that all has been recorded. As Lindlof points out, it is easier to notice these problems and do something about them if they are caught very soon after the event (Lindlof, 1995, p. 210).

The previous chapter also pointed out that transcribing tapes – writing out their content word for word – is a lengthy process. Transcribing machines are available, which have a foot control and headphones. This ensures the audibility of the tape is maximised and the tape can be stopped while you type it up, or write it out. It is worth enquiring whether your department or institution has such a machine to which you can be given access, as this will speed up the process of transcription.

The transcribing machine is particularly useful for oral history, where a full account of the interview is necessary. For interviews based on interview guides you can be more selective – often informants digress from the question and then it is only necessary to transcribe what is relevant, summarising more tangential material.

When transcribing from tapes, remember to record exactly the quotations and key phrases which you judge to be significant. The value of an ethnographic account is to let the informants speak directly to the reader. This makes the report more lively and interesting to read. If every account is summarised second-hand then the report will be 'sanitised' and dull. The value of using open-ended questions is that it allows informants to express themselves more freely than in a structured format. It is important therefore that such fullness should not be lost at the analytical stage. Look particularly for *unexpected* information and *contradictory* views. People often hold opinions which are not entirely consistent and these should be carefully noted – not edited out.

The written transcript will become your working document: so, when typing up transcripts, remember to leave wide margins to allow you to add your own comments

191

and codes or indexes of the data. A word-processor makes it easy to change the layout, make corrections as you listen and save the transcription on to disk.

Analysis with computers

Although research methodology textbooks which explain the use of computers in data analysis have been mostly orientated towards survey or quantitative research, the pattern is now changing. A growing number, including the Miles and Huberman sourcebook quoted earlier, contain detailed instructions on how to use computer programs for ethnographic or qualitative research.

As with the analysis of survey data, whether you use this technology or not is going to depend on a number of factors:

- your current level of computer literacy
- the availability of computers and software
- the time at your disposal for learning new software, and
- the availability of technical support from staff and fellow students as you learn.

Computer programs can take much of the drudgery out of ethnographic analysis by providing efficient means to store, code and sort data. If you are working on a team, it may be that one member could take on this area of expertise as their particular contribution.

Even without dedicated software, some progress is possible. Dey (1993, p. 81) suggests a simple and highly effective use of word-processor packages in his 'user-friendly' guide to qualitative data analysis using computers. He shows how researchers can store all their information, yet concentrate on analysing only what is relevant for the particular purpose of the study on hand. A full transcript is typed up on a word-processor and saved in one file. A second file is then created and the full transcript is edited to provide only the essential information, which is then saved separately as a summary.

Remember to make backups of your files whenever using the computer. Everyone knows this is good advice but rarely gets round to following it until after they have experienced a disaster. It is really frustrating to lose vital data at a critical time, or to find your disk has become infected with a computer virus.

Beginning the analysis

Keep in mind that the data are being analysed to provide a report for the client organisation which will summarise the information collected, present conclusions and make recommendations. The best way to think about analysis for practical social research is to work backwards from the final use of the material through the stages of categorisation and dissection.

How will the data be presented?

The chapter on the client report (Chapter 10) explains how the data has to be presented in sections which bring together the relevant themes. Resist the easy path of giving a blow by blow account of each question or lengthy undigested information on individuals. Instead the report should compare and contrast informants, putting together a 'story' which pulls together the various threads of the research.

Example 8.1
A student agreed to evaluate the training programme for volunteers used by an organisation providing support to victims of violent crime. Initially the student found it difficult to bring together her results and presented a series of life-history accounts of those she had interviewed. She radically altered her approach later, however, and was able to group responses around a number of themes which emerged from the interviews, as in the extract below.

Reasons for becoming a volunteer

All six respondents said that they wanted to become involved in their local community and that the organisation appeared to offer a viable avenue for such community involvement. Jayne, for example, felt that:

> *'This seemed an ideal voluntary group because you would be actually working with people face to face in the community as well as deal with other agencies also working in that community'.*

One of the respondents, Gloria, had been a victim of crime and a visit by a volunteer had prompted her to become a volunteer herself, as she felt that it was a worthwhile organisation which met a real need in the community. Indeed, she considered her voluntary work as *'free time well spent'*.

Claire, Michael and Karen had all chosen the organisation from a Community Action Handbook (for students) which detailed a number of voluntary organisations. It was their intention to do something 'useful' for the community whilst gaining experience of community work for a future career such as social work or community care. (Daniels, 1992)

(*Note*: The student used pseudonyms for her informants, and in this extract the name of the group has been deleted.)

In such an example, where the number of informants is low, tables are unnecessary as information can be more simply summarised in words. As pointed out in Chapter 6, remember that with a small sample raw figures should be given rather than percentages, which can be misleading. For example, to talk of 20 per cent of the sample holding a particular view may sound quite impressive. But if your sample is only five, you are talking about just one person!

With a larger sample, presenting information using tables or graphs is helpful as these communicate basic informa-

tion quickly. An explanation can then expand on the data
by illustrating it with relevant examples.

Example 8.2

A student who was asked to produce a report for a
community housing development interviewed residents
before and after they moved into their new homes.
She summarised the information collected on their
expectations of the development as follows.

EXPECTATIONS

As can be seen by the table below, overall expectations
can be grouped into two main areas:

> Better life
> Community spirit
> Social life

and

> No gangs
> Better neighbours
> Better environment
> Better housing

The expectations of the respondents are to have a better quality of life than is being experienced at their present
home. As one respondent said: '*I just wanted to better
myself and my life*'.

One resident told me how he was looking forward to
having a garden after living in a flat, and that
'*There'll be no stairs or lifts*'.

Another respondent living in a flat told me how he
'*couldn't wait to get the key and walk through our front
door and not onto a landing*'.

An elderly woman could only describe the new home
as '*Heaven*'. She would be able to manage her hus-
band's wheelchair without struggling in and out of the
door.

The '*friendly atmosphere*' was something else being

Table 8.1 *The expectations of respondents (multicoded)*

Expectations	Number
Better life	8
Community spirit	6
Better environment	4
No gangs	2
Better neighbours	2
Social life	2
Better house	4
Children's play area	1
Don't know	1
Total responses	30
Total sample	14

looked forward to, where people '*help each other*' and the '*community spirit develops*'.

Others wanted an area '*free from gangs*' and '*no druggies*', and with improved housing, free from draughts and damp. (Lightfoot, 1994)

Case studies

Individual informants may provide examples – either typical or extreme – illustrating important themes which have emerged from the data. Case studies are valuable in putting 'flesh on the bones' of the research. They remind the reader that the client organisation is working with real people whose lives are unique.

Such examples are illuminating not only to the client organisation, but can even be useful at a further stage if the report is used to present a case to policy-makers or to support a funding application. The reader in this case is more removed from the service users, so case studies can be effective ways of showing how problems impact on people's lives and how the client organisation is working to improve their conditions.

As in Example 8.1, it is necessary to use pseudonyms for your informants to preserve their anonymity. Details may have to be omitted to make them less identifiable. Informants should be given a name, rather than being referred to as 'Subject A' or 'Subject B', which turns them into objects. Direct quotations should be used so that the person (not the 'case') speaks as directly as possibly – as a human being.

Plummer (1983, p. 107) comments on Strauss and Glaser's distinction between a case *history* and a case *study*. A case history, he says, uses documents to tell 'a good story' in depth whereas the case study uses the personal document for a wider purpose, which may be theoretical – or in our case, to illustrate the work of the client organisation. As Strauss and Glaser put it:

> The research goal in a case history is to get the fullest possible story for *its own sake*. In contrast, the case study is based on analytic abstractions and constructions for purposes of description, or verification and/or generation of theory. There is no attempt at obtaining the fullest possible story for its own sake. (Strauss and Glaser, 1977, p. 183)

Example 8.3
The student in Example 8.1 decided to add case studies of the victims of crime whom the client organisation was supporting. She included background information on the crime itself and details of the victim's dealings with the organisation. She added direct quotations on the victim's feelings about the client group and how it had dealt with him or her.

Case studies may be considered at the start of the project when the research is being designed, although at that stage it is not always clear what criteria should be used for selecting a sample. It is worth being aware of the possibility of using information from individuals in this way during the interview process. Some interviews yield more information than others and you may be feel that some of the material provided by informants is too

197

important to be lost in the general account. An example of this is provided below.

Example 8.4
Two students interviewed people who had attended a centre for the visually impaired, in order to evaluate the usefulness of the skills they had been taught. As well as analysing the interviews, they also presented four case studies, one of which is included here:

> James attended the centre for 2 years and 7 months. He is in his late 50s and has been registered as blind since the late 1980s. The thought of starting at the centre made James feel 'very uncertain'. He found he had many questions to be answered such as, 'what will the staff be like?' and 'what will I be asked to do?' However, on reflection, James said 'I didn't take into account that the staff had dealt with hundreds of people like me before'.
>
> Immediately after starting the programme of rehabilitation, James felt his 'confidence increase'. He still uses the skills he learned at the centre, which he feels has enabled him to become 'more independent'. James has since worked on a voluntary basis at the centre instructing in Braille, Moon and computers. He has an interest in writing but knew he would need 'to go on to further education in order to pursue a career in journalism'.
>
> He is now undertaking a course in journalism, however, which he hopes will eventually lead to a career in freelance writing. James comments on what he feels the centre provided for him. 'I would not be able to do half of this course if it were not for the centre. It was a milestone in my life.' (Ashton and Ainsbury, 1993)

How can transcripts be transformed into a report?

To answer this question it is important to consider first how researchers 'make sense' of data. Because an open-ended set of questions has been used, the information

198

generated may not be quite what was expected. Nigel Barley gives an instructive and amusing account of real life ethnographic research in Africa among the Dowayo tribe, a fieldwork experience which was fraught with frustrations at the levels both of collecting and interpreting data.

> Dowayo explanations always ended up in a circle I
> came to know well. 'Why do you do this?' I would ask.
> 'Because it is good.'
> 'Why is it good?'
> 'Because the ancestors told us to.'
> (Slyly) 'Why did the ancestors tell you to?'
> 'Because it is good.'
> (Barley, 1983, p. 82)

Hopefully your information will be more easily interpreted than this! The stages for making sense of data suggested below are:

- to organise the material through coding
- to produce a data matrix to summarise responses
- to construct tables where appropriate.

Organising material – coding

Open-ended questions produce a mass of data which has not been pre-coded. Coding after the event is then necessary to categorise the replies and to find order among what may seem like chaos. Categorisation is required to allow comparisons between informants and to show how widespread certain feelings and attitudes may be (as in the example of the group above who worked with victims of violent crime).

Different researchers use different practices. Whyte talks of *indexing* his field-notes, by pencilling index codes in the margin of the transcripts.

> I do not consider it advisable for the researcher to determine his or her indexing categories before he or she starts

the field study . . . After eight or ten interviews, the researcher should have the feel of the situation sufficiently to develop a reasonably adequate indexing system. At this point, we might reread the first interviews and pencil the appropriate indexing categories on the margins of each page. (Whyte, 1984, p. 117)

Each answer to a question, then, will have a number of codes attached to it according to the range of responses which have been given. The codes can be descriptive or conceptual – based on the themes which have emerged from the research. As Robson indicates:

A code is a symbol applied to a group of words to classify or categorise them . . . Codes are retrieval and organizing devices that allow you to find and then collect together all instances of a particular kind. (Robson, 1993, p. 385)

Codes facilitate taking apart the data like building blocks and putting them together again in a different way. Codes can be given numeric values (as one would do for computer analysis) or shorthand indices (as Whyte does). A simple method of coding can be to use different coloured highlighters to pick out comparable text. Alternatively scissors and paste can be used. With highlighters, there is a problem in the limited range of colours. If using scissors and paste, then it is worth following Riley's (1990, p. 27) practical advice and avoid cutting up the only copy. Use multiple copies and do not start to cut up until reference information has been written on the transcripts. As little piles of slips accumulate, then collect them together in a simple filing system: Riley suggests old envelopes will do.

Traditionally, file cards have been used to store information in a form which is easily retrievable, although the computer is now also being used for this task. Dey's (1993) 'user-friendly' guide uses humour to put over some of the applications of the computer for this stage of research and you may find this much more accessible than some of the weightier tomes dealing with this topic. If there is time it is worth looking into computer methods of data organisation and analysis. However, if the sample is fairly small then the manual methods of segmenting and categorising data will be adequate.

Data matrix

The data matrix introduced in previous chapters is an ideal way of putting together the summarised data in coded or indexed form (or on little pieces of paper). The matrix by definition includes all the informants. It provides an 'at a glance' way of noting responses and making comparisons. It enables the quantification of results so each individual is put in context.

The matrix summarises but does not supplant the interview transcripts. It is necessary to keep the original data intact, of course, as the matrix will be useful mainly for reference – it cannot contain all the depth of information which has been collected. After comparing responses on a topic, you may then wish to refer back to individual transcripts to pick out a quotation in detail.

Example 8.5
Example 8.2 showed how a student presented her data in a table. To see how she was able to summarise her interview data, an extract from her data matrix is presented in Table 8.2 (this was in fact submitted as an appendix to her methodology report). The questions were as follows:

Q1: How long have you been in your present house?
Q2: How did you hear about the housing co-operative?
Q3: How many live in your present house?
Q4: What are the problems with living here?
Q5: What are your expectations of the new housing?

In this example, the informants are listed as the columns, the questions as rows, though it could just as easily have been the other way round.

The matrix is particularly valuable for team projects

Table 8.2 Data matrix

Respondents

	1	2	3	4
Q1	12 yrs	4 yrs	30+ yrs	22 yrs
Q2	Granddaughter organised it all	Local press	Neighbour-hood centre	Local press
Q3	One	One adult + 2 kids (husband will come with us to new home)	One	Two – married couple
Q4	House damp. Had a fire in the entry to flats, don't feel safe	Want a better class of people Locals don't mix. Kids play round the garages	Want a bungalow. Can't manage the stairs	Medical – husband in wheelchair, it's difficult to manage
Q5	Just can't wait to get key and walk through front door. No more lifts, no more getting stuck in them when they break down.	Just want somewhere decent for me and the kids away from the druggies and smackheads	Greenery and trees	Heaven – just to get my husband out

(Lightfoot, 1994)

where each member may have interviewed a number of people in depth. The matrix allows the team to pool information and work co-operatively.

Example 8.6
One pair of students used a huge sheet of card to draw out a large and complex matrix. They proudly carried this around with them as concrete evidence of data collected and covered the tutor's floor with it during supervision sessions. As well as its symbolic

1. *Counting* – categorising data and measuring the frequency of occurrence of the categories
2. *Patterning* – noting of recurring patterns or themes
3. *Clustering* – grouping of objects, persons, activities, settings, and so on with similar characteristics
4. *Factoring* – grouping of variables into a small number of hypothetical factors
5. *Relating variables* – discovery of the type of relationship (if any) between two or more variables
6. *Building of causal networks* – development of chains or webs of linkages between variables
7. *Relating findings to general theoretical frameworks* – attempting to find general propositions that account for the particular findings in this study

Figure 8.1   Tactics for drawing conclusions from qualitative data

significance, there was a practical value to the matrix. It became obvious at an early stage that the two students were summarising their data quite differently – one in much greater detail than the other. It was useful to sort this out at a preliminary stage as the reported results would have been distorted if different methods of data recording were being used.

Quantifying qualitative research

Ethnographic research is usually regarded as qualitative, but that does not mean that statistical analysis becomes irrelevant. In Example 8.2 the student presented her data in a frequency table which clearly showed the client the trends within her sample of interviews. Robson (1993, p. 401) suggests a variety of tactics for providing some form of numerate analysis of ethnographic data, which are reproduced in Figure 8.1.

Oral and life history

At the beginning of this chapter the transcription of tapes was treated as a non-problematic method of reproducing data. Oral historians, however, have pointed out that the transcript is but a pale reflection of the original interview. Gestures, accent, tone can all be lost in transcription. Yow indicates some ways in which the original speech can be retained. For instance:

> You may be writing down 'goin'' and 'havin'' many times as well as 'ain't' and bad grammar in such phrases as 'spoke to him and I'. If that is what was said, write it. (Yow, 1994, p. 229)

Punctuating and creating sentences to convey the meaning to the reader is another pitfall to be aware of. People rarely speak in polished sentences. Non-standard punctuation should be used to convey the reality of spoken conversation – short sentences, unfinished sentences and so on. Yow suggests that dashes can be useful in making a sentence understandable, words that the narrator has emphasised can be underlined, while parentheses (brackets) may be used to convey non-verbal gestures or a distinct change in the voice. The following example is adapted from a student project.

Example 8.7
Did you like the fact that you knew lots of the villagers?

Mrs Brown: Oh – I thought it was lovely – of course, I was a different person then – I was young then. We lived up by there (points to photographs on her lap). There was an elderly couple transferred next door to us on a temporary basis but this elderly couple didn't want to go back afterwards because they wanted to stay by us. We loved them. They was really lovely people. (Speaks softly and smiles).

(Bergquist, 1993)

As well as making transcripts, the original oral history tapes should be preserved. These are a source for future historians. In addition, because the interviewer is also recorded, it is possible for a listener to detect bias in the way the questioning was conducted. Finally, as Lummis (1987, p. 88) points out, the tape is the sole way in which accent, 'itself historical evidence', can be accurately recorded. Accent defines geographical communities which may be losing their specific identity and in some societies, such as Britain, it is also a strong indicator of social status.

In analysing the data, then, the process of indexing and matrix construction as outlined above will be necessary steps. According to Yow (1994) the historian's model of analysis is as follows:

> If the researcher is using a collection of life histories, usually gathered around a theme such as a particular occupation or movement, then it is the common meanings of the shared experience that are sought.

This is contrasted to a social science model which concentrates on significant life experiences as an organising framework. It is important, however, not to neglect any evidence which is contrary to the 'common meanings' which emerge in the data. Lummis cautions that a decision must be made to:

> take account of all the evidence available, even those cases which are contrary to one's thesis. I have found this a valuable discipline even in analysing a few interviews. (Lummis, 1987, p. 106)

Writing an oral history

Writing an oral history account is more difficult than writing about ethnographic data. Students sometimes find it hard to find the right tone and language for the report and can be confused about how to use their data. Consideration

of the question, Who is the audience?, may help to resolve these problems.

Local community groups, organisations and families can
all be recipients of applied research reports using oral
history methodology. So aim to use language which is accessible to those who are the audience, and aim to tell a
story. Be clear what the purpose of the report is and focus on the areas relevant to this.

Once the material has been indexed the data can be
grouped into themes and generalisations drawn (but note
any dissenting voices). This should help you avoid a common and difficult problem in this kind of research: how
to use quotations illustratively without distorting the trends
and underlying patterns which you have discovered. Social
anthropology used to be criticised for what was dubbed
'butterfly-collecting'. Unusual or dramatic illustrations were
'pinned' on to the text like exotic species to brighten up
the account. Obviously you want to use quotations which
are illuminating and interesting, perhaps even humorous.
But there is a need to avoid biasing the evidence by its
presentation – presenting a village full of droll characters,
perhaps, or a school of ardent scholars and upright teachers.

One solution has been to publish the interviews as directly
as possible, which according to Lummis reduces history
to personal retrospective testimony. However, it is not quite
that simple: 'the extracts all have to be selected and edited and are inevitably shaped by the compiler's conscious
and unconscious purposes' (Lummis, 1987, p. 186).

Nevertheless, this is the approach advocated by some
feminist methodologists who are keen to let their informants be heard with as little interpretation as possible. Sherna
Gluck (1985) conducted two interviews with an American
woman who had been active in the suffrage movement.
The account is presented by Nielsen in a collection of
'exemplary readings' and she comments on it as follows:

> Gluck's work . . . has a celebratory tone, thus reflecting the
> importance of history as inspirational and visionary for fu-
> ture generations. This story reflects 'the personal is politi-
> cal' theme of feminist inquiry. There is no sharp distinction

---

- Is misinformation (unintended) given?
- Has there been evasion?
- Is there evidence of direct lying or deception?
- Is a 'front' being presented?
- What may the informant 'take for granted' and hence not reveal?
- How far is the informant 'pleasing you'?
- How much has been forgotten?
- How much may be self-deception?

Plummer (1983, p. 103)

Figure 8.2   A brief checklist of dimensions of bias

between [the informant's] personal and public life. Gluck's documentation is minimally edited and without censorship. (Nielsen, 1990, p. 116)

The account of the informant is presented in the first person as a biography, with news clippings inserted in various places to provide historical context. However, the questions that Gluck asked are not published and we do not know whether the account has been polished up, edited or led in particular directions through the influence of the interviewer. The biography may be more direct than a story illustrated with direct quotes, but it is still not problem-free.

Perhaps the best advice for you is to get hold of some good oral history accounts and see how the writer has presented the evidence. These should help with style and language, though the specific interests of your audience still need to be taken into consideration.

Using other sources

Cross-checking is vital in oral history. Yow (1994: 172) reminds us that 'Nobody tells another person everything . . . oral history is selective.' Do not, therefore, rely exclusively on your informants but search out other sources of information. Plummer provides a useful checklist of questions to ask of a life history account – see Figure 8.2.

Plummer calls such cross-checking 'validity checks' and suggests consulting official records for 'factual data'. Community or organisation magazines, newspapers, club records, minutes, diaries, school log-books and so on can also be important ways of verifying information and can spark off new areas of inquiry, if this research is conducted at the same time as the interviewing. Historical context is supplied by reference to events of the time or by comparisons with similar groups or communities elsewhere about whom published information is available.

The problem you will face on a research project is the lack of time to do all this adequately, so you either have to limit the number of people you interview and spend more time with written records or negotiate a division of labour in your group whereby one person takes responsibility for researching archival material and photocopying maps, document and photographs.

Incidentally, colleagues in history departments collaborating on oral history projects have stressed the importance of using a variety of sources. For sociologists the tendency is to regard the informants' own accounts as the primary source of data and, provided that informants give accounts which are consistent, sociologists usually tend to feel confident that the material is valid. Cross-checking will undoubtedly strengthen the value of a project, however, and some attempt should be made to widen the source of evidence, even if it is restricted by time-constraints.

Validity and reliability

Validity and reliability are concepts which in the past were most closely identified with 'scientific' research. This in turn, as we saw in Chapter 2, was usually defined as research based on a positivist approach which yielded data from the experiment or the survey.

Nowadays such an approach is widely challenged by writers on the methodology of social research. Silverman, for instance, argues:

It is an increasingly accepted view that work becomes scientific by adopting methods of study *appropriate* to its subject matter. Sociology is thus scientific to the extent that it uses appropriate methods and is rigorous, critical and objective in its handling of data. (Silverman, 1993, p. 144)

Validity and reliability are the two key concepts in a discussion of rigour. For your purposes, you will need to consider these issues as you design, carry out and analyse your research. They will also be important topics to be dealt with in your methodology report.

Silverman argues that the concern with reliability shown by quantitative methods textbooks needs to be expressed also in qualitative research. That is, the issue of whether each informant understands the questions in the same way and whether answers can be coded without the possibility of uncertainty. He proposes that it is important for ethnographers to pre-test an interview schedule and compare how at least two researchers analyse the same data.

Hammersley (1991) notes that the natural sciences replicate research (through experiments) to discover whether the same results can be reproduced. This, he argues, is much more difficult in ethnography but that does not mean that we have to abandon the concept of truth or validity as a criterion for assessing research findings. Instead he proposes three steps in assessing the validity of what he terms ethnographic 'claims' or arguments (Hammersley, 1991, pp. 61–2). Claims include how terms are defined, the way facts are described, explained or predicted, and how values are presented through evaluation and prescription. The steps are as follows.

1. *Plausibility*: is a claim plausible – is it likely to be true given our existing knowledge?
2. *Credibility*: is a claim credible – is it likely that the ethnographer's judgement is accurate, given the nature of the phenomena, the circumstances of the research, the characteristics of the researcher and so on?
3. *Evidence*: if we are unsure about plausibility or

credibility, do we have the evidence to convince us of validity?

To assess the validity of an ethnographic study, therefore, you need to ask how plausible or credible each claim is in the light of existing knowledge. If found to be high in plausibility or credibility, then a claim may be accepted. However, if you judge claims to be lacking in plausibility or credibility, then you need to look at the evidence provided by the writer to support them.

Robson argues that prolonged involvement with a project and persistent observation are ways in which credibility can be enhanced, but also recommends peer debriefing:

> Exposing one's analysis and conclusions to a colleague or other peer on a continuous basis can assist in the development of both the design and analysis of the study. The exercise of being explicit in formulating something for presentation to a peer fosters subsequent credibility.   (Robson, 1993, p. 404)

Triangulation, using evidence from different sources, different methods of investigation and different investigators is also seen as an important way of fostering credibility. Most writers on ethnographic methodology agree that triangulation is the major way of validating qualitative research. Silverman too agrees that the use of multiple methods increases validity but adds a note of caution. Triangulation should not be used to 'adjudicate' between conflicting accounts – that is, to show who is lying and who is not. All accounts are relative to the context in which they were given and are the product of social interaction.

If you interview the staff of an organisation and the service users it is possible that you may receive quite different accounts of what is happening. Your job is not to decide whom to believe, but rather to understand *why* the accounts differ – that is, to place them in the context of the social position of the informant and make sense of them that way.

Conclusion

Analysing ethnographic data means organising and creating order out of a mass of information. It is important to keep in mind the final report and the way material can be presented for your audience to understand. The data matrix is a useful device for summarising information and allowing comparison. To retain the richness of your data it is good to use direct quotations as well as summarised data – this allows your informants to speak for themselves. Case studies have been recommended as a way of making your audience aware of the human dimension of policies and service provision, while oral and life history methods also have a contribution to make to applied research. Finally, validity and reliability are important criteria for judging the quality of research, as they were for the survey.

9
Documentary and Other Sources

Finally, we look at other sources of information which may be considered to supplement, rather than take the place of, the survey or ethnographic methods detailed above. In addition to published data such as census information there are organisational records of particular relevance to evaluation studies, and various personal records such as diaries and biographical texts which can provide an insight into individual experience. Lastly there are 'unobtrusive measures' based upon observation as well as observational methods themselves.

Available data

Despite the attraction of gathering data from primary sources – that is, informants contacted personally by the researcher through interview or questionnaire – do not overlook the usefulness of secondary sources of information. These are records made or collected by others, and cover a wide range of material. Chief advantages are greater speed and lower cost of retrieval, compared to primary data gathering. The chief disadvantages are that material recorded by other people for other purposes may not be entirely suitable for current needs, and there are questions about the existence of any inherent bias in the material which might threaten its validity.

Singleton *et al.* (1988, p. 326) call such materials 'available data', and classify them broadly under five headings:

- public documents and official records (including Census data)
- private documents
- mass media
- physical, non-verbal materials
- social science data archives.

Of these sources, probably the first four are the most likely to be used in an applied project. Social science data archives are valuable sources of information but more appropriate for post-graduate research. Whether such data are readily available will be for you to discover, but the idea of available data is a liberating one because it means that your research should not be limited by what you can directly undertake through primary contacts.

Official records

Example 9.1
On a project evaluating a luncheon club for the elderly (those over 60 years of age) in a particular neighbourhood, students wished to estimate what percentage of the elderly population used the lunch club. They found that the local library had copies of the relevant census data for the area, and they were easily able to calculate that the club was catering for around 10 per cent of the local elderly population. It was serving about 80–100 meals per day. The students concluded that there was scope for expanding the meals service to accommodate more of the area's large population of elderly people, but that the existing facilities could not cope with an increase in numbers without rebuilding.

As the Census of Population is such an important tool for local authorities in planning how to meet the needs of local residents, and for social scientists in addressing issues of inequalities in welfare across the country, you are likely to find that analyses of census data are available to meet your project requirements without the necessity of working directly with census tables.

For example, Forrest and Gordon (1993) produce a classification of the 366 local authority areas of England ranked in order of census variables and two derived indices of material and social deprivation. If this national picture is not sufficiently precise for your needs, you may find that City or County Council Planning Departments also produce maps and tables of census indicators broken down to electoral ward level, which should be adequate for local purposes (see, for example, Central Policy Unit, Liverpool City Council: 1993).

Documents from organisations

An especially fruitful source of available data comes from documents not intended for public consumption but produced by organisations as a record of their activities. These include any of the written records, files, registers, accounts, inventories, job descriptions, organisation charts, constitutions, minutes, or other documents which proliferate in organisations.

The reason for such proliferation can be traced to Weber's (1947) discussion of bureaucracy, which has been influential in much later theorising and research about formal organisations. Weber saw bureaucracy as a feature of modern organisation, where consistency and reliability of administration was obtained through rational organisation of structure, and in particular the reliance upon written records (the 'bureau') and impersonal decision-making in administration.

Organisations rely on written records, and the extent (and condition) of their records can be used as indicators of the degree of their bureaucratisation. For Pugh and Hickson (1976) written records represented the aspect of 'formalisation' in a bureaucracy, so that in their research they enquired about written 'rules, procedures, instructions and communications'. By establishing the presence or absence of these, they derived a measure of the formalisation of an organisation as shown by, for example:

- number of handbooks
- organisation chart
- written terms of reference or job descriptions
- written operating instructions available to direct worker
- manual of procedures or standing orders   (Pugh and Hickson, 1976, p. 72)

Pugh and Hickson's research covered service as well as manufacturing organisations, but they studied no organisation with fewer than 250 employees and no voluntary organisation. The client organisations you are likely to be working with at the community level are much less likely to be highly bureaucratised. However, you may still find that they keep a variety of organisational records, reports and publicity materials. Furthermore, you should consider that the *absence* of written records also needs to be explained.

Access to records

Access to the organisation is negotiated as the first stage of research, but you may find that when it comes to making use of organisational records this has to be treated as a further stage. There may be a requirement to renegotiate, and to be sensitive to the concerns of the organisation's managers.

Example 9.2
On the same luncheon club project used in Example 9.1 students wished to interview the volunteers who helped with the meals. Staff were fully occupied preparing and serving meals at lunchtime, and went home as soon as lunch was over, so the students wanted to find out from the organisation the volunteers' names and addresses so they could interview them later.

The co-ordinator was unwilling to allow access to this confidential information. Further negotiation established that the co-ordinator would approach the volunteers to see if they were willing to be interviewed, and if they were, to pass on their names. So the issue was resolved through involving the staff in the decision to participate.

Using organisational records

Example 9.3
A study for a local voluntary organisation to document and evaluate the use of its building used records of room bookings (taken with permission from the programme supervisor's diary) to depict the range and variety of users. Bookings for the six rooms available were on a weekly, fortnightly, monthly, bi-annual, annual or casual basis. The list of monthly users was broad and varied, including the following:

1918 Club
Alcoholics Anonymous
Animal Rights
British Cactus and Succulent Society
Elvis Presley Appreciation Society
Free Church Women's Council
Light Rail Transit Association
MSF Trade Union
Northern Counties Athletic Association
Peoples' Dispensary for Sick Animals

(Jenkins, 1993)

The list of room bookings was subsequently used as a sampling frame for a telephone sample survey of user groups. The survey demonstrated not only that the rooms had the strong attractions of being cen-

trally located and cheap to hire, but also that the kind-
liness of staff and the guiding philosophy of the host
organisation were attractions to its users – who could
not readily think of anywhere else they could meet if
that organisation were not there.

This example illustrates how organisational records could
be used to establish some important factor – in this case,
the wide range of external groups and organisations using the facilities. While the information was 'available' in
the sense of being capable of being discovered in written
form (as well as in unwritten form in the mind of the
supervisor), it required an investigative effort to extract
it and to present it. At that stage it could serve not just
as a corrective to oral accounts which might be partial,
but also as a new form of record for the organisation,
which could use it to assess its range of contacts.

Personal documents

In contrast to organisational documents, individuals may
produce their own personal documents in terms of diaries and letters. Although these may have been written for
a limited circulation, they are not 'public' in the sense of
being readily accessible by all. Personal documents also
go beyond written sources to include photographs and
other mementoes.

Scott (1990, p. 187) points out that snapshot photogra-
phy, whose heyday was from 1910 to the 1950s, became
part of family life, with each photograph kept carefully
in the family album. In contrast, the modern era of improved cameras and colour film has in an age of comparative affluence rendered the photograph disposable.

Old photographs and mementoes can be particularly
valuable in backing up or validating written records, as
well as providing a stimulus for reminiscences (Plummer,
1983, p. 28).

'The world is crammed full of personal documents,'
says Plummer, in which

for the sociologist, the human document is 'an account of
individual experience which reveals the individual's actions
as a human agent and as a participant in social life' Blumer,
1939, p. 29. (Plummer, 1983, p. 13)

So an oral history project concerned with the life of a
community could search out such personal documents as
it records on tape the voices and experiences of the informants. As a source of data these documents may be
used descriptively as illustration, or as material for content
analysis. But, as shown in Chapter 8, it is also worth thinking
of how such documents could be used at a second stage
for exhibition and feedback to the group of informants.

Example 9.4
A community study team held a tea party as a 'thank
you' for the informants (and their wives or husbands)
who had agreed to be interviewed in the study. On
this occasion one of the attenders spontaneously
produced photographs of many years past, which
circulated round the tables as individuals identified
themselves and others on the photographs, providing in turn more information on further aspects of
community life such as the local factory's holiday camp.

Example 9.5
In another project tracing the experiences of former
students at a college of education, personal photographs and mementoes were copied to provide a
display. Informants were invited back to the college
for a reunion party and were able to view the display and talk about their memories with each other
before the material went on general display in the
college for contemporary students. Particularly interesting for the informants was the opportunity to re-
visit rooms in the college they had once occupied,
and of which they had photographs in their former
state.

The diary as research record

Diaries are usually thought of as records and interpretations of past events. But there is a role for the diary as a method of prospective data collection. This has been employed successfully in a number of studies of health care, where informants are asked to keep a diary of how they feel, and what they do in response to symptoms (Robinson, 1971). The advantage of this method is that the diary is kept for a specific research purpose, so the material it contains is directly relevant to the study. Also, as a contemporaneous record it does not rely on people's memory to say how they felt over a period in the past, such as the previous fourteen days.

You too can keep a diary and use it in your reports. In Chapter 4 it was suggested that the fieldwork diary should be part of the research plan. Evidence from the diary, as a record of your visits and contacts with the organisation, your informants, and anyone else connected with the research can then be included in the methodology report (see Chapter 11). In this report the intention is to amplify the client report and to give you the opportunity to reflect on research in practice and on your own learning experience.

Although the diary could be presented as a factual account of meetings and fieldwork events, it is much more interesting to read if it contains comments and evaluation of feelings and insights as the research progresses. Keeping such a diary for yourself is a good discipline as it provides a record to supplement a fallible memory, it enables you to pinpoint when new ideas arrived, and it allows you to 'let off steam' about the inevitable frustrations of the exercise.

Example 9.6
Some of this comes through from a couple of entries in the fieldwork diary of a student engaged on an evaluative study of a centre for autistic adults.

Thursday 5 November

Activities continued until lunch. At lunch the staff and the service users sit down together and enjoy a three course meal which is (usually) cooked in the kitchen by the service users and the instructor who is in the kitchen that day. I talked to K. [staff member] during lunch, much to the delight of one of the service users who is convinced that we are having a love affair!!! K. thought it would be fun to bring a video camera in and make a video (?!) After lunch everyone helps to clear the tables and then sits chatting until the hour is over. One of the service users entertained us doing impressions of everyone, and telling us all who he thought we looked like. He thought I looked like Su Pollard? I hope not (no offence, Su!) One of the service users has taken rather a fancy to me, he keeps touching my hand and wanting a hug. He has to be dealt with firmly so that he does not go too far, but I'm not very good at getting cross, so it is something I shall have to work at and I daresay I shall get the confidence after I have made a few visits.

Tuesday 9 November

I went to see A.J., who is the technician in the Psychology Department, to see whether it would be possible for me to borrow the departmental video camera for a day. He told me that one of the other members of staff had the machine at the moment, and sent me off to ask them if I could borrow it. The member of staff said that he was not actually using the machine at the moment, and promised that he would try and remember to bring it in for me, though I must get authorisation from the head of department first. Went to see the head of department. He said fine, but that if I wanted to edit the video after shooting, I would have to go to the AVA department to ask for help. I saw one of the AVA department staff that evening and asked them. They told me that the best policy would be to get the acting head of the Sociology department to ask on my behalf. I said I would go and see him. I saw him, he saw the boss at AVA, the boss said Yes, I said Phew!! All systems go now, that is if the person with the video camera remembers to bring it in.

Mass media

For projects which are essentially operating at the local level, you may find that the mass media have little to offer in the way of coverage or analysis. Indeed, one of the delights of conducting projects with community groups and organisations is in finding out about activities which are mostly out of sight and unreported, but which nevertheless can have a lot to offer the community and the users of the services. Good news of this kind is seldom newsworthy in itself.

However, there are two ways in which the media may be relevant to your project. The first is where the client organisation does achieve some publicity, either through some special activity or special client, or because current events give it a prominent focus. The second is where it is not so much the organisation, but the service that it provides which becomes topical through political and media debate about a social problem of the moment – teenage pregnancy, sex education, youth crime or whatever.

Example 9.7
A documentary study of a local tragedy was able to draw on a wide assortment of reporting in the national press, where the event and its aftermath were described, pictured and analysed. The coverage itself became an issue, as many local people felt that some popular newspapers had been intrusive and unfair in their reporting. The project was undertaken at the request of a relative of one of the victims of the tragedy, and sought to piece together his eye-witness account with the media coverage and the records of the subsequent judicial enquiry to provide a more balanced account. In this case the press coverage of the tragedy was not simply a source of information on the event, but had to be analysed for its content

221

which contributed to the upset of the victims' families and that of other survivors.

Example 9.8
An example of the second type of media relevance comes from a project undertaken in collaboration with a Well Woman Centre, which sought to find out from school children what their needs were in respect to health. The study was done through the co-operation of local schools, asking pupils to discuss the issues in class and to fill in a short questionnaire. But at the same time the whole issue of sex education in schools became a moral and political 'hot potato', when the media picked up on frank explanations of sexual behaviour given to children in one particular school, and the Government Minister for Education felt impelled to intervene.

The subsequent debate in the media, including the editorials and the letters pages, provided a useful background against which the study could be set. The study's findings were also a contribution to the debate by showing what children's own perceived needs for information were.

Depicting the scene

There is a recommendation in Chapter 10 for the use of photographs in the client report to illustrate the settings where the research took place. By providing a view of the buildings and the activities, this can give the reader a visual indication to supplement the verbal descriptions. In some cases it may be possible to draw upon published photographs, such as picture postcards which offer a representation of the area studied.

Example 9.9
In a project based in a local hospital, the students included a postcard view of the hospital exterior – the only view available commercially. Its strongly

geometric, high-rise, modern design presented an impersonal front, in contrast to the human activity and emotions which the study reported inside the building.

Objects such as buildings are worth studying for what their design, ornamentation and location has to say about the significance and status of what goes on inside (Macdonald, 1993). This applies whether the building in question belongs to the Royal College of Physicians or the local voluntary organisation you may be working with. The latter is likely to be on a much more modest scale, utilising non-purpose built premises, in an out-of-the-way part of town.

Unobtrusive measures

'Unobtrusive measures' is the name given by Webb *et al.* (1966) to all non-reactive research in social science, that is to say, research which does not alter the situation under study, as interviews and questionnaires surely do. Pride of place goes to what they call 'physical trace' measures based upon changes to objects through use. These can be either erosion (wear and tear) or accretion (deposit or addition of other substances). Their book is a rich source of ideas about possible measures whose outstanding advantage is their 'inconspicuousness' (Webb *et al.*, 1966, p. 50).

The authors are aware that there are problems in interpreting the data, and problems too in the selective survival of the physical traces as different objects or geographic areas experience different rates of wear and restoration. However, they argue that non-reactive measures are a useful supplement to the traditional approaches of interviews and questionnaires. Applied to community research, you could compare different areas in terms of the amount of graffiti or litter, or the number of derelict properties, or even the number of satellite television dishes. The British system of car registration, including a letter for the year, allows you to calculate the age (newness) of cars in the area – except in the few cases of personal registrations, which are themselves an indicator of status. These could be used as alternatives to reputational measures of an area's desirability, in which you would ask residents to rate different areas in terms of their social attractiveness.

Observation

Webb *et al.* go on to discuss further examples of non-reactive research, archives and private records which we have considered above. They also discuss 'simple observation', by which they mean surreptitious observation (Webb *et al.*, 1966, p. 131) where the observer conceals the fact that recordings are being made. We have already chosen to discard covert research as a method to be used in collaborative research, but would like to suggest that participant observation, with all the risks of reactivity producing changes in the behaviour of the observed, is still worth including in your research strategy.

It can often be overlooked in focusing on interviews and questionnaires that these methods involve extended periods in the field when you are actually observing what goes on as you work.

Example 9.10
Students conducting a questionnaire survey of elderly people for an evaluation of a community centre became concerned that the information they had managed to collect by questionnaire would be inadequate. On discussion with their supervisor, it transpired that they had attended the centre on numerous occasions and could give a detailed account of its activities from memory. This led to a decision to build on the observation more systematically to document the processes of interaction at the centre.

Observation, according to Whyte (1984, p. 83), is often given a low status in social research because of the priority given to the verbal content of social interaction. Yet it can be used fairly readily to record basic aspects of behaviour. Observation of groups may be based on trying to discover the pattern of social activity by seeing who initiates actions and inferring from this the leadership roles.

Bales's (1950) Interaction Process Analysis develops observation to classify actions and words in terms of giving and receiving opinions, agreement and disagreement, thus analysing small group relationships. However, structured observation of this kind is difficult to employ, as

> interaction process analysis is so complex that it takes considerable training for observers to reach a point at which reliability scores are high enough to warrant confidence. (Whyte, 1984, p. 89)

None the less, a simplified observational scheme based upon specifying who initiates activity and who responds to others may be sufficient to identify leaders in group activity, and back up (or contradict) information received verbally about group membership and behaviour.

Situated observation

Observation is typically situated by place and time. Boundaries for observation are set by the physical surroundings, whether this is a work area, a rest room, or an open public area. Goffman's (1959) notion of 'front stage' and 'back stage' draws attention to the way in which people present themselves differently before an audience of outsiders and among their fellows.

Studies of patients in medical settings (Silverman, 1993, p. 42) point out the fairly mundane fact that different areas of a hospital are reserved for different activities – and make the more interesting point that the demeanour of patients changes in the different areas.

Activities in the same place of observation can vary significantly at different times according to the planned and unplanned schedule of events, and the personnel present. So to understand life on the hospital ward for young children, it is necessary to observe at different times: during parental visiting; at mealtimes; at treatment times; and at late evening when parents and staff may be few in number, yet children's interactions continue unabated (Hall, 1977).

Bogdewic, in Crabtree and Miller (1992), offers the advice of *mapping* the territory to be observed at an early stage in the research.

> This map provides one context for the interactions you observe. It enables you to consider differences, such as the difference between group space and personal space ... It helps you see where you are spending your time and where you are not. Last, the exploration required to draw the map is one way of becoming familiar with the setting. (Bogdewic, 1992, p. 55)

Bogdewic (1992, p. 53) also provides a template for observation by suggesting the following categories for recording:

- Who is present?
- What is happening?
- When does this activity occur?
- Where is this happening?

However, his final two categories:

- Why is this happening?
- How is this activity organised?

are not pure observational categories, because they are based upon the observer's inferences about the structuring of behaviour. As Whyte (1984, p. 84) insists, 'We cannot observe *why* anyone does anything'.

Conclusion

The case for using available data, unobtrusive measures and simple observation is that such methods are relatively easy to use and provide a quick entry into the research field. With the exception of observation, these methods avoid the problems of reactivity associated with traditional research techniques. Observation is a term covering a variety of styles, as many commentators have noted (for example, McNeill, 1990, pp. 81–2), from complete non-participant observation through to complete participation, with varying degrees of reactivity.

In each case the suggestion is that the methods outlined above should be regarded as supplements to the researcher's practice rather than as the sole method. Their disadvantage lies in the lack of control, as the researcher does not know, for example, the conditions under which organisational records have been created. And, following Whyte's comment above, nor does the researcher know the reason behind the generation of the evidence which is collected or observed. He or she may have a shrewd guess at the reason, but that is a notion that then has to be tested by other available data, or in other circumstances, or by triangulation against other methods.

PART III

10
Presenting the Client Report

In this chapter you are taken through the different stages of writing a report for your client organisation. For the client, this is the outcome of your project, so it is important that the report meets their needs. Various types of report are explained and suggestions made about presentation and content. Where recommendations are made, they should be grounded in the evidence you have collected from informants. Findings which could be interpreted as unfavourable to the organisation or to persons within it require sensitive handling. Finally, we comment briefly on some of the implications of using the client report for academic assessment.

One report or two?

Because the emphasis throughout has been upon applied research, it is suggested that two reports are appropriate for different audiences – one for the client organisation as a record of the project findings, and the second for the student's academic department which gives details of the methodology used. The client report is intended to be easily understood by organisation members and to focus on results. But there will be issues of research practice and methodology which are not appropriate for this audience, yet still need discussing as an integral part of the research experience. That is why it is suggested that the

231

client report is complemented by a methodology report. These two reports address different issues and different readers – and will therefore be written in different styles.

For students undertaking a group project collaboratively, it makes sense for only one joint report to be produced for the client. The report therefore is a matter for teamwork (see Chapter 1: Teamwork and Group Projects) and will integrate the work of all the team members.

Whether or not the student works as a member of a team, each individual, we suggest, is also responsible for producing an individual report on the methodological issues which have arisen. This is explained in detail in the Chapter 11.

Type of report

The nature of the client report will depend on the type of research negotiated and completed. As projects may differ widely in purpose, in methodology and in the type of organisation being studied, there can be a wide diversity in the client reports.

To give a flavour of the different kinds of projects that can be undertaken and the different types of report produced, we offer the list below. It is illustrated with actual examples. However, the list is not exhaustive or prescriptive – organisations are always coming up with new needs, so students and tutors can devise fresh ways of meeting them.

1. *Evaluation* – using interviews, questionnaires and observations to evaluate a service provided by an organisation.

    Example 10.1
    Members and staff of a mental health day care centre were interviewed to discover if the existing service was meeting the needs of current and potential members. The outcome was a report summarising the results of the interviews in terms of the characteristics and opinions of

members and staff. The study was used to provide evidence for negotiation by the organisation with the local council over the future
provision of services.

2. *Community survey* – using a structured schedule and
   doorstep interviews to conduct a survey of residents
   in a local area.

Example 10.2
Residents of an inner-city area were interviewed
about their awareness of the facilities provided
by a local Community Association, including their
City Farm. The report analysed the level of knowledge and use of the facilities together with attitudes towards future use. This enabled the
Association to rethink the scope of their services
and how they should be promoted.

3. *Publicity* – to investigate publicity needs and devise
   new promotional materials.

Example 10.3
Existing and potential service users of a therapeutic community for hard drug users, together with
referral agents, were asked to assess existing
leaflets produced by the organisation. The outcome
was a report on how people had heard about
the community and what they thought were its
important features, together with a draft layout for
a new publicity leaflet incorporating these findings.

4. *Documentary* – to discover and list the usage of facilities provided by an organisation.

Example 10.4
On the basis of observation, use of records and
personal interviews a report was prepared for a
charity which analysed the usage of its building
by the many groups based there, as well as an

appraisal by residents of the accommodation facilities offered. This material then formed the basis for publicity and was used by the manager to familiarise new recruits and potential funding bodies with the scope of this charity.

5. *Oral history* – to involve older members of a group or community in producing a record of their history.

Example 10.5
A village society wished to maintain a sense of community identity at a time of threat from outside forces for redevelopment, by means of recording the past experiences of long-term residents. The outcome was a report bringing together childhood and working life reminiscences. The study provided the focus for a programme on local radio.

6. *Documentary history* – to collect published and unpublished materials and prepare a documentary report to meet identified needs.

Example 10.6
An organisation set up to support local residents following a community tragedy wished to provide a particular family with a historical record of the tragedy and its aftermath as it affected one family member. Eye-witness accounts, media coverage and judicial inquiry reports were used to produce the report, which has been presented to the family as a memorial.

7. *Market Research* – to interview members of the general public on their knowledge of and attitudes to aspects of an organisation's work.

Example 10.7
A team of students interviewed shoppers in local shopping centres about people's attitudes to

volunteering. The report detailed their knowledge of local opportunities for volunteering, and was supplemented by interviews with individual volunteers. This was done to assist a community organisation which recruits volunteers in making its publicity more effective.

8. *Needs assessment* – to provide evidence of need in a specific area to support a group's application for funding to provide community facilities.

Example 10.8
Interviews with lone parents provided evidence to produce a report on the specific needs of this group and the likely benefits to come from the provision of facilities. The organisation used the report to support their application for the funding of a day centre for the children of lone parents.

A product as project outcome

Additionally, you may wish to create an identifiable product as a tangible result of the project, such as a publicity brochure or a video for the organisation. However, this would still need to be accompanied by a report explaining how and why the product was designed or re-designed in the case of a leaflet, or in the case of a video, the principles underlying the production and the research which went into making it.

Guidelines for report writing

The aim of the client report is to communicate the findings clearly and concisely. There are two issues to consider:
• what you have found out, and
• how it should be presented.

The data analysis stage will have already enabled you to select findings and issues to discuss in the report. But presentation is also important. If you look at reports produced by large organisations – company reports or the annual report of your own institution, for example – you will see how graphic design has been used to make the information stand out, and how such things as tables, photographs, charts, highlighted quotes, paragraph headings and the use of space are all part of the presentation. You cannot hope to rival these in terms of a glossy report with professional design, but there are ideas there which can be borrowed on a smaller scale to make your report more effective.

Length is another important feature. A short, 30-page readable report has more impact than a 100-page exhaustive analysis of a questionnaire. In fact, a long report is likely to indicate that not enough time has been spent sifting through the data to pick out the important issues and findings. So do set enough time aside for writing and getting other people's comments on your draft.

Be prepared to make revisions to your drafts

It is unlikely you will be able to write the report at one sitting. Most authors, as we do, write several drafts. For the first draft concentrate on setting the main points down on paper, using second and later drafts to put them in logical order and make them readable. If you start jotting down points at the data analysis stage, this has the beneficial effect of spreading the writing time for the report over a longer period.

When working in a team it makes the best use of time if each member takes responsibility for producing one section of the report. But in this case it is also sensible to appoint one of the group as the editor, who will bring the separate drafts together and give them a coherent feel and style.

Do try if at all possible to get comments on the draft back from your organisation before you commit yourself to the final version. Besides maintaining contact with the organisation, this allows them to comment on any elements where they may feel there are inadequacies and allows you to flag up any points which you think may be particularly important or contentious.

As well as seeking the advice of your tutor, you could ask a relative or friend to read your work – particularly if they do not know much about your project. If what you have written is not clear to them, it may not be clear to your client in the organisation either.

User-friendliness

The suggestions below are offered to help you through this report writing stage, which can be time-consuming, but they are not intended to be a straight-jacket. What really appeals to readers is the variety and freshness of the reports based on original work.

It may be argued that the style to adopt in order to present a professional image of competence is that of the 'scientific report' such as is found in academic journals or textbooks. We, however, place greater emphasis upon the report being 'user-friendly', readable and informative to the client – and addressed to a wider, non-specialist audience which is not concerned with the technicalities of social science. The end result may sound more like journalism than academic work – but there is still the second methodology report in which to display academic skills.

> *From the very outset, put yourself in the practitioner or user's place.*

This practical advice for report writing is given by Morris *et al.* (1987, p. 20). Users will accept or reject your findings according to whether the information is:

> Relevant
> Practical
> Useful
> Credible
> Understandable
> Timely

Consult this checklist as you write your report.

Structure of the report

Thinking of the different parts which go to make up the final report, we can identify the following elements:

- Cover
- Preface
- Abstract/Executive Summary
- Background to the Research
- Findings
- Conclusion and Recommendations
- Appendices.

Front cover

The front cover should give at least the following information:

- Title of the report
- Subtitle, if required
- Name of the client organisation
- Author(s)
- Date
- Your academic department
- Name of the academic institution you belong to.

Your own institution may have laid down strict criteria

for the cover of your work, so check any regulations that apply. Aim to make the cover look professional in its appearance – that is, well set out and balanced on the page. It sets the tone for what follows.

Preface

Acknowledgements and thanks It is good practice to thank the academic members of staff, including your tutor, who have helped you (and after all they will be marking the finished work); the staff in the organisation you have been working with and the service users you have interviewed. For this last group a general word of thanks may be appropriate, rather than picking out individuals by name. This is essential when confidentiality and anonymity have to be respected.

Visual impact Where possible, include a *photograph* and/ or *map* of where you have been conducting your research. It adds visual attraction to the report and interests the reader. A photo may show the exterior or interior of a building, a shot of the research team posing – perhaps with some staff or service users, or you could have a picture of yourself engaged in interviewing.

Always check first with your client that it is acceptable to take photographs, and that any people in the photograph besides yourself agree to you using it in the report. There are some organisations where it would be regarded as intrusive or unethical to photograph vulnerable people.

Example 10.9

A project for an organisation helping women victims of domestic violence involved students in interviewing women in a refuge. The location of the refuge is highly confidential. Not even the male supervisor of the women students was allowed to know where it was, and obviously no photographs were possible.

Where photographs are available, they can be added to with drawings and diagrams at other places throughout your report. They help to break up text and can often say more than a written description. For instance, in a report dealing with the facilities provided in a centre a photograph is an effective way of showing the reader what service users have been discussing.

Contents page The contents page is a useful guide to the reader about the structure of the report. It should set out the page numbers as well as the section headings and be neatly formatted to create a good impression. Page numbering in the text can be left to your word processor to format automatically, but remember that if you alter the draft (or even change the font) the page references may need to be updated on your contents page.

Abstract/executive summary

Begin your report with a brief summary. In contrast to a dissertation, where conclusions come at the end, a report should *begin* with a concise summary of your findings. This is to grab the attention of the reader and 'flag up' what is to follow. Recognise that for some readers this summary may be the only part they wish to read.

For those who will read the whole report, the summary directs attention to key areas that are explained in detail later on. Aim for brevity at this stage – short sentences or even pithy phrases preceded by a number, asterisk or 'bullet'. One page is better than two. Half a page is best of all.

If you have done an evaluation project you can also include a summary of recommendations at this point – your reader will then want to read on and find out *why* these recommendations have been made. A good idea again borrowed from official reports is to put a page reference after each recommendation (in brackets) to mark where each item is discussed in the main report.

Background to the research

The client organisation Near the beginning of your report, give a short summary of the client organisation's activities. Obviously your client knows what the organisation does but this allows you to show that you too understand the key issues, including the *ethos* and *objectives* of the client. Moreover there will be other readers of the report: apart from your tutor and external examiner, who may not be familiar with the client organisation, the report may be used later by the client for other purposes – publicity or funding applications, for example, where a clear statement of the organisation is essential. The description of the organisation written into the original research agreement provides a base to start from, but this can now be amplified by your own experience of working with it.

Origins of the research You may think it worth while to spell out briefly how the project came to be negotiated, and to mention your prior interest and involvement, if relevant. The *context* of the research could also be described – such as developments in the voluntary sector or changing perspectives in the organisation itself or new philosophies of care, which led to the opportunity for your project to be undertaken.

Aims of the project Outline the research proposal which was agreed between you and the client. Use your research brief (see Chapter 4) to state the objectives of the research carried out.

Example 10.10
A student undertaking an evaluation of the volunteer training programme of a victim support centre wrote as follows.

Initially there were two main objectives of the research:

(i) The first consisted of a comparative account of two schemes which were located in different geographical areas and portrayed very different socio-economic environments. The aim was to establish whether characteristics of the volunteers differed in relation to the area they worked in, with variables such as age and gender, for example, being considered.

(ii) The second objective entailed an evaluation of the service provided from both a client and volunteer perspective.

(Daniels, 1992)

Research methods   It is important to explain clearly your methods of research. Aim to sound 'professional' (that is, you know what you are doing) without lapsing into technical jargon. Use terms that your reader can understand.

Technically accurate methodology is important in giving the report *credibility*. Morris *et al.* note: 'If people do not *trust* the results of the evaluation, it goes without saying that they will not use the information' (1987, p. 29).

Credibility, they add, is at least equally affected by the evaluator's style of working and reporting.

Methodologically, an evaluation is credible if data are collected in ways that the potential users perceive to be valid, reliable, and objective. Validity in this sense is not simply the technical validity of a scientific research study, but a validity that reflects organizational sensitivity. The evaluator must communicate a clear sense of 'what's going on' and how the organization 'works' from the user's experience. A careful analysis of data from multiple sources adds to the evaluation's validity. Detailed accounts from qualitative studies, direct observations and interviews, indicate the evaluator's understanding of users' experiences and varied points of view. (ibid., p. 30)

Example 10.11

From the same evaluation of the volunteer training programme in Example 10.10, the student continued:

> Thus, through the in-depth loosely structured interviewing of a volunteer sample of eight and a client sample of six it was hoped that the two aims would be met. It was also agreed that a small number of ex-volunteers might be contacted to establish why they left the organisation.
>
> (Daniels, 1992)

However, the project did not work out as envisaged. As is often the case, fieldwork problems arose and the student accounted for these in a following section entitled 'Reassessment of Aims of the Research'. Here she covered such issues as changes in the sample size, and an alteration of the focus to include a different set of informants, namely full-time members of staff.

Findings

This section is the main part of your report. Aim to *tell a story* rather than just listing results, as you did in the Summary. Use a variety of ways of presenting your findings – through the tables, charts and graphs which have been discussed in the previous chapters as well as through straightforward text.

Begin by clarifying the sources of your information, whether through observation, interviews, questionnaires, documents or a mixture of sources. Where you have used sample surveys, show the nature of the sample you actually achieved – its size and its make-up in terms of age, gender and other relevant variables.

When you have numerical information, present this in tables and remember to *label* your tables and *number* them in sequence. The labels should clearly indicate what the table is explaining. Show which questions produced the information – this can be by a direct quote or in the brief explanation of the table which should always be given below. If you are presenting statistics on the tables, do not expect the reader to have to interpret the statistics – this is your job.

In your commentary draw attention to the most interesting or significant results, rather that just reiterating the information in the table. An effective way of illustrating a point is by inserting one or two short direct quotations from informants. These can be taken either from responses to open-ended questions or from recorded interviews.

Selection and interpretation

If you have conducted a questionnaire survey or in-depth interviews using a structured guide, it would be dull in the extreme to present the responses as a list of consecutive items. Instead, think of grouping answers around *themes* and of ordering these themes according to their priority for your report.

It is possible to find reports of questionnaire surveys which do simply take each question in turn and display the results. Such a presentation does not make good reading or make proper use of the data. Each question does not require equal treatment, as some questions may be intrinsically more interesting and worth longer discussion than others.

More useful and revealing is the situation where you *cross-classify* the results of one question against another, or against the characteristics of your informants, to discover if the different variables are related in some way to each other (see Chapter 6). Similarities and contrasts can then be brought out, using direct quotations, which in the case of in-depth interviews may be several lines in length.

When presenting the results of your investigations, be sure to distinguish between what your informants have told you and believe to be true, and what you have been able to establish as fact from your own observations. Give thought too to how you are to interpret or explain your results, and whether there are possible different reasons for what you have discovered which need to be considered.

Example 10.11
A study of patients' relatives discovered that relatives of patients who had died were less satisfied with the amount of information that had been given them than relatives of patients still receiving treatment. The students explained:

We could interpret this dissatisfaction as being due to any of a number of reasons – the unhappy outcome of the disease; relatives reflecting more as time has passed; or perhaps the staff may not be as forthcoming with information as death becomes more likely. (Morgan and Nixon, 1994)

Conclusions and recommendations

Conclusions Sum up your findings and your interpretations of the results. Reference can be made to other studies or published statistics if these are relevant. Be sure to highlight among the results those issues which are of particular concern to your client organisation – and indicate whether the results bear out these concerns or not. Remember that your client may be as interested in negative findings as they are in positive ones.

Example 10.12
A study of the recruitment of volunteers, using a multiple choice question, found that people had been attracted to becoming volunteers in a variety of ways,

but *none* had been recruited through the publicity materials produced by the organisation concerned.

Recommendations   Not all reports will require a section for recommendations. Oral and documentary histories, for example, will not, though most other types of report listed earlier include some form of evaluation of service or 'fact-finding' exercise, and may therefore make recommendations for action. According to Robson,

> The most important aspects are that recommendations should:
>
> (a) be clearly derived from the data; and
> (b) be practical (i.e. capable of implementation).
> (Robson, 1993, p. 421)

This means that recommendations arise best from the people you have interviewed rather than from some 'expert' knowledge of your own which you have acquired over a few months. Rooting recommendations in their source – the informants or 'true experts' – gives them more credibility. Such recommendations are 'practical' if they suggest attainable improvements to the service, although you may need to indicate that these changes would require extra funding or a shift in priorities, that is, that there are costs attached to them.

Robson also argues that is helpful to distinguish:

(a) findings   – information about the situation
(b) interpretations   – explanations offered about the findings
(c) judgements   – values brought to bear on the data
(d) recommendations   – suggested courses of action.

(Robson, 1993, p. 421)

This is sound advice for students who have in the main been trained to write standard academic essays which are organised around findings, interpretations and judgements. There is a case for separating out the recommendations, with interpretations and judgements being included in the conclusions. In this way the results of your research are analytically distinguished from the issue of what to do about those results. The organisation is then free to assess your evidence separately from your recommendations.

Example 10.13
Two students were asked to evaluate a training programme for the visually impaired by interviewing people who had completed the programme. On the basis of the informants' responses, the recommendations were as follows:

- An introductory tape may be useful in order to dissipate any unnecessary fears clients have before starting at the Day Centre.
- Information about the clients' previous employment history would be beneficial to both client and Manager. This could aid decision making for selection of programmes tailored to individuals.
- For Braille and typing, tuition time could be extended.
- Clients felt it would be helpful to synchronise the Centre's timetable with other educational establishments.
- Because some clients lived alone, a cassette tape would be a more efficient way of providing information on holidays and other matters than the current written information.
- A newsletter would be a useful way of keeping former clients up to date with information about the Centre.

(Ashton and Ainsbury, 1993)

Appendix

Supplementary material Appendices can be used to provide the detailed material which underpins your findings.

This would be too much for every reader, but provides the information to check your interpretation of the results and so enhances its credibility. Here you could explain your methodology in greater detail. You should always provide copies of your research instruments – questionnaire(s), interview schedule or *'aides-mémoire'*, as well as any other information given to your informants. You may also display tables or statistical data which were left out of the main body of the report, or present case studies in full here.

References It is unlikely that you will have a great list of references in the client report. Most can be kept for the methodology report (see Chapter 11). But, as in any piece of academic work, all quotations from other writers must be attributed. Follow the standard procedure which your academic institution applies. The Harvard system (as used in this book) is a well-known example. Here in the text the author's surname and date of publication (in brackets) is given, and full details of the publication are given in an alphabetical list of authors at the end of the work. This is much easier to read than the alternative of on-page footnotes, or numbered end-notes.

Style of the report

Language and presentation

Aim to use language which is accessible to the ordinary reader – write in clear, lively English and avoid jargon. If you need to use technical or scientific terms, think about including a *glossary* in your appendix.

Morris *et al.* (1987, pp. 34–6) make a number of useful suggestions for increasing the impact of what you write in a report:

- shorten sentences by cutting out deadwood
- use active verbs as much as possible
- use familiar words ('help' not 'facilitate')
- personalise your text by using everyday expressions.

The following are examples of useful simplifications (taken from Inman, 1994).

Avoid	*Prefer*
accommodate	hold, contain
assistance	help
commence	begin, start
demonstrate	show
discontinue	stop
endeavour	try
establish	set up
inform	tell
numerous	many
participate	take part
request	ask
revealed	said
sufficient	enough

Example 10.14

A draft report was originally written as follows (27 words):

> A large proportion of residents in the survey sample (see fig. 14), prioritised young people as the most neglected group in terms of welfare and leisure facilities.

It could be rewritten and simplified thus (20 words):

> Young people were the ones our informants believed were most in need of welfare and leisure facilities (see Fig. 14).

Finally, write shorter sentences and shorter paragraphs and use space effectively. There is no point cramming words on to a page – a solid wall of text is discouraging to read. So, as you edit, cut down the paragraphs to cover just a single idea. Even one-sentence paragraphs can be effective as long as they are not overdone.

Focus on important points

Use section headings to break up the report into manageable chunks. Ensure that the headings clearly indicate the content of the section.

Example 10.15
One report evaluating the facilities at a day centre had the following headings:

> Goals and Values
> Functions
> Reasons for Attendance
> Communication
> Day Centre Users

This is rather plain and boring. It could have been given more content to attract the reader's attention, as follows:

> HOW TO ACHIEVE 'NORMALISATION'
> WHAT THE CENTRE PROVIDES FOR ITS MEMBERS
> LONELINESS – THE REASON FOR ATTENDANCE
> THE BENEFITS OF COMMUNICATION
> WHO ARE THE CENTRE USERS?

Formatting

Changes in font through choice of typeface and size of print can be an effective way of giving your report visual appeal and directing the reader to the most important points. But do not overdo it, otherwise it can become a distraction rather than an aid. Marshman and James (1994, p. 133) provide the following guidelines:

Heading or Sub-heading	In reports it is often most effective if you can have a title in the left margin (in one font) and the text to the right (in another font). Achieving this effect with a word processor is quite simple: put in the title first, then indent the main text and switch font.

Figure 10.1   The report style

- Restrict yourself to one or two font types
- Use fonts in contrasting pairs, serifed and sans-serif
- Vary the properties of text – using bold, italics, and so on – to give emphasis and variety, rather than using additional fonts.

Section headings, for instance, should stand out clearly. Boxes can be used to highlight text – for quotations or case studies, perhaps. Quotations may also be indented. Asterisk a set of key points or use 'bullets'. *Italics give emphasis* as do CAPITAL LETTERS, underlining and **BOLD**.

A particularly useful method of setting out your work is the Report or Minutes Style, with a section heading in the left margin and the main text indented right in parallel, as in Figure 10.1.

Pagination

The contents page assumes that the report pages are numbered. This should be continuous throughout the document, beginning on page 1 after the contents page. If in word-processing the report you separate it into a number of sections for convenience, remember to start each section with the correct page number. Try to avoid having a page end with the first line of a paragraph or start with the last line of a paragraph. This is something you can check on the final draft before printing, and correct by minor alterations to line spacing and page margins.

Length of the report

It is much more difficult to set an absolute word length for this kind of report than it is for a dissertation. You are aiming to be comprehensive but concise, and an effective report communicates information quickly to busy readers. 'The shorter the better' is a good guide. Less is more.

Where the client report is to be submitted for academic assessment the number of words should be checked with your supervisor; there may be regulations in your academic institution which affect this. If the supervisor is satisfied that you have worked hard on your project and produced a report which reflects that accurately, then number of words becomes an irrelevant criterion for assessment.

Should you still want some indication of suggested length – and we recognise that students do often like the security of fixed limits, then without being prescriptive we would say that in our experience reports of around 30–35 pages including tables and graphs are quite adequate, and much lengthier presentations are to be discouraged.

Dealing with potential problems with the report

We have earlier suggested that it is good practice if your client can read a draft of the report before you present the final version. This will ensure that any factual errors can be eliminated and that the client's interest in your work is maintained. Consultation on the draft may also be the opportunity for handling a particularly sensitive and tricky issue:

> *What should you do if in the course of your research you have collected critical or hostile information about your client (whether this is about the organisation itself or named persons within the organisation)?*

It would be unethical as well as improper to ignore such information and present a rosy picture of the organisation because you do not want to upset people. On the other hand, you should beware of being over-critical on the basis of limited and partial information. Some of the unfavourable impressions you observe or are given may be about personalities in the organisation and are not really relevant to the issues you are researching. But others may directly impinge on the quality of services provided.

You may find it helpful to discuss problems of this kind with your supervisor, to decide what importance to give such information. The criticisms should be reported in some way. But no one likes to be criticised. Your informants may have an axe to grind, and the rest of your report may be discredited by your readers if you present unsubstantiated criticism as fact.

One way of dealing with this situation is to have a meeting with the client and raise these uncomfortable issues verbally in a tactful way, along with other items for discussion in the rest of the draft. This does appear to work. You may find that your client is already aware of the problems and has taken steps to deal with them, or has a different version of events to offer as a corrective to the views of your informants.

Remember your report has been 'commissioned' by the client and if criticisms have to be made you should aim to do this as tactfully and skilfully as possible while remaining true to your informants. You should look for the most constructive way to get the points over. However, you should remind yourself that you are a relative newcomer to the scene and may have only a partial understanding of what is at issue.

Such difficulties are quite common, but are part of the learning experience of the project – a useful way of discovering how such problems can be dealt with in the real world. These are issues you should discuss at greater length in your methodology report. This would be the place to present the issues and the dilemmas and to show how the process of dealing with them has been addressed.

A more extreme problem occurs when circumstances that could not have been anticipated make fieldwork so difficult that little direct evidence is collected on which to write the report. The organisation you are working with may undergo a radical change during the research period, with your organisational contact moving on elsewhere. Or the co-operation you were relying on for the distribution of questionnaires does not take place, and few returns are made. Or, despite earlier assurances, it proves impossible for one reason or another to gain access to interview the target informants.

Obviously such problems would need to be discussed with your supervisor as early as possible. Tutors are aware that research of this kind does have its hazards and that students should not be penalised for problems beyond their control. These problems may be minimised, however, if the careful procedures for negotiation explained in the earlier chapters are followed and students keep in regular contact with tutors.

The tutor also has a role to play in following up any problems as they arise with the client organisation. Often a phone call may be sufficient to disentangle some crossed lines of communication and provide required reassurances, but occasionally a further visit to the organisation is required to propose or negotiate revisions to a research plan which in practice has become unworkable.

While revisions to research plans are commonplace, complete breakdowns of projects are fortunately rare. In such cases the second methodology report still provides you with the opportunity of describing and analysing the problems that have occurred, even if the client report is much curtailed.

Assessment criteria

Although the primary focus of the client report is the client organisation and its needs, it is also suggested that this report can be assessed for academic purposes as part of your work as a student. As well as any subject-specific skills which have been tested by the type and nature of the research undertaken, there are other skills developed through the practical work which may also be assessed. Here are some examples.

- **Practical skills** – you have completed the agreed field-work in a competent manner (or explained changes which may have occurred in the fieldwork plan).
- **Analytical skills** – you have made sense of the data col-lected and been able to evaluate the organisation in the light of the evidence.
- **Presentation skills** – you have presented a clearly writ-ten report with tables, charts and diagrams to summar-ise the evidence. Oral history reports may also aim to provide photographs and documents to supplement the text.
- **Policy skills** – you have shown that you can deal with issues requested by the client and present relevant rec-ommendations where appropriate. Oral history reports will not, however, be concerned with policy skills. Such reports are descriptive and analytical rather than being aimed at producing policy recommendations.

Teamwork and group reports

Where a team has collaborated to produce the client re-port, this does create a problem: how should marks for the report be allocated to individual team members? You may feel that the simplest method of giving the same mark to all members of the team is unfair to the members of the team who have done much more or less than others.

One of the issues for a team, we have suggested ear-lier, is to manage the contributions of members so that there is a fair equivalence and no one feels exploited. Some marking schemes would extend that idea of collec-tive responsibility to the allocation of marks. For example, the team is given the responsibility for dividing up the aggregate marks to reward individual contributions. A mark of 60 per cent for a team project with four members would give 60 x 4 = 240 marks for redistribution among the individuals in proportion to their effort.

Another alternative is to require you to provide in ad-dition to the report a detailed breakdown of your indi-vidual contribution to each stage of the research and report writing – perhaps on a standard rating scale given to each of the team members – and then to adjust the individual marks accordingly.

Our preference is for simplicity, and for using the methodology report to distinguish the different contributions among a team. But there are no hard and fast rules, it is a case of developing an assessment strategy which matches the objectives of applied research and is agreed to be fair by you as students and by the examiners.

Ideally one would like also to include in the assessment some feedback from the client organisation. It is gratifying to be asked, as students have been, to present their findings in person to the organisation's staff and management committee, and to receive their thanks directly. But the timescale for academic assessment is typically brief, and we have not yet found a workable and reliable way of formally incorporating the client's view into assessment.

Conclusion

The client report sets out the findings of the research project which you negotiated with the client organisation. As such it is the principal outcome of your research. It needs to be well-structured and clearly presented, drawing attention to significant findings but avoiding jargon.

You should ensure that it covers all aspects of your project work so that the organisation – and your academic assessors – have a clear idea of what you have achieved. Where recommendations are made, these should be presented in such a way that they can be seen to arise out of the information that has been collected.

Findings which could be construed as critical of the organisation concerned need to be handled carefully and responsibly. How you deal with this – and other problems arising in the course of the research – is one subject of the methodology report, introduced in Chapter 11.

11
Presenting the Methodology or Reflexive Report

This chapter concentrates on the writing of a report for the academic department, rather than for the client organisation. The reason for proposing this methodology report is to supplement the client report by recording the insights derived from the practice of research. The aims are to provide context, reflexive remarks and evaluation of learning. Advice is given on content and presentation and some possible criteria for assessment.

Methodology or reflexive report

In applied research, the client report communicates the findings of the research to the organisation concerned. Why then should you be advised to produce a second report?

There are two reasons. Because the client report focused on the needs of the organisation, it may not contain sufficient academic content to meet the requirements of your subject. Second, and more positively, a methodology report allows the researcher to *reflect* on the process of research. This shows how the research methods of the textbooks were actually employed to meet the circumstances of the particular situation and what has been learned from this.

This second report is an academic report because it is written to demonstrate subject-specific skills and competencies, but it is probably better termed a *methodology* report because it focuses upon:

- *methodology* – the overall approach to studying the research topic, and the constraints, dilemmas and ethical choices involved; and upon
- *methods* – the particular research techniques which have been employed, adapted and revised, and the success or otherwise of these choices.

The client report is a public document, which under the kind of research agreement suggested in Chapter 3 becomes the property of the organisation to do with as they like. But the methodology report is a private document for academic assessors, in which you can be both more frank and more personal in your evaluation of your own efforts (and those of your colleagues if you worked in a team).

The two reports therefore stand together and complement each other as product and process, as project and evaluation, as the 'official' and 'unofficial' accounts of research. In much the same way academic research published in books and journals is occasionally enlivened by 'behind the scenes' accounts of how the research was actually done (Platt, 1976; Bell and Newby, 1977; Bell and Roberts, 1984). As has been argued in Chapter 2, many feminist methodologists in particular emphasise the importance of writing about research as it actually happens, rather than presenting it as a 'hygienic' process (Kelly, 1988; Maynard, 1994).

Reasons for the methodology report

Against this background, there are a number of pragmatic reasons for a methodology report. Some have to do with supplementing the client report, others stress the independent value of the methodology report in terms of its demonstration of learning.

1. *To enable the study to be set in a sociological context.*

   Example 11.1
   A student was asked to evaluate a booklet prepared for patients at a hospital. He did this by
   interviewing patients who had used the booklet, and finding out which sections they found
   helpful and what other information they would
   like to have had in the booklet. The client report was well received by the hospital staff, but
   did not go into the wider social issues concerning the role of information and information control
   on doctor/patient relationships. The methodology
   report provided the opportunity to discuss these
   issues as the context within which the actual
   research was undertaken.

2. *To report problems and dilemmas in the conduct of the
   research.*

   Example 11.2
   In an evaluation study of a voluntary training
   centre, two students came across criticism by
   clients of one particular staff member. It would
   have been inappropriate to record this in the client
   report as it would have breached the undertaking given not to identify individuals, and the
   students did not have sufficient knowledge to
   substantiate the criticism. Nevertheless, as discussed in relation to the client report, such information could not be ignored. The students
   had to represent the views of the people interviewed fairly and, after discussion with their
   supervisor, mentioned the issue in conversation
   with the organisation's director. (The organisation was already aware of the problem.) The handling of sensitive information such as this can
   be explained in the methodology report.

3. *To allow individual assessment within group projects.*

Where students work collectively in a team, a common mark may be awarded for the client report, but if students submit an individual methodology report then they can also receive an individual mark. Where different amounts of work have been done, the methodology report allows a record of work to be submitted in terms of the research diary. The methodology report also enables subjective evaluation of what students have learned as individuals.

4. *To report details of work done but not evident in the client report.*

Example 11.3
Two students began a project for a voluntary organisation. As the study unfolded, it became clear that the initial focus had not been tightly enough defined, and that the organisation could not provide access to the people it wanted information on, who were carers in the Chinese community. A decision was taken to abandon the project, and restart with another organisation on a better negotiated project. The methodology report explained the effects of this false start on the timescale of the eventual project. Though the initial project had been aborted, it had still contributed to learning about social research.

5. *To 'go behind' the methods textbooks to disclose the pleasure and the pain of actual research.*

Example 11.4
Three students had decided to conduct a doorstep interview sample survey as part of their investigation of the actual and potential use of a community centre. A random sample was selected

on the basis of textbook methods. Whereas the client report mentioned the number of contacts and non-responses, the methodology report was more outspoken on the difficulties of interviewing in an inner-city area in the middle of January, and on the amount of time required to contact even a modest number of informants.

6. *To present evidence of personal learning.*

One of the objectives of encouraging students to undertake applied research is to develop their personal skills. So the methodology report allows you to include your own self-assessment of what you have learned through carrying out the project – and possibly what you would not do again.

Content of the methodology report

There are three main areas for a methodology report:

- context
- reflexivity
- evaluation.

Context

Providing context means searching out material to show an understanding of the general issues or context surrounding the research. In relation to community, voluntary and non-profit organisations such issues may have to do with:

- the needs of service users
- the development of statutory, commercial or voluntary services to meet such needs
- legislative changes affecting provision of services
- public opinion, stereotyping and moral panics
- the political economy of care and community action.

Giving context can be seen as a way of putting back in the social context which the client report has left out, either because it was not relevant to the particular study or because the organisation is already familiar with it.

Example 11.5
A student who investigated the effects of lack of child care on career opportunities for single mothers supplied background information in her methodology report comparing the level of child care provision in Great Britain with that in other countries. This highlighted one source of the problem – lack of government investment.

Ideally, providing context means being able to demonstrate a methodical, balanced and well-researched accumulation of topic-based material. The client organisation is likely to be a good source of information, either having copies of relevant reports and studies which can be borrowed, or knowing where such information can be found locally or nationally.

Another source of background material is your institution's library or the local library, which may hold census data on your particular geographical area of study. Also there are a number of organisations which conduct studies and provide information on the voluntary sector itself. In the UK, for example, there is the Volunteer Centre, and the Association for Research into the Voluntary and Community Sector (ARVAC).

However, a sense of proportion is needed: setting the context is only a small part of an applied research project. It is impossible to achieve in 1000 words what dissertation students do in 10 000–15 000 words. In addition, if the client organisation is very innovative or specialist, very little contextual material may be available.

Given the constraints on time which mean you must give priority to the most important report – that for the client – it may not be possible to go into the depth suggested here.

Reflexivity

By reflexivity is meant the capacity to stand back from the detail of the chosen research methods, and to consider the social situations in which they are used. You will be aware that your actions influence the responses of your respondents, and those responses in turn affect how you carry through the research.

The unintended effects of doing research

The well-known 'Hawthorne effect' (Roethlisberger and Dickson, 1964) describes how the act of doing research in a social setting can change participants' attitudes and behaviour. Without comparative material, however, you may find it difficult to estimate the effect of the intrusiveness of different techniques on the responses and behaviour of your informants. But there are some pointers which may assist in your sensitisation to such effects.

For example, you should consider the following:

- Did the questions asked elicit answers different from those expected?
- Did the results from face-to-face interviewing match up with the results obtained from using a questionnaire?
- Did informants treat the researcher differently at the end of the research involvement than at the beginning?

Example 11.6

A student evaluating the work of a day centre for people with mental health problems made the following comments in her methodology report.

It is possible that due to the fact that the service users knew and liked the interviewer their responses may have been different from the ones they would have given had they been interviewed by someone they did not know. The Hawthorne Effect is an experimental effect which was observed to take place by Elton Mayo in 1927. Mayo found that when people know that they are being observed, or that an experiment is being carried out, it directly affects their behaviour.

This effect may have taken place with the service users and the staff at the centre especially since many of them were particularly fond of the interviewer, and may have been answering in the way they thought she would want them to. Being aware of this problem, I tried to ensure that no indication was given to the interviewees as to what the expected answers to any of the questions were.

Role relationships

To get to a position where informants would be comfortable in an interview, you may first have spent a period of time with them, observing their activities and getting to know them as individuals. It was pointed out earlier that this is particularly important when vulnerable individuals are being studied. However, getting to know people before the formal research begins does not eliminate all the problems, as two students who were interviewing adults with learning difficulties found out.

Example 11.7
One of the students wrote in her methodology report:

The question of validity was raised by S——, who runs the Club. She had been nearby while we were interviewing and told us, after we had finished, that what one informant had told us for a couple of the questions was untrue. This was because he didn't want us to know the real reasons for him coming to the club (to find a girlfriend). Another informant also made up the whole of the interview as he was sitting with his friends and thought it would be amusing. He did, however, give us a second interview which we took as being valid. S—— after these

264

two incidents offered to check all the interviews we had done at the Club to see if most of them were true. We felt that this would have gone against the confidentiality we owed to our informants. After all, if the informants had not had learning difficulties we would have taken what they had said at face value.

Other questions to be considered are:

- Who did my informants take me to be?
- What role did they put me into?

You may have adopted the student role to gain access to the information, or you might have stressed the role of independent researcher for the client organisation (with the consequent results from your research in developing or changing service delivery).

Example 11.8
A student conducted a research project involving the perceptions of doctors about the services provided by a counselling agency. In her methodology report she made the following remarks.

My neatly designed plan was soon demolished as I telephoned some 20 doctors without booking a single interview. Research was not as simple as the textbooks suggested. Getting past the practice managers was a feat in itself! I was feeling really discouraged and frustrated. I had been introducing myself as a student who was doing research for my degree. I finally hit on the key to success by following the advice of my supervisor and introducing myself as a 'researcher for the counselling agency which is offering a *free* counselling service for doctors' patients'. After this change of approach I booked 10 doctor interviews and felt quite delighted with my progress and what I had learned from this experience.

265

Furthermore, the traditional academic role of 'outside enquirer' may be questioned or modified as you or your informants develop a more personal style of interaction.

Example 11.9
In a study of a day centre for people with mental illness, students' relationships with the members developed well beyond the impersonal scientific model to encompass such things as:

- joining in with members in the activities provided
- attending the centre's fund-raising open day
- selling (and buying) items of hand-crafts at a sale of work in the centre.

Example 11.10
In a study of a luncheon club for the elderly, students' activities included:

- joining in the afternoon dance
- on one occasion of staff shortages, helping with serving the meals.

In a study of how researchers actually conduct research in organisations (Bryman, 1988b), researchers were reported as sometimes providing informants with a 'listening ear' (Crompton and Jones, 1988, p. 70). As Bresnen elaborates: 'I did do rather a lot of sympathetic listening to catalogues of problems, and suggested reasons for them and possible solutions' (Bresnen, 1988, p. 44). Crompton and Jones stress that the 'listening ear' requires the absolute importance of guarantees of confidentiality. In their own research, they emphasised their *independence* from informants. Bresnen, on the other hand, describes himself as involved *interactively* in responding to what he is told – though concerned lest he cause any disruption or 'aggravation'.

For feminist researchers such as Oakley, interactive research is seen as a move away from the traditional hierarchical relationship between researcher and researched and a step towards a more equal relationship. Repeated

interviewing means that a long-term relationship can develop instead of the interview being a one-off affair. Interviewing women about childbirth, Oakley (1981) often
found that interviewees took the initiative in defining the
interviewer–interviewee relationship as something beyond
the limits of question asking and answering. Hospitality
was normal and friendship developed so that:

> four years after the final interview I am still in touch with
> more than a third of the women I interviewed. Four have
> become close friends, several others I visit occasionally, and
> the rest write or telephone when they have something salient
> to report such as the birth of another child. (Oakley, 1981,
> p. 30)

Example 11.11
In a methodology report of a project largely based
on repeated in-depth interviews, a student commented:

> I call them *'MY'* respondents because by the time
> I had interviewed them I felt that I had known them
> all my life. I was welcomed into homes like a long
> lost friend and have an open invitation to take myself
> and my family back any time. I felt none of the
> resentment I was expecting about the 'professional'
> coming into the area to take and give nothing in
> return. These people were eager to help in any way
> they could.

Finally on role relationships, researchers need to be aware
of how informants might wish to voice or to conceal criticisms of their organisation. Informants may seek to enlist
the support of the researcher in their interpretation of
events within the organisation. To quote Bresnen again:
'a good many of the comments made were in the form
of analyses of the situation for which "someone was to
blame"' (Bresnen, 1988, p. 44).

   In making such comments, the informant is implicitly
asking the interviewer to accept their view of the situation. Bresnen notes that the idea of complicity can be

taken further as the interviewee pumped him for information about the organisation, when he 'could easily have slipped into the reverse role of key informant' (Bresnen, 1988, p. 44).

The opposite situation occurs when informants are hesitant about admitting 'discrediting things that the interviewer suspects' (Lawrence, 1988, p. 101). Lawrence suggests techniques for handling the problem of unwillingness to reveal unpalatable facts to an outsider by using comparisons to 'lower the threshold'. For example, the interviewer might phrase a question thus:

> *We know that such a problem has been reported in other studies, is this a problem you experience here?*

The methodology report, then, is the place where you can discuss how the data may have been influenced because of the way you interpreted your role, how informants saw you – and how you saw the informant's role and how they saw themselves.

From design to practice

Your carefully thought-out research plan probably went through several revisions – in the light of the things which were planned but which could not be accomplished, and of unforeseen changes which had to be made as the opportunity arose. As Buchanan *et al.* (1988, p. 55) argue, 'the practice of field research is the art of the possible'. The tidiness and orderliness of design are usually replaced by the fuzziness and compromise of practice. Taking the opportunities that arise to gather information from *new contacts* may lead to useful insights.

Example 11.12
Students investigating the use and potential of a community centre originally concentrated on summer play activities for children and services for the elderly, which they thought were the appropriate activities for a centre

to provide. However, after making contact with a nearby school and talking with the head teacher, they discovered that there was a need for supplementary tuition for bilingual youngsters in the area.

This was a facility which the community centre could organise. The new contact, the head teacher, had not been originally seen as part of the research sample. But as the result of this encounter the research design was considerable altered.

Sometimes the research plan may become blocked because of difficulties of access. People may not be at home for doorstep interviews or cannot be contacted for reasons of privacy.

Example 11.13
To complete an evaluation of a mental health day centre, students wished to seek the opinions of prospective members, currently in the care of a hospital. Staff at the centre believed that access for interviews could be given, and despite the advice of the supervisor the students made a number of attempts to liaise with the hospital staff to gain permission for interview.

Finally it was accepted by all that Research Ethics Committee permission (see Chapter 5) would be required before interviews could take place, and the research timetable did not allow sufficient time for that permission to be secured. In retrospect, this was a problem that should have been noticed on first drawing up the research agreement, when a decision could have been made either to seek permission or to omit this aspect of the study.

The methodology report is the place for these decisions, changes, opportunities, disappointments and disasters to be recorded. The report is a private document, but will show assessors what has been learned by doing rather than learning from the textbook. As Bechhofer (in Worsley, 1992) points out:

There is usually a tidiness and order to written research accounts – a sanitized quality which fails to reproduce the messy
reality of the research-process even in the hands of the most
experienced and rigorous exponent – that paradoxically should
remind us of what research is *really* like.   (Worsley, 1992,
pp. 114–15)

Not all this 'messy reality' can be, or should be, tidied
up in the client report. It is important to record in that
report the number of informants *actually* contacted as well
as the number hoped for, and what steps were taken to
search out alternative sources of information if the original plans were unworkable, or produced too little information. The client organisation will respect honest attempts
to find out information – and may already have some
experience of precisely those difficulties which were encountered.

The difference with the methodology report is that here
these problems can be examined as indicators of:

• how the 'sanitised' version differs from reality
• what was learned from engaging in practical research
• what initiative was shown in revising the research plans.

Handling problems

A problem which causes practical and ethical difficulties
is the handling of criticism and conflict within the organisation being researched. The previous chapter includes
suggestions about how this can be handled informally
through verbal feedback and mentioned sensitively in the
client report. The methodology report is the place for a
full discussion of what the issues were, how they arose,
and how they were handled.

Example 11.14
In a study which produced a documentary account
for a family of a relative's death in a community
tragedy, the student was working from an eye-witness

account which contained material the student felt could be construed as derogatory. He wondered whether this material should be omitted as not essential to the main story. So he interviewed the eye-witness to clarify the story. The informant was insistent that he wanted his account to go forward as originally dictated, feeling that this was true to his perception of events at that time. In the light of this discussion, the student left the material in but made it clear that this was only one eye-witness's account.

Example 11.15
In another study based in a hospital, the commencement of fieldwork revealed serious communications problems between staff on the hospital wards and staff in the out-patient department. This had a direct effect on the fieldwork in that it was much more difficult to arrange interviews in the out-patient department. However, the research itself was not the prime cause of the problems, but merely brought into the open a pre-existing situation.

It was decided that it would not be appropriate to refer to such a situation in the client report, as this was not directly relevant to the study. Nevertheless, in its effect on data gathering and in its contribution to an understanding of the hospital as a social organisation, it did constitute material for the methodology report.

The fieldwork diary

The fieldwork diary (see Chapter 4) provides evidence of your contribution to the research. Diaries, it has been suggested earlier, can be used in many ways. The fieldwork diary may be a record of research events – telephone conversations, interviews, meetings – a notebook for new ideas or questions to be answered as they occur, and a place for recording your feelings.

What is the most useful way to use it? Some students

271

list dates of meetings and keep entries to the minimum. Example 11.16 is an extract from such a diary.

Example 11.16

5 November – pilot interview with Sr Smith. Whilst there I also met and spoke to Walter, a pensioner living in a hostel for the homeless.

8 November – pilot interview with Revd Brown

12 November – interview with AJ from the Housing Community. He also has links with the —— Community (another housing trust). Gave me a list of people and organisations involved with housing and homelessness in the city. I telephoned LS and arranged an interview for 16th Nov.

16 November – interviewed LS from —— Homes.

24 November – met with supervisor to discuss progress so far. Need to see the client to sort out next stage

19 December met with —— (the client) to discuss the questionnaire.

However, the diary can also be used to itemise the frustrations and problems which arise – as a way of letting off steam! The next extract is from a student who successfully completed her research. However, the initial stages were fraught with problems concerning her sample of informants.

Example 11.17

27 October – Looked up addresses, very few on the phone. Spent a miserable afternoon trying to find someone in. Met Mrs X miserable, moaning old biddy. Didn't get much from her, but it's a start. Went to the tower blocks (apartments) – most depressing place I've ever been to – no wonder they want to get out as soon as possible.

28 October – Went to the General Meeting. Got 23 out of the 150 postal interviews. 16 per cent response rate. Didn't think it would be this bad. J asked people to meet me after to make appointments. 18 came to

see me. Felt a lot better. Made arrangements to either see them or ring to make appointments. Thank God. Growing sense of frustration at getting nowhere. People don't know why or what I'm doing – do I? Apathetic response to the questionnaire doesn't help. I want to put my suggestions forward to the committee but don't feel I should really get involved.
29 October – Two more interviews achieved, feel things moving now.

This project did go from strength to strength as the aims of the research were renegotiated with the client and the size of the sample grew. Without the fieldwork diary, the student might have forgotten the teething problems. Instead, she provided a very cogent account of them and the subsequent developments in her report.

The fieldwork diary may be included as an Appendix to the methodology report. It serves to document the work undertaken, and to provide information for assessment about the extent of the fieldwork operations, both individually and collectively if a team has been involved. To show that keeping the diary need not be onerous or boring, this section closes with another extract from the diary of a student who completed a first class piece of work. The extract has its amusing side – and it also shows the *insights* that the diary can contain.

Example 11.18
5 November – At 4.15 it was time for the service users to go home. Here beginneth the nightmare. At the beginning of the day I had put my bag into Bill's office so that none of it would go walkabout. Bill left early that day and had not told me so my bag, my money, my train ticket, door keys etc were locked in Bill's office. This is the point at which I discovered that no one else had a key to the room. Good bye bag. My whole life was locked into that one room . . .
Fiona drove me home. What an angel. I hope John is in a good mood tomorrow. We are meant to go to the other training place for the morning but we are

273

going to have to take a major detour to the centre on the way.

One thing I noticed about the centre in comparison with the one at home was that the staff did not talk about the service users in a humiliating way in front of them. The staff seemed to be more friendly with the service users, they joked with them on an equal level.

Evaluation

The section on evaluation in the methodology report is the most personal of all. How does what has been learned from doing applied research differ from what is learned in other academic courses? Specifically this relates to the kind of transferable skills which were outlined in Chapter 1, but it also allows an evaluation of the experience of applied research as it affected you, and what has been learned of the voluntary and community sector through involvement with it.

As the methodology report is for restricted circulation rather than a public document, the discussion can be frank. It may be used to evaluate the experience of teamwork, where this has been the method of working.

In teamwork the client report is an amalgam of the various contributions of individual team members. The team has to ensure that whatever arrangements for sharing the work are made, they are agreed by all to be fair, and remain flexible. Over the course of a project lasting two semesters or eight months, it is likely that the team will have to make allowances for temporary illness of team members (or their children), and to recognise that individual deadlines for other academic work may affect research plans.

In the methodology report, the different strengths that team members brought to the project can be credited – or problems of co-operation and frictions may be mentioned (without being too personal!). The experience of team work is a relevant issue – was it an experience found to be beneficial or would you have liked to have changed certain elements of it?

Example 11.19
Comparing the methodology reports of a successful team project involving two students is interesting. The first student, who was about twenty years older than the other noted:

> C—— is a very approachable and sociable person and despite the large age gap between us we seemed to complement each other, enough for us to undertake the project. It was also convenient, from the safety and time aspect, that I had the use of a car to convey us both around the necessary institutions. However, we seemed to have the enthusiasm to progress in this project as a team and that was of vital importance for both the success of the project and for us, the researchers.

The other student commented independently:

> The two other factors that perhaps contributed to the response we received from all our informants was the fact we were both female and that we were of different ages (I'm 21 and B—— is in her forties) ... The older informants saw B—— more as a mother figure and responded well to her, I seemed to get a better response from those of a similar age to myself due perhaps to the fact that I was seen as part of their peer group ... This shows that working in a team with mixed ages is beneficial, where one of us didn't get a satisfactory response the other did.

Written or oral report?

The assumption so far has been that the methodology report is a written report, like the client report. However, an oral presentation (or viva examination) could be combined with a written report with certain advantages.

- Explaining research outcomes and processes using summary points and diagrams (on overhead projector) provides evidence of another transferable skill.
- When done in a student seminar, this can serve to interest others in doing applied research themselves.
- It is interactive, allowing students to be questioned on aspects where further clarification would be helpful.

The disadvantages are that student presentations may:

- create anxiety on the part of the students, so that they perform less effectively than in a written report.
- be more difficult to assess objectively.
- be inconvenient to schedule with the attendance of examiners and other students, if they take place during the normal examination period.

The first difficulty can be overcome by preparation and practice, the second by using a checklist as would be done for interviews, the third by making it a regular part of the assessment process.

Even if the methodology report is not presented orally, you may find as practical researchers that you are invited to talk to the client organisation about your main report at an interim or final stage. So practice in oral presentation may well be desirable in any case.

Assessment criteria

As with the client report, the assessment of the methodology report should be geared to what it seeks to test. For example, there are considerations such as the following.

- **Context** – you have located the research in the context of other academic work on similar themes, as shown, for example, in a bibliography.

- **Reflexivity** – you have analysed the practical problems which arose in the research, and outlined the solutions adopted for them. Decisions which would now be revised in the light of experience are discussed alongside alternative strategies, and you show an understanding of your own role in the research and how it affected others.
- **Methodology** – you are aware of current debates in research methodology and have been able to apply this to the practice of research.
- **Ethics** – you are sensitive to all involved in the research process, use appropriate language, and have applied the guidelines of the appropriate professional body.
- **Initiative and learning** – you have demonstrated initiative in progressing the research, taking decisions and making contact with the client and informants. You have worked as a full member of the team (where appropriate) and not over-relied on the tutor or other group members. You can show evidence of personal learning from the research experience.

Finally, there is the relative weighting of the two reports. As the client report is the external 'product' of the course, and you will have spent most time on it, it seems appropriate for this to receive a higher weighting than the methodology report.

What this will be in practice is for your institution, department and supervisor to determine. In our experience a weighting of 70 per cent for the client report (compared to 30 per cent for the methodology report) appears reasonable and is acceptable to students as a fair balance.

Where the client report has taken up substantially more time and energy at the expense of the methodology report there is a case for increasing the weighting proportionately. Conversely, in those rare situations where the research programme had to be substantially modified or curtailed because of unforeseen problems and the client report is fairly slim, then a comprehensive methodology report may be used to remedy the situation and would therefore deserve a greater proportion of the final total marks.

Conclusion

In this chapter some of the elements of a good methodology/reflexive report have been discussed. This really is the place for individual understanding, creativity and flair to shine through. It is the opportunity for you to write about the 'messiness' of research behind the 'sanitised' client report – the problems which arose and how they were resolved.

- Given a second chance, would it all be done differently?
- Or would just some elements be changed?
- What have you personally learned from this research project?

There are not many places in a degree course when comments like this can be made and where you can reflect on individual progress. Make the most of it!

Appendix A:
Statement of Ethical
Practice

Sociologists, in carrying out their work, inevitably face ethical, and sometimes legal, dilemmas which arise out of competing obligations and conflicts of interest. This statement points to a set of obligations to which members should normally adhere as principles for guiding their conduct. Departures from the principles should be the result of deliberation and not ignorance. The statement is meant, primarily, to inform members' ethical judgements rather than to impose on them an external set of standards. The statement does not, therefore, provide a set of recipes for resolving ethical choices or dilemmas, but recognises that often it will be necessary to make such choices on the basis of principles and values, and the interests of those involved.

Professional integrity

Members have a responsibility to:

1. safeguard the proper interests of those involved in or affected by their work.
2. report their findings accurately and truthfully.
3. consider the effects of their involvement and the consequences of their work or its misuse for those they study and other interested parties.
4. recognise the boundaries of their professional competence and not accept work they are not qualified to carry out.
5. satisfy themselves that the research they undertake is worth while and that the techniques are appropriate.
6. be clear about the limits of their detachment from and involvement in their areas of study.

279

7. avoid claiming expertise in areas outside their true competence.
8. have regard for the reputation of the discipline when dealing with the media.

Responsibilities towards research participants

Sociologists, when they carry out research, enter into personal and moral relationships with those they study, be they individuals, households or corporate entities. Although committed to the advancement of knowledge, sociologists should be aware that that goal, in itself, does not provide an entitlement to override the rights of others. Members should, therefore,

1. satisfy themselves that a study is necessary for the furtherance of knowledge.
2. be aware that they have some responsibility for the use to which their research may be put.

Relationships with research participants

Sociologists have a responsibility to:

1. ensure that the physical, social and psychological wellbeing of research participants is not adversely affected by research.
2. protect the rights of those they study, their interests, sensitivities and privacy.
3. recognise the difficulty of balancing conflicting interests, characterised by disparities of power and status.
4. ensure a relationship of trust wherever possible (with powerless as well as more powerful research subjects).
5. obtain, as far as possible, the freely given informed consent of those studied.
6. explain as fully as possible what the research is about.
7. explain who is undertaking and financing the research.
8. explain why it is being undertaken.
9. explain how the results will be disseminated.
10. ensure that participants are aware of their right to refuse to participate for whatever reason.
11. indicate how far participants will be afforded anonymity and confidentiality.

12. ensure that respondents can reject the use of data-gathering devices such as tape recorders and video cameras.
13. ensure that films or recordings are not shown to people other than those to whom the participants have agreed.
14. be aware that consent may need to be renegotiated over time during the course of field research (especially in prolonged studies).
15. be careful not to disturb the relationship between gate-keepers and participants.
16. anticipate and guard against any harmful consequences for the participants arising from the research (having obtained consent does not absolve researchers from this responsibility).
17. minimise the disturbance to those participating in the research.
18. be particularly careful when research participants are particularly vulnerable because of their age, social status or powerlessness.
19. avoid intruding on the personal space of the ill, or those too young or too old to participate.

Covert research

There are serious ethical dangers in the use of covert research but covert methods may avoid certain problems, where participants change their behaviour because they know they are being studied, or when access is closed by powerful or secretive interests. Covert methods violate the principles of informed consent and may invade the privacy of those being studied. Participant or non-participant observation in non-public spaces or experimental manipulation of participants without their knowledge should be resorted to only where it is impossible to use other methods to obtain essential data.

Covert researchers should:

1. safeguard the anonymity of research participants.
2. ideally obtain consent to the research after it has been concluded (prior to publication).

Appendix A

Anonymity, privacy and confidentiality

Social researchers should:

1. respect the anonymity and privacy of research participants.
2. keep personal information concerning research participants confidential.
3. decide whether it is proper or appropriate to record certain kinds of sensitive information.
4. anticipate threats to confidentiality and anonymity.
5. store data in a secure manner.
6. be aware of their obligations under the Data Protection Act.
7. use pseudonyms or other technical means to break the link between identifiable individuals and the data.
8. advise participants who may be identifiable from a combination of attributes that are unique to them that it may be difficult to disguise their identity.
9. ensure that research colleagues also respect guarantees of confidentiality and anonymity.
10. be aware that research data given in confidence do not enjoy legal privilege (that is, they may be liable to subpoena by a court).
11. honour guarantees of privacy or confidentiality given to organisations as well as to individuals and small groups, unless there are clear and compelling grounds not to do so.
12. avoid any actions which may have deleterious consequences for sociologists who come after them or which might undermine the reputation of sociology as a discipline.

Adapted from British Sociological Association 'Statement of Ethical Practice' (1991) as abbreviated by Harvey and MacDonald (1993) and reproduced by permission. The full document and the associated 'Guidelines for Good Professional Practice' are available from the BSA.

Appendix B:
Agreement for Research

LIVERPOOL INSTITUTE OF HIGHER EDUCATION

INTERCHANGE

The following is the outcome of a meeting on [date] between
Irene Hall, Lecturer, and [name], student at the Department
of Sociology, Liverpool Institute of Higher Education and
[name], Team Manager, of [name and address of organisation].

*(All parties may comment on the agreement and if any section needs
to be altered a fresh agreement will be issued. Please contact Irene
Hall, the Project Supervisor, with comments at the Sociology Department, Liverpool Institute of Higher Education, Tel.)*

1. **Project agreement** between Irene Hall and [name of student]
   of the Department of Sociology, Liverpool Institute of Higher
   Education and [name and organisation].

2. **Duration of project**: The project will run from October
   1995 to Easter 1996: fieldwork to be completed by December 1995.

3. **[Name of organisation]** has developed a Day Centre which
   members with mental health problems can use. The Centre
   also supports Care in the Community clients based in flats
   and a residential house. The Centre operates according to
   [organisation's] Action for Independence aims and philosophy which include providing individually tailored services
   based on the principle of normalisation.

4. **Proposed project**: [Student] will evaluate the services provided by the Day Centre, focusing particularly on the process
   of setting up groups. She will interview staff and service

283

users face-to-face interviews with a schedule agreed with [Team Manager].

If possible, [Student] may also be able to interview past service users about their reasons for not currently using the Centre.

5. **Project outcome:** [Student] will produce a report which will be available in draft form by Easter and in its final form at the beginning of May. [Organisation] will have the right to use this report as it wishes, with due acknowledgement being made to the student and to L.I.H.E.

   [Student] will submit this report to L.I.H.E. as part of assessment for her degree along with an account of the methodology involved.

6. **Attendance:** [Student] will commit the equivalent of one half-day per week in the first term for fieldwork and a similar amount of time in the second term for analysis and writing reports.

7. **Expenses:** The payment of travel expenses will be provided by [organisation]. [Student] will be responsible for providing a typed copy of her reports to L.I.H.E. as part submission for her degree.

8. **Supervision:** Irene Hall will be available weekly for supervision throughout the course of the project.

9. **Confidentiality:** [Student] will work to the British Sociological Association guidelines on ethics and will respect the confidentiality of the information given. Due attention will be given to anonymity and she will conduct the research in a sensitive manner.

10. **Acknowledgements:** At any time when the report or any part of it is used, proper acknowledgement should be made to the student by name, to the Liverpool Institute of Higher Education and to Interchange.

Ageement for Research

SIGNED _____
(Organisation)

SIGNED _____
(Student)

SIGNED _____
(Supervisor)

DATE _____

A copy of this agreement will be sent to Interchange.

Appendix C:
Oral History Consent Form

1. Have you any objections to the Oral History Project using your contribution in the following ways:

   (a) as a source which might be published?   YES / NO

   (b) for educational use?
      (e.g. in school teaching pack)   YES / NO

   (c) for broadcasting purposes?
      (e.g. in local radio programme)   YES / NO

2. Have you any objections to your name being mentioned?

      YES / NO

3. Do you wish to apply any other restrictions to the use of your material?

      YES / NO

WE HOPE TO LET YOU SEE A COPY OF ANYTHING THAT MIGHT BE PUBLISHED WHICH IDENTIFIES YOU.

Signature of informant_____

Address _____

_____

_____

Name of interviewer_____

Date of interview _____

Main topics covered _____

_____

_____

Use of documents

If you are given photographs or other documents you need to give a written receipt and keep a copy for yourself. There needs to be a clear undertaking about when the material will be returned as well as how it will be used. We include a receipt form below.

PROJECT (NAME) RECEIPT

1. The following article(s) has/have been lent to the project.

_____

_____

_____

_____

2. Use to which _____ will be put.

_____

_____

_____

3. Date by which the article(s) lent will be returned

_____

4. Name of informant _____

   Signature _____

   Date _____

5. Name of interviewer _____

   Signature _____

   Date _____

Bibliography

Abbott, A. and Wallace, C. (1990) *An Introduction to Sociology: feminist perspectives* (London: Routledge).

Anderson, K., Armitage, S., Jack, D. and Wittner, J. (1990) 'Beginning Where We Are: Feminist Methodology in Oral History', in J. McC. Nielsen (ed.) *Feminist Research Methods: exemplary readings in the social sciences* (Boulder, Colo.: Westview).

Arber, S. (1993) 'Designing Samples', in N. Gilbert (ed.) *Researching Social Life* (London: Sage).

Ashton, D. and Ainsbury, F. (1993) 'A New Beginning', unpublished report, Liverpool Institute of Higher Education.

Bailey, A. (1990) 'Personal Transferable Skills for Employment: The Role of Higher Education', in P.W.G. Wright (ed.) *Industry and Higher Education: collaboration to improve students' learning and training* (Buckingham: Society for Research into Higher Education and Open University Press).

Bales, R.F. (1950) *Interaction Process Analysis* (Reading, Mass.: Addison-Wesley.

Barley, N. (1983) *The Innocent Anthropologist* (Harmondsworth: Penguin).

Bechhofer, F. (1992), 'The Research Process', in P. Worsley (ed.) *The New Introducing Sociology* (Harmondsworth: Penguin).

Belbin, R.M. (1981) *Management Teams: why they succeed or fail* (London: Heinemann).

Bell, C. (1978) 'Studying the Locally Powerful: Personal Reflections On a Research Career', in C. Bell and S. Encel (eds) *Inside the Whale* (Sydney: Pergamon).

Bell, C. and Newby, H. (1977) *Doing Sociological Research* (London: George Allen & Unwin).

Bell, C. and Roberts, H. (1984) *Social Researching* (London: Routledge & Kegan Paul).

Benney, M. and Hughes, E.C. (1977) 'Of Sociology and the Interview', in M. Bulmer (ed.) *Sociological Research Methods* (London: Macmillan).

Bergquist, A. (1993) 'Oral History', unpublished report, Liverpool Institute of Higher Education.

Bibliography

Blaikie, N. (1993) *Approaches to Social Enquiry* (Cambridge: Polity Press).

Blumer, H. (1939) *Critiques of Research in the Social Sciences: 1: an appraisal of Thomas and Znaniecki's The Polish Peasant in Europe and America* (New York: Social Science Research Council).

Bogdewic, S.P. (1992) 'Participant Observation', in B.F. Crabtree and W.L. Miller (eds) *Doing Qualitative Research* (Newbury Park: Sage).

Bourque, L.B. and Clark, V.A. (1994) 'Processing Data: The Survey Example', in M.S. Lewis-Beck (ed.) *Research Practice* (London: Sage).

Brannen, J. (1992) *Mixing Methods: qualitative and quantitative research* (Aldershot: Avebury).

Bresnen, M. (1988) 'Insights On Site: Research into Construction Project Organisations', in A. Bryman (ed.), *Doing Research in Organisations* (London: Routledge).

Bryman, A. (1988a) *Quantity and Quality in Social Research* (London: Unwin Hyman).

Bryman, A. (1988b) *Doing Research in Organisations* (London: Routledge).

Bryman, A. (1992) 'Quantitative and Qualitative Research: Further Reflections On Their Integration', in J. Brannen (ed.) *Mixing Methods: quantitative and qualitative research* (Aldershot: Avebury).

Bryman, A. and Cramer, D. (1990) *Quantitative Data Analysis for Social Scientists* (London: Routledge).

Buchanan, D., Boddy, D. and McCalman, J. (1988) 'Getting In, Getting On, Getting Out and Getting Back', in A. Bryman (ed.) *Doing Research in Organisations* (London: Routledge).

Bulmer, M. (1977) *Sociological Research Methods* (London: Macmillan).

Bulmer, M. (1978) *Social Policy Research* (London: Macmillan).

Bynner, J. and Stribley, K.M. (1979) *Social Research: principles and procedures* (London: Longman/Open University Press).

Caldwell, P., Crotty, A. and Meehan, J. (1993) 'Volunteering', unpublished report, University of Liverpool.

Callaghan, A. (1993) 'Evaluation of Parish Links', unpublished report, Liverpool Institute of Higher Education.

Central Policy Unit, Liverpool City Council (1993) *Key Statistics Liverpool Wards 1971/81/91* (Liverpool: Liverpool City Council).

Clegg, F. (1989) *Simple Statistics* (Cambridge: Cambridge University Press).

Bibliography

Converse, J.M. and Presser, S. (1994) 'Survey Questions: Handcrafting the Standardized Questionnaire', in M.S. Lewis-Beck (ed.) *Research Practice* (London: Sage).

Cramer, D. (1994) *Introducing Statistics for Social Research: step-by-step calculations and computer techniques using SPSS* (London, Routledge).

Crompton, R. and Jones, G. (1988) 'Researching White Collar Organisations: Why Sociologists Should Not Stop Doing Case Studies', in A. Bryman (ed.) *Doing Research in Organisations* (London: Routledge).

Daniels, C. (1992) 'Service Evaluation for Victims of Crime', unpublished report, Liverpool Institute of Higher Education.

Davidson, J.O'C. and Layder, D. (1994) *Methods, Sex and Madness* (London: Routledge).

Denzin, N. (1970) *The Research Act in Sociology* (London: Butterworth).

de Vaus, D.A. (1991) *Surveys in Social Research*, 3rd edn, (London: UCL Press).

Dey, I. (1993) *Qualitative Data Analysis* (London: Routledge).

Dixon, B.R., Bouma, G.D. and Atkinson, G.B.J. (1987) *A Handbook of Social Science Research* (Oxford: Oxford University Press).

Douglas, J.D. (1976) *Investigative Social Research: individual and team field research* (Beverly Hills, Calif.: Sage).

Education for Enterprise (1992) *Personal Skills for Working Life: a self-assessment guide* (Middlesbrough: Educational Development Services, Teesside Polytechnic).

Erickson, B.H. and Nosanchuk, T.A. (1992) *Understanding Data*, 2nd edn (Buckingham: Open University Press).

Everitt, A., Hardiker, P., Littlewood, J. and Mullender, A. (1992) *Applied Research for Better Practice* (London: Macmillan).

Feuerstein, M.-T. (1986) *Partners in Evaluation: evaluating development and community programmes with participants* (London: Macmillan).

Fielding, N. (1993) 'Qualitative Interviewing', in N. Gilbert (ed.) *Researching Social Life* (London: Sage).

Finch, J. (1984) 'The Ethics and Politics of Interviewing Women', in C. Bell and H. Roberts (eds) *Social Researching: politics, problems and practice* (London: Routledge & Kegan Paul).

Forrest, R. and Gordon, D. (1993) *People and Places: a 1991 census atlas of England* (Bristol: School for Advanced Urban Studies).

Freedman, D., Pisani, R., Purves, R. and Adhikari, A. (1991) *Statistics*, 2nd edn (New York: Norton).

Gilbert, N. (1993) *Researching Social Life* (London: Sage).

Bibliography

Glaser, B.G. and Strauss, A.L. (1967) *The Discovery of Grounded Theory: strategies for qualitative research* (Chicago: Aldine).

Gluck, S.B. (1985) *Five American Suffragists Talk About Their Lives* (New York: Monthly Review Press).

Goffman, E. (1959) *The Presentation of Self in Everyday Life* (Garden City, NY: Doubleday).

Graham, H. (1984) 'Surveying Through Stories', in C. Bell and H. Roberts (eds) *Social Researching* (London: Routledge & Kegan Paul).

Guba, E.G. and Lincoln, Y.S. (1989) *Fourth Generation Evaluation* (Newbury Park, Calif.: Sage).

Guirdham, M. and Tyler, K. (1992) *Enterprise Skills for Student* (Oxford: Butterworth-Heinemann).

Hakim, C. (1992) *Research Design: strategies and choices in the design of research* (London: Routledge).

Hall, D.J. (1991) 'The Research Imperative and Bureaucratic Control: The Case of Clinical Research', *Social Science and Medicine*, 32(3), 333–42.

Hall, D.J. (1977) *Social Relations and Innovation: changing the state of play in hospitals* (London: Routledge & Kegan Paul).

Hall, D.J. and Hall, I.M. (1995) 'Voluntary Organisations and Higher Education: Development Through Exchange', Occasional paper in sociology and social policy, Department of Sociology, Social Policy and Social Work Studies, University of Liverpool.

Hammersley, M. (1989) *The Dilemma of Qualitative Method: Herbert Blumer and the Chicago Tradition* (London: Routledge).

Hammersley, M. (1991) *Reading Ethnographic Research* (London: Longman).

Hammersley, M. (1992) *What's Wrong with Ethnography: methodological explorations* (London: Routledge).

Harding, S. (1987) *Feminism and Methodology* (Milton Keynes: Open University Press).

Harvey, L. and MacDonald, M. (1993) *Doing Sociology: a practical introduction* (London: Macmillan).

Hellevik, O. (1989) *Introduction to Causal Analysis: exploring survey data by crosstabulation* (London: George Allen & Unwin).

Hessler, R.M. (1992) *Social Research Methods* (St. Paul, Minn.: West).

Hoinville, G., Jowell, R. and Associates (1977) *Survey Research Practice* (London: Heinemann).

Hornsby-Smith, M. (1993) 'Gaining Access', in N. Gilbert (ed.) *Researching Social Life* (London: Sage).

291

Bibliography

Howard, K. and Sharp, J.A. (1983) *The Management of a Student Research Project* (Aldershot: Gower).

Inman, C. (1994) *The Financial Times Style Guide* (London: Pitman).

Jaeger, R.M. (1990) *Statistics: a spectator sport*, 2nd edn (Newbury Park, Calif.: Sage).

Jayaratne, T.E. (1993) 'The Value of Quantitative Methodology for Feminist Research', in M. Hammersley (ed.) *Social Research: philosophy, politics and practice* (London: Sage).

Jenkins, S. (1993) 'Description and Appraisal of Services', unpublished report, University of Liverpool.

Kelly, L. (1988) *Surviving Sexual Violence* (Cambridge: Polity).

Kolakowski, L. (1993) 'An Overall View of Positivism', in M. Hammersley (ed.) *Social Research: Philosophy, politics and practice* (London: Sage).

Krueger, R.A. (1994) *Focus Groups: a practical guide for applied research*, 2nd edn (Thousand Oaks, Calif.: Sage).

Kuhn, T.S. (1964) *The Structure of Scientific Revolutions* (Chicago: University of Chicago Press).

Lavrakas, P.J. (1987) *Telephone Survey Methods: sampling, selection and supervision* (Beverly Hills, Calif.: Sage).

Lawrence, P. (1988) 'In Another Country', in A. Bryman (ed.) *Doing Research in Organisations* (London: Routledge).

Lee, D. and Newby, H. (1983) *The Problem of Sociology: an introduction to the discipline* (London: Hutchinson).

Lee, R.M. (1993) *Doing Research on Sensitive Topics* (London: Sage).

Lightfoot, G. (1994) 'Report for Housing Co-operative', unpublished report, Liverpool Institute of Higher Education.

Lincoln, Y.S. and Guba, E.G. (1985) *Naturalistic Inquiry* (Newbury Park, Calif.: Sage).

Lindlof, T.R. (1995) *Qualitative Communication Research Methods* (Thousand Oaks, Calif.: Sage).

Lummis, T. (1987) *Listening to History* (London: Hutchinson).

McCrossan, L. (1991) *A Handbook for Interviewers*, 3rd edn (London: HMSO).

Macdonald, K. (1993) 'Exemplar B: Building Respectability', in N. Gilbert (ed.) *Researching Social Life* (London: Sage).

McNeill, P. (1990) *Research Methods*, 2nd edn (London: Routledge).

Malec, M.A. (1993) *Essential Statistics for Social Research*, 2nd edn (Boulder, Colo.: Westview).

Marsh, C. (1982) *The Survey Method: the contribution of surveys to sociological explanation* (London: George Allen & Unwin).

Bibliography

Marsh, C. (1988) *Exploring Data: an introduction to data analysis for social scientists* (Cambridge: Polity).

Marshman, A. and James, M. (1994) *Desktop Publishing with PagePlus 3* (Leyburn: I/O Press).

May, T. (1993) *Social Research: issues, methods and process* (Buckingham: Open University Press).

Maynard, M. (1994) 'Methods, Practice and Epistemology: The Debate About Feminism and Research', in M. Maynard and J. Purvis (eds) *Researching Women's Lives from a Feminist Perspective* (London: Taylor & Francis).

Maynard, M. and Purvis, J. (1994) 'Doing Feminist Research', in M. Maynard and J. Purvis (eds) *Researching Women's Lives from a Feminist Perspective* (London: Taylor & Francis).

Mies, M. (1993) 'Towards a Methodology for Feminist Research', in M. Hammersley (ed.) *Social Research: Philosophy, politics and practice* (London: Sage).

Miles, M.B. and Huberman, A.M. (1994) *Qualitative Data Analysis*, 2nd edn (Thousand Oaks, Calif.: Sage).

Miller, W.L. and Crabtree, B.F. (1992) 'Primary Care Research: A Multimethod Typology and Qualitative Road Map', in B.F. Crabtree and W.L. Miller (eds) *Doing Qualitative Research* (Newbury Park, Calif.: Sage).

Morgan, E. and Nixon, C. (1994) 'Relatives and Their Needs', unpublished report, University of Liverpool.

Morris, L.L., Fitz-Gibbon, C.T. and Freeman, M.E. (1987) *How To Communicate Evaluation Findings* (Newbury Park, Calif.: Sage).

Moser, C.A. and Kalton, G. (1971) *Survey Methods in Social Investigation*, 2nd edn (London: Heinemann).

Navarro, A. (1992) 'Methodological Report', unpublished report, Liverpool Institute of Higher Education.

Newell, R. (1993) 'Questionnaires', in N. Gilbert (ed.) *Researching Social Life* (London: Sage).

Nicholson, R.H. (1986) *Medical Research with Children: ethics, law and practice* (Oxford: Oxford University Press).

Nielsen, J.McC. (1990) *Feminist Research Methods: exemplary readings in the social sciences* (Boulder, Colo.: Westview).

Nolan, B. (1994) *Data Analysis: an introduction* (Cambridge: Polity).

Northledge, A. (1990) *The Good Study Guide* (Milton Keynes: Open University).

Norušis, M.J. (1988) *The SPSS Guide to Data Analysis for SPSS/PC+* (Chicago: SPSS Inc).

Oakley, A. (1981) 'Interviewing Women: A Contradiction in Terms?', in H. Roberts (ed.) *Doing Feminist Research* (London: Routledge & Kegan Paul).

Oakley, A. (1993) *Essays on Women, Medicine and Health* (Edinburgh: Edinburgh University Press).

Ong, B.N. (1993) *The Practice of Health Services Research* (London: Chapman & Hall).

Oppenheim, A.N. (1992) *Questionnaire Design, Interviewing and Attitude Measurement*, new edn (London: Pinter).

Parker, H., Bakx, K. and Newcombe, R. (1988) *Living with Heroin: the impact of a drugs 'epidemic' on an English community* (Milton Keynes: Open University Press).

Pawson, R. (1991) 'Approaches to Teaching Social Research Methods', in J. Gubbay (ed.) *Teaching Methods of Social Research: report of a conference at City University* (Norwich: Sociology Curriculum Project, University of East Anglia).

Platt, J. (1976) *Realities of Social Research: an empirical study of British sociologists* (London: Sussex University Press).

Plummer, K. (1983) *Documents of Life: an introduction to the problems and literature of a humanistic method* (London: Unwin Hyman).

Popper, K. (1961) *The Poverty of Historicism* (London: Routledge & Kegan Paul).

Posovac, E.J. and Carey, R.G. (1989) *Program Evaluation: methods and case studies*, 3rd edn (Englewood Cliffs,NJ: Prentice-Hall).

Pugh, D.S. and Hickson, D.J. (1976) *Organisational Structure in its Context* (Farnborough: Saxon House).

Reinharz, S. (1979) *On Becoming a Social Scientist* (San Francisco: Jossey-Bass).

Rickford, F. (1995) 'Clubbing Together in the Community', *Guardian*, 29 March, p. 22.

Riley, J. (1990) *Getting the Most from your Data: a handbook of practical ideas on how to analyse qualitative data* (Bristol: Technical and Educational Services).

Robinson, D. (1971) *The Process of Becoming Ill* (London: Routledge & Kegan Paul).

Robson, C. (1993) *Real World Research* (Oxford: Blackwell).

Roethlisberger, F.J. and Dickson, W.J. (1964) *Management and the Worker* (New York: John Wiley).

Rose, D. and Sullivan, O. (1993) *Data Analysis for Social Scientists* (Buckingham: Open University Press).

Rose, G. (1982) *Deciphering Sociological Research* (London: Macmillan).

Rossi, P.H. and Freeman, H.E. (1993) *Evaluation: a systematic approach*, 5th edn (Newbury Park: Sage).

Salamon, L.M. and Anheier, H.K. (1992) 'In Search of the Non-Profit Sector. 1: The Question of Definitions', *Voluntas: Inter-*

national Journal of Voluntary and Non-Profit Organisations, 3(2), 125–51.

Scanlon, J. (1993) 'Challenging the Imbalances of Power in Feminist Oral History', *Women's Studies International Forum*, 16, 6, 639–45.

Scott, J. (1990) *A Matter of Record* (Cambridge: Polity).

Searle, J. (1991) 'Intentionalistic Explanation in the Social Sciences', *Philosophy of the Social Sciences*, 21, 3, 332–44.

Shaw, C.R. (1968) *The Jack Roller: a delinquent boy's own story* (Chicago: University of Chicago Press).

Silverman, D. (1993) *Interpreting Qualitative Data* (London: Sage).

Singleton, R., Straits, B.C., Straits, M.M. and McAllister, R.J. (1988) *Approaches to Social Research* (New York: Oxford University Press).

Skeggs, B. (1994) 'Situating the Production of Feminist Ethnography', in M. Maynard and J. Purvis (eds) *Researching Women's Lives from a Feminist Perspective* (London: Taylor & Francis).

Stacey, M. (1969) *Methods of Social Research* (Oxford: Pergamon).

Stanley, L. (1990) *Feminist Praxis: Research, theory and epistemology in feminist sociology* (London: Routledge).

Stanley, L. and Wise, S. (1993) *Breaking Out Again: Feminist ontology and epistemology*, 2nd edn (London: Routledge).

Strauss, A. and Glaser, B. (1977) *Anguish: a case history of a dying trajectory* (Oxford: Martin Robertson).

Tate, A. and Thompson, J.E. (1994) 'The Application of Enterprise Skills in the Workplace', in S. Haselgrove (ed.) *The Student Experience* (Buckingham: Society for Research into Higher Education and Open University Press).

Tilley, A. (1994) 'Methodology and Evaluation', unpublished report, Liverpool Institute of Higher Education.

Torkington, N.P.K. (1991) *Black Health – a political issue* (London and Liverpool: Catholic Association for Racial Justice / Liverpool Institute of Higher Education).

Torrington, D., Weightman, J. and Johns, K. (1989) *Effective Management: people and organisations* (Hemel Hempstead: Prentice Hall).

Tuckman, B.W. (1965) 'Development Sequences in Small Groups', *Psychological Bulletin*, 63, 384–99.

Wallace, W. (1979) 'An Overview of Elements in the Scientific Process', in J. Bynner and K.M. Stribley (eds) *Social Research: principles and procedures* (London: Longman/Open University Press).

Wallace, W.L. (1971) *The Logic of Science in Sociology* (Chicago: Aldine-Atherton).

Walsh, A. (1990) *Statistics for the Social Sciences: with computer applications* (New York: Harper & Row).

Webb, E.J., Campbell, D.T., Schwartz, R.D. and Sechrest, L. (1966) *Unobtrusive Measures: nonreactive research in the social sciences* (Chicago: Rand McNally).

Weber, M. (1947) *The Theory of Social and Economic Organisation* (Glencoe, Ill.: Free Press).

Weber, M. (1949) *The Methodology of the Social Sciences* (Glencoe: Free Press).

Weber, M. (1968) *Economy and Society – an outline of interpretative sociology* (New York: Bedminster).

Weiss, C.H. (1972) *Evaluation Research: methods for assessing program effectiveness* (Englewood Cliffs,NJ: Prentice-Hall).

Wellings, K., Field, J., Johnson, A.M. and Wadsworth, J. (1994) *Sexual Behaviour in Britain: the national survey of sexual attitudes and lifestyles* (Harmondsworth: Penguin).

Westover, B. (1986) 'To Fill the Kids' Tummies: The Lives and Work of Colchester Tailoresses 1880–1918', in L. Davidoff and B. Westover (eds) *Our Work, Our Lives, Our Words* (London: Macmillan).

Whyte, W.F. (1984) *Learning from the Field* (Beverly Hills, Calif.: Sage).

Worsley, P. (1992) *The New Introducing Sociology* (Harmondsworth: Penguin).

Young, K. (1991) '*Shades of Green*', in Jowell, R., Brook, L. & Taylor, B. (eds) *British Social Attitudes: the 8th Report* (Aldershot: Dartmouth Publishing).

Yow, V.R. (1994) *Recording Oral History: a practical guide for social scientists* (Thousand Oaks, Calif.: Sage).

Index

Index

303